FrontPage

A Tutorial to Accompany Peter Norton's®

Introduction to Computers

 **Glencoe**
McGraw-Hill

New York, New York   Columbus, Ohio   Woodland Hills, California   Peoria, Illinois

MW00717654

FrontPage® 2000
A Tutorial to Accompany
Peter Norton's® Introduction to Computers

Glencoe/McGraw-Hill

A Division of The **McGraw·Hill** Companies

Send all inquiries to:

Glencoe/McGraw-Hill
936 Eastwind Drive
Westerville, OH 43081

ISBN: 0-02-804191-7
Development: FSCreations, Inc.
Production: Lithokraft II

The clip art and photos used in the Webs *My Web* and *ComCon2* on the Student Data Disk are imported from the Corel MEGA GALLERY, copyright 1996 Corel Corporation. All other photos and graphics are from the Microsoft Clip Art Gallery.

Peter Norton, Peter Norton's stylized signature, and Peter Norton's crossed-arms pose are registered trademarks of Peter Norton.

FrontPage 2000, Internet Explorer, Outlook, Word, and *Microsoft* are registered trademarks of Microsoft Corporation. All other trademarks and service marks are the property of their respective owners. Glencoe/McGraw-Hill is not associated with any product or vendor mentioned in this tutorial.

1 2 3 4 5 6 7 8 9 083 05 04 03 02 01 00

PREFACE

Microsoft FrontPage® 2000, one of the instructional tools that complements *Peter Norton's® Introduction to Computers,* covers the basic features of FrontPage® 2000, Microsoft's popular Web development and maintenance program. Glencoe and Peter Norton have teamed up to provide this tutorial and its ancillaries to help you become a knowledgeable, empowered end user. After you complete this tutorial, you will be able to build Webs based on FrontPage templates and wizards, customize them to suit your preferences, and comprehend the intricate workings of this powerful program. You will also develop a better understanding of how the World Wide Web functions and its role in today's workplace.

STRUCTURE AND FORMAT OF THE *FRONTPAGE 2000* TUTORIAL

Microsoft FrontPage® 2000 covers a range of functions and techniques and provides hands-on opportunities for you to practice and apply your skills. Each lesson in *Microsoft FrontPage® 2000* includes the following:

■ **Contents and Objectives.** The Contents and Objectives at the beginning of each lesson provide an overview of the FrontPage 2000 features you will learn.

■ **Explanations of important concepts.** Each section of each lesson begins with a brief explanation of the concept or software feature covered in that lesson. The explanations help you understand "the big picture" as you learn each new FrontPage 2000 feature.

■ **FrontPage in the Workplace.** FrontPage in the Workplace, which appears in the margin at the beginning of each lesson, presents a real-world overview on how the lesson material may be applied within an organization.

■ **New terms.** An important part of learning about computers is learning the terminology. Each new term in the tutorial appears in bold italic type and is defined the first time it is used. As you encounter these words, read their definitions carefully. If you encounter the same word later and have forgotten the meaning, you can look up the word in the Glossary.

■ **Hands On activities.** Because most of us learn best by doing, each explanation is followed by a hands-on activity that includes step-by-step instructions which you complete at the computer. Integrated in the steps are notes and warnings to help you learn more about FrontPage.

■ **FrontPage Basics.** This element appears in the margin next to Hands On activities. FrontPage Basics lists the general steps required to perform a particular task. Use the FrontPage Basics as a reference to quickly and easily review the steps to perform a task.

■ **Hints & Tips.** This element appears in the margin and provides tips for increasing your effectiveness while using the FrontPage program.

■ **Another Way.** This element appears in the margin and provides alternate ways to perform a given task.

■ **Did You Know?** Read each Did You Know?, another element that appears in the margin, to learn additional facts related to the content of the lesson or other interesting facts about computers.

■ **Web Note.** Web Notes that appear in the margin contain interesting facts and Web addresses that relate to the content of the lesson and to your exploration of the World Wide Web.

■ **Illustrations.** Many figures are provided to point out the specific features on the screen and illustrate what your screen should look like after you complete important steps.

■ **Using Help.** Each lesson contains one or more Using Help activities in which you access the Microsoft Explorer Help feature to explore lesson topics in more depth.

■ **Self Check exercises.** To check your knowledge of the concepts presented in the lesson, a self-check exercise is provided at the end of each lesson. After completing the exercise, refer to Appendix D: Answers to Self Check to verify your understanding of the lesson material.

■ **On the Web.** At the end of each lesson, an On the Web section focuses on a specific feature of the World Wide Web. Many of the sites you will visit contain additional information about Web page design or the FrontPage program.

■ **Summary.** At the end of each lesson, a Summary reviews the major topics covered in the lesson. You can use the Summary as a study guide.

■ **Concepts Review.** At the end of each lesson are three types of questions: Matching, Completion, and Short-Answer questions. When you complete these exercises, you can verify that you have learned all the concepts and skills that have been covered in the lesson.

■ **Skills Review.** The Skills Review section provides simple hands-on exercises so you can practice each skill you learned in the lesson.

■ **Lesson Applications.** The Lesson Applications provide additional hands-on practice to apply your problem-solving skills and to refine your skills using FrontPage 2000.

■ **Projects.** The projects at the end of each lesson apply your skills creatively to a real-world situation. The Projects give you an opportunity to develop the critical-thinking skills you need in the workplace. In addition, the Project in Progress offers the opportunity for you to build on your work from lesson to lesson.

■ **Case Study.** The Case Study is a capstone activity that allows you to apply the various skills you have learned throughout the tutorial.

■ **Portfolio Builder, Command Summary, and Answers to Self Check.** These appendices provide a wealth of information. The Portfolio Builder gives an overview of portfolios and provides tips on creating your personal portfolio. The Command Summary reviews the mouse and keyboard techniques for completing Internet Explorer tasks. Answers to Self Check exercises found within each lesson are provided in Appendix D.

■ **Glossary and Index.** A Glossary and an Index appear at the back of the tutorial. Use the Glossary to look up terms that you don't understand and the Index to find specific information.

■ **Student Data Disk.** Attached to the inside back cover of this tutorial you will find a disk called the FrontPage 2000 Data Disk. This CD contains FrontPage 2000 files for you to use as you complete the hands-on activities and the end-of-lesson activities. You must copy the files from the FrontPage Data CD to a Zip disk, to a folder on your hard drive, or to a network drive. Instructions for copying these files are provided in the following section entitled "Copying Files from Your FrontPage Data CD."

MOUS CERTIFICATION PROGRAM

The Microsoft Office User Specialist (MOUS) program offers certification at two skill levels—"Core" and "Expert." FrontPage 2000 is approved courseware for the MOUS program that will aid you in fully understanding the skills required for the Microsoft FrontPage 2000 "Core" certification exam. Obtaining MOUS certification can be a valuable asset in job searches and workplace advancement. For more information about the Microsoft Office User Specialist program, visit www.mous.net.

Before beginning a course of study toward a specific certification, make sure to check on the availability of the exam and the location of your local testing center at www.mous.net. This text is correlated to the Core level certification exam objectives; however, the availability of the exam is solely determined by Microsoft and Microsoft's testing agent.

ABOUT PETER NORTON

Peter Norton is a pioneering software developer and an author. *Norton Utilities, AntiVirus*, and other utility programs are installed worldwide on millions of personal computers. His books have helped countless individuals understand computers from the inside out.

Glencoe teamed up with Peter Norton to help you better understand the role computers play in your life now and in the future. As you begin to work in your chosen profession, you may use this tutorial now and later as a reference book.

REVIEWERS

Many thanks are due to the following individuals who reviewed the manuscript and provided recommendations to improve this tutorial:

Pat Fox
Florida Metropolitan University
Orlando College—North
Orlando, Florida

Billy Hix
Motlow College
Tullahoma, Tennessee

CONTENTS

CONTENTS

CONTENTS

CONTENTS

COPYING FILES FROM YOUR FRONTPAGE DATA CD

CD-ROMs can hold hundreds of megabytes of data. As their name implies (Compact Disk-*Read-Only* Memory), you cannot modify the data they contain. You must copy the files from the FrontPage 2000 Data CD to a folder on a hard disk, network drive, or a Zip disk then remove the *read-only* attribute so you can work with them. Due to the large number of files and the storage space required, a hard disk, network drive, or a Zip disk is the recommended media on which you should store the data files and your solutions as you work through this tutorial. Using the following instructions, you should copy the files from your FrontPage 2000 Data CD into a folder named *FrontPage Student Data Disk* that you'll create on your destination drive. After the files are copied, it is a simple matter to remove the read-only attribute.

1. **Insert the FrontPage 2000 Data CD into the CD drive of your computer.**

2. **Click Start** ▯Start **, point to Programs, and click Windows Explorer.**

The Exploring window opens.

3. **Click the drive icon that represents your CD drive in the Folders panel of the Exploring window.**

The CD contains ten folders that now appear in the Contents panel, as shown in Figure 1.

4. **Click Select All on the Edit menu.**

The folders in the Contents panel appear highlighted.

5. **Click the Copy button** ▯Copy **.**

6. **Scroll up, if necessary, and click the appropriate drive icon (and folder, if necessary) where you want to store your FrontPage files.**

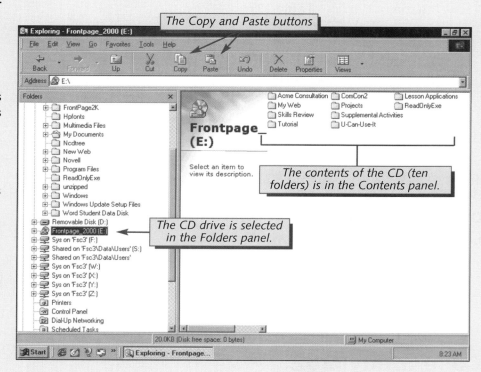

The Copy and Paste buttons

The contents of the CD (ten folders) is in the Contents panel.

The CD drive is selected in the Folders panel.

Figure 1 ◄
Contents of the FrontPage 2000
Data CD

If you are copying the FrontPage 2000 Data CD folders and files onto your hard drive or a network drive, navigate to the drive and folder where you want to store the files. If you are copying files to a Zip disk, insert a disk in your disk drive. Then create a folder for the FrontPage 2000 Data CD folders and files: Click the drive icon; click the folder name if necessary; click the file menu; then point to New and click Folder. Type FrontPage Student Data Disk as the folder name. Click this newly created folder in the Folders panel of the Exploring window, and go to step 7.

7. Click the **Paste button** ![Paste](.) .

A Copying box will appear on the screen to indicate the progress of the copying process. In a few moments all of the files will be copied to your *FrontPage Student Data Disk* folder.

To use and save changes to the files copied from the CD, you must remove the read-only attribute of the files. To simplify this process, a program has been provided for this purpose—it is located within the *ReadOnlyExe* folder within your new *FrontPage Student Data Disk* folder.

8. Double-click the *ReadOnlyExe* folder.

The folder opens revealing a file named *ReadOnly*.

9. Double-click the *ReadOnly* file.

A Browse for Folder window opens.

10. Double-click the drive containing your *FrontPage Student Data Disk* folder within the Browse for Folder window.

11. Click the *FrontPage Student Data Disk* folder to select it.

Your screen should look similar to Figure 2.

12. Click the **Select button** in the Browse for Folder window.

The Remove Read-Only Attribute dialog box appears indicating that the read-only attribute has been removed and your files are ready to be accessed by FrontPage 2000.

13. Click **OK**.

14. Right-click the *ReadOnly-Exe* folder in the Folders list, click ⌊Delete⌋, then click Yes in the Confirm Delete Folder dialog box.

You are now ready to begin the FrontPage 2000 tutorial!

Figure 2 ◀
Browse for Folder window
of *ReadOnly* file

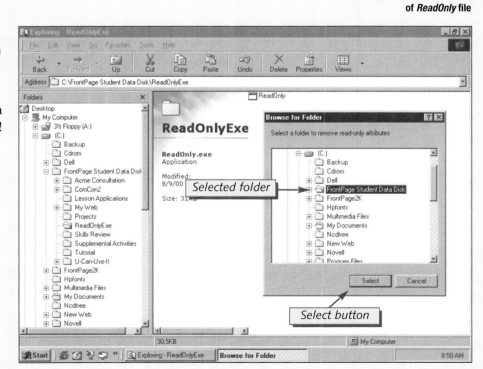

FrontPage 2000

FrontPage 2000 Basics

CONTENTS

OBJECTIVES

After you complete this lesson, you will be able to do the following:

■ Define a Web and its components.
■ Use your mouse to point, click, double-click, right-click, select, and drag.
■ Start FrontPage 2000.
■ Name the main features of the FrontPage window.
■ Understand the FrontPage menu bar and toolbars.
■ Open an existing Web in FrontPage 2000.
■ Use the Views bar to examine a Web in Page, Folders, Reports, Navigation, Hyperlinks, and Tasks views.
■ Switch between the Normal, HTML, and Preview tabs in the Page view.
■ Print the structure of a Web from Navigation view.
■ Create and delete a task in the Tasks view.
■ Mark a task as completed and view a task history.
■ Print a Web page including a custom footer.
■ Use Help to find features new to FrontPage 2000.
■ Close a Web and exit FrontPage 2000.
■ View a Web using your Web browser.

Microsoft FrontPage is a powerful Web site creation and management tool. The multiple views that FrontPage provides allow you to effectively design and update your Web site.

Lesson 1 provides you with the basic skills you need to view and print the contents of a Web site using FrontPage. You will learn how to open an existing Web, navigate through the Web's pages, assign tasks, close a Web, and quit the program. Also, you will become familiar with the online Help system, a feature that will teach you more about FrontPage and that will assist you with problem solving.

FrontPage

INTRODUCING MICROSOFT FRONTPAGE

FrontPage 2000 is Microsoft's Web publishing software program. Using FrontPage you can create, collaborate, modify, publish, and otherwise manage Web sites.

If you have ever *surfed* the Web, you have first-hand experience viewing and navigating over the Internet. The **Internet** is a worldwide network of computers that allows users to share information in the form of text, graphics, images, video, and audio. A **network** is a collection of computers that permits the transfer of data and programs between users. In a sense, the Internet is a *super network*.

The **World Wide Web** is a part of the Internet that connects specially formatted documents. These documents are called **Web pages** and are stored in a special language known as **Hypertext Markup Language (HTML)**. When you use a **Web browser**, such as Internet Explorer or Netscape Navigator, you are using a program that reads these HTML documents. The browser displays text and graphics in a format that is easy to view and read.

With FrontPage 2000 you create and maintain a **Web**—a group of Web pages—without having to learn the complexities of HTML. These Webs can range from a few pages that share an individual's hobby or interests to huge sites where businesses display product catalogs, take online orders, provide technical support, and more.

USING THE MOUSE

Microsoft FrontPage is just one of many programs, or **applications**, that requires **operating system** software such as Windows 95 or Windows 98. Soon after you turn on your computer, several **icons** or pictures appear. The icons represent items on a disk, and the screen is the **desktop.** The **taskbar**, the bar across the bottom of the desktop, contains **buttons** that you can click to perform various tasks. Click the Start button 🔲Start to show the Start menu. On the Start menu, you can click to open any program installed on your computer, including Microsoft FrontPage.

You will use the **mouse** extensively in Microsoft FrontPage. The mouse is the key to the graphical user interface because it lets you choose and manipulate on-screen objects without having to type on the keyboard. Although the mouse is the most popular pointing device, you may also use several other pointing devices. **Trackballs** have buttons like the mouse, but instead of moving the mouse over the desktop, you spin a large ball. Laptops often employ either a small **joystick** in the middle of the keyboard or a **touch-sensitive pad** below the keyboard. Each of these devices, however, lets you point to items on the screen and click buttons to perform actions on those items.

Your mouse probably has two or three buttons. Whenever the directions in this tutorial say *click*, use the left mouse button. If the directions say *right-click* or *click the right mouse button*, use the right mouse button.

You can perform several actions with the mouse:

■ If you roll your mouse slowly in a wide circle over different parts of your screen, you'll notice a symbol will appear that looks like an arrow ⌐. This symbol is called the *mouse pointer,* or more simply, the *pointer*. Moving the mouse to position the pointer on the screen is called *pointing*. Table 1.1 shows several shapes you may notice as you point to objects on the screen.

TABLE 1.1	COMMON POINTER SHAPES
Pointer Shape	**Description**
⌐	Normal Select (arrow pointer)
+	Fill Handle Select (crosshair pointer)
⌐?	Help Select (What's This? pointer)
⌐⌛	Working in Background
⌛	Busy
+	Precision Select (drawing)
I	Text Select (editing)
⊘	Unavailable
↕	Vertical Resize
↔	Horizontal Resize
↖	Diagonal Resize 1
↙	Diagonal Resize 2
✥	Move Object
⟨ᵐ⟩	Hyperlink Select

■ To *click* the mouse, point to an object and quickly press and release the left mouse button.

■ To work with an object on the screen, you must usually *select* (or *choose*) the item by clicking the object—pressing and quickly releasing the mouse button.

■ To *double-click*, point to an object and click the left mouse button twice in rapid succession without moving the pointer.

■ To *right-click*, point to an object, press the right mouse button, and then quickly release it.

■ To *drag* (or *drag-and-drop*), point to an object you want to move, press and hold the left mouse button, move the mouse to drag the object to a new location, and then release the mouse button.

STARTING MICROSOFT FRONTPAGE

Before you can start Microsoft FrontPage, both FrontPage 2000 and Windows 95, 98, or 2000 must be installed on the computer you are using. The figures in this tutorial use Windows 98; if you are using a different version of Windows, the information on your screen may vary slightly.

Warning Be sure to use the FrontPage Data CD (located on the inside back cover of this tutorial) to create the Student Data Disk for this tutorial. Refer to the section in the front of this book entitled Copying Files From Your FrontPage Data CD for instructions, or ask your instructor.

Launching FrontPage

1. Click the Start button and point to Programs.

2. Click Microsoft FrontPage.

Launching Microsoft FrontPage

In this activity, you will launch FrontPage 2000 using the Start menu and recognize the program's opening window components.

1. Turn on your computer.

Note If you are prompted for a user name and/or password, enter the information at this time. If you do not know your user name and/or password, ask your instructor for help.

The Windows operating system boots the computer. Your screen should resemble Figure 1.1. If the Welcome to Windows screen appears, click its Close button ☒ to close the window.

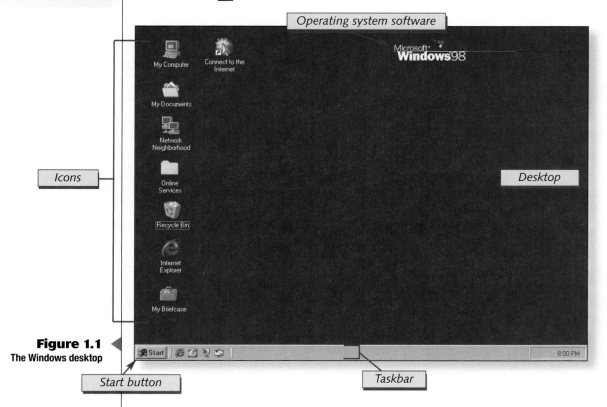

Figure 1.1
The Windows desktop

Double-click the title bar to maximize a window.

Windows allows users to customize the appearance of the desktop; that is, to choose the specific background colors and icons they wish to see. Due to these selections, your desktop may appear slightly different than Figure 1.1.

2. Click the Start button 🏁Start on the Windows taskbar, point to Programs, and click Microsoft FrontPage.

The empty Microsoft FrontPage window appears on the desktop as shown in Figure 1.2.

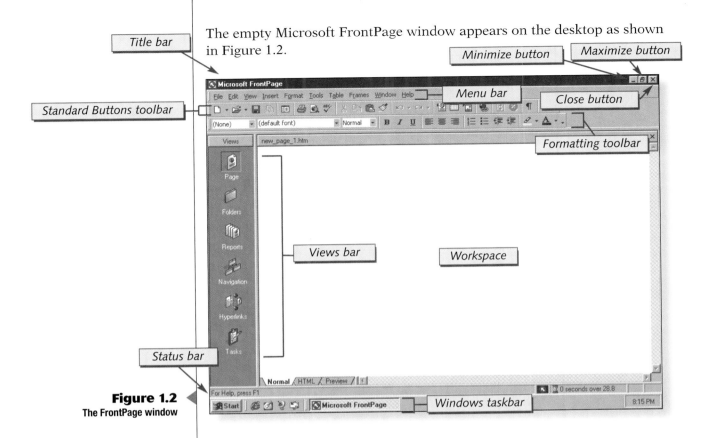

Figure 1.2
The FrontPage window

3. Click the **Maximize button** ☐ if the window is not maximized.

4. If you don't see the Standard buttons toolbar or Formatting toolbar as shown in Figure 1.2, click **View**, point to **Toolbars**, and click to check the missing toolbar.

5. If you see any extra toolbars, click **View**, point to **Toolbars**, and click to uncheck the extra toolbar to remove it from the screen.

EXPLORING THE FRONTPAGE WINDOW

In the next few activities, you will learn how to identify and use the components of the FrontPage window. As you can see in Figure 1.2, FrontPage contains many standard Windows elements, including a title bar, a menu bar, and toolbars. These items should seem familiar to you if you have used other Windows application programs.

Note *When this tutorial mentions a toolbar button, a picture of the button is displayed within the text. For example, when a step instructs you to click the Start button*  *, the button will be illustrated as shown here.*

Understanding the Menu Bar

As shown in Figure 1.2, the FrontPage *menu bar* appears below the title bar. The menu bar displays some of the menu names found in most Windows applications, such as File, Edit, and Help. FrontPage also includes menus and commands specific to the creation of Web pages, such as the Frames menu or the Open Web command on the File menu.

The menus list the commands available in FrontPage. You can display the list in several different ways. The most common way is to click the menu name to display the commands. If you prefer to use the keyboard, you can press [Alt] on your keyboard and then press the underlined letter in the menu name to display that menu. For example, to display the File menu, you would press [Alt] and then the letter F ([Alt] + F).

When you click a menu in the FrontPage window, the *short menu*, a list of the most commonly used commands, appears. If you keep your pointer on the menu for a few seconds or if you click the double arrow at the bottom of the menu, an *expanded menu* appears. This expanded menu shows all of the commands available on the menu; the expanded menu includes commands that are used less frequently as well as the common commands. Figure 1.3 shows both versions of FrontPage's Insert menu—as a short menu and as an expanded menu.

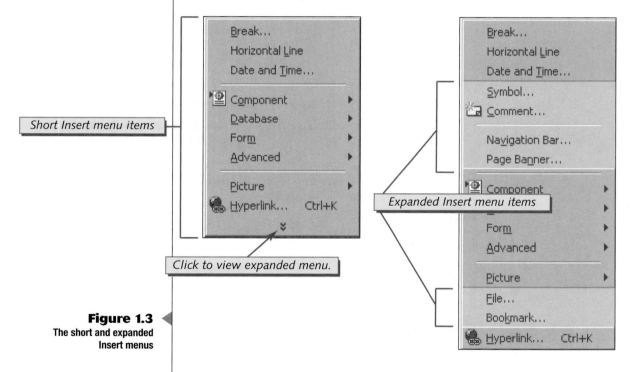

Short Insert menu items

Click to view expanded menu.

Expanded Insert menu items

Figure 1.3
The short and expanded
Insert menus

As you can see in Figure 1.3, nine commands appear on the initial Insert menu. These nine commands are considered to be the commands that users issue most often from this menu. The expanded menu shows six additional commands that are not used as frequently. (These six additional commands can be identified by their lighter gray background.) After you issue one of the additional commands shown on the expanded menu, that command is added to the short menu. This *adaptive menu* feature allows menus to be customized for each user.

After you display a menu, you can choose a command using either the mouse or the keyboard. To choose a command using the mouse, click the command you want. To choose a command using the keyboard, press the underlined letter of the command. For example to choose the Open command from the File menu, press the letter O while the File menu is displayed.

 *Although these lessons emphasize the mouse method for performing most commands, the Command Summary Appendix lists the keyboard actions for the commands.*

Table 1.2 provides a brief description of the menus available on the FrontPage menu bar.

TABLE 1.2	THE FRONTPAGE MENU BAR
Menu	**Contains Commands that Let You . . .**
File	Control your Web page files by opening, previewing, saving, publishing, and printing them.
Edit	Rearrange the elements within your Web page by copying, moving, and deleting them.
View	Change the appearance of your screen display.
Insert	Insert various elements into your Web page, such as pictures.
Format	Change the appearance of the text within your Web page or add background graphics.
Tools	Customize toolbars and commands and set page options.
Table	Draw, insert, and format a table.
Frames	Edit your Web pages that are organized in Frames. (A Frames page allows you to partition the browser window to display multiple pages on screen at the same time.)
Window	View Web pages individually in separate windows.
Help	Access FrontPage's online Help system and the Microsoft Office on the Web for assistance and support.

Working with Toolbars

Below the menu bar is the Standard buttons toolbar, as shown in Figure 1.2 on page 7. A *toolbar* contains buttons for many of the most frequently used commands, such as opening or printing a file. Although you can access these commands by clicking the command on one of the menus, using the buttons on the toolbar as a shortcut is often more convenient. You can quickly identify any command button by pointing to the button and reading the short description or *ScreenTip* that appears under the pointer. Table 1.3 provides a description of actions available from the Standard buttons toolbar.

TABLE 1.3	THE FRONTPAGE STANDARD BUTTONS TOOLBAR	

Button	Name	Action
	New Page (File menu)	Creates a new Web page.
	Open (File menu)	Opens a Web page.
	Save (File menu)	Saves the current page.
	Publish Web (File menu)	Publishes files in the current Web.
	Folder List (View menu)	Displays or hides the Folder List.
	Print (File menu)	Prints the current page or View.
	Preview in Browser (File menu)	Displays the current page within a Web browser, such as Microsoft Internet Explorer.
	Spelling (Tools menu)	Checks spelling on the current page or all pages in an open Web.
	Cut (Edit menu)	Removes items from the current page to the Clipboard from where they can be pasted into another location.
	Copy (Edit menu)	Copies selected items from the current page.
	Paste (Edit menu)	Completes a Cut or Copy action by inserting the contents of the Clipboard.
	Format Painter	Copies formatting and applies it to selection.
	Undo	Reverses your last command or text entry.
	Redo	Reverses the action of Undo.
	Insert Component (Insert menu)	Inserts your selection (such as a spreadsheet or picture) from a drop-down menu.
	Insert Table (Table menu)	Inserts a new table into your current page.
	Insert Picture From File (Insert menu)	Inserts a picture into your current page.
	Hyperlink (Insert menu)	Inserts hyperlink at the location you select.
	Refresh (View menu)	Refreshes the current page or view.
	Stop	Stops loading a page.
	Show All (Format menu)	Shows or hides page elements.
	Microsoft FrontPage Help (Help menu)	Provides an Answer Wizard, Contents, and Index to answer your questions about Microsoft FrontPage.
	More Buttons	Allows you to customize the toolbar by adding additional buttons or removing existing buttons. Also lets you reset the toolbar to display default buttons.

The Formatting toolbar appears directly below the Standard buttons toolbar. This toolbar contains buttons that change the appearance of your Web page. For instance, using the Formatting toolbar, you can modify the font, text size, text style, alignment, color, and other features of your Web page. You will learn more about formatting your Web page in later lessons.

 *If your Standard buttons toolbar and Formatting toolbar share one row below the menu bar, you can display them as two separate toolbars by clicking Customize on the Tools menu. On the Options tab, deselect the* Standard and Formatting toolbars share one row *option.*

OPENING A FRONTPAGE WEB

You can view the contents of an existing Web by opening it in FrontPage 2000. Several FrontPage features can only be seen when you are actually working on a Web. Webs can be stored on disks or on network drives. To be accessible over the Internet, Webs are typically stored on network drives.

Opening a Web

In this activity, you will open a Web from your Student Data Disk.

1. Click the drop-down arrow on the Open toolbar button .

A menu appears with two options: Open and Open Web.

2. Click Open Web 📄.

The Open Web dialog box appears.

3. Click the drop-down arrow beside the *Look in* text box.

4. Click the drive that contains your Student Data Disk.

5. Double-click the *FrontPage Student Data Disk* folder.

6. Double-click the *U-Can-Use-It* Web. Your screen should look similar to Figure 1.4.

 *For a detailed illustration of the FrontPage toolbars, see Appendix C: Toolbar Summary.*

Figure 1.4
The Open Web dialog box

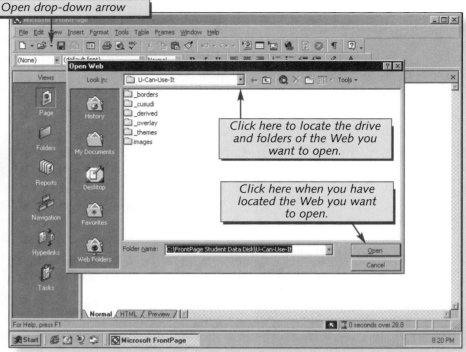

Open drop-down arrow

Click here to locate the drive and folders of the Web you want to open.

Click here when you have located the Web you want to open.

Opening a Web

1. Click the drop-down arrow on the Open tool-bar button, and click Open Web.

2. Locate the folder containing the Web within the Open Web dialog box.

3. Click the folder to highlight it, then click Open.

4. If necessary, double-click the desired page in the Folder List to make it appear within Page view.

7. Click **Open**.

8. Click the **Page view icon** 🗐, if necessary.

The Web opens. The *U-Can-Use-It* company Web should appear similar to Figure 1.5.

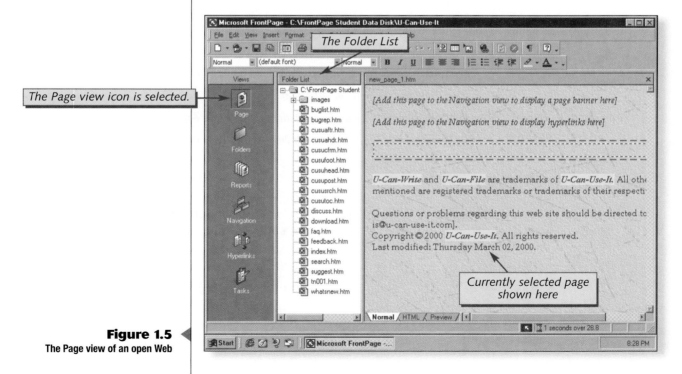

The Folder List

The Page view icon is selected.

Currently selected page shown here

Figure 1.5
The Page view of an open Web

USING WEB VIEWS

Using the **Views bar** on the left side of the FrontPage window, you can view and manage a Web in a number of ways. The Views bar contains six icons. Table 1.4 shows the purpose of each of the icons in the Views bar.

TABLE 1.4	THE VIEWS BAR
Icon	**Purpose**
Page	Used to create and edit Web pages.
Folders	Shows how the content of the Web is organized, similar to Windows Explorer.
Reports	Lets you analyze and troubleshoot Web components.
Navigation	Lets you control the sequence in which pages are displayed in the Web.
Hyperlinks	Checks the status of pointers in your Web to other pages and files.
Tasks	Lets users plan and collaborate on the development of complex Webs.

The Page View

When you are designing and modifying the pages in your Web, you will most likely stay in the Page view. The other views are used for organizing, checking, and controlling the way these pages work within the Web.

Using the Page View

1. Open the Web.

2. Click the Page icon, if necessary, in the Views bar.

3. Double-click any file in the Folder List to view it.

Using the Page View

In this activity, you will examine the different tabs within the Page view.

1. **Click the Page view icon** 🔲 **then click the Normal tab, if necessary.**

To the right of the Views bar is the Folder List. Here you find the pages that make up the Web.

2. **Double-click *index.htm* in the Folder List.**

The index page appears in the editing window as in Figure 1.6.

You will learn more about the various objects—buttons, graphic images, text boxes, and so on—in later lessons. There are three tabs at the bottom of the editing window. By default, the Normal tab is selected. You will most often be within this tab when you enter text and edit objects on a page. The tabs change the appearance of the Web page in the editing window.

3. **Click the HTML tab.**

The editing window now shows the HTML code that underlies the Web page. Experienced Web designers often write all or part of a Web page directly in HTML.

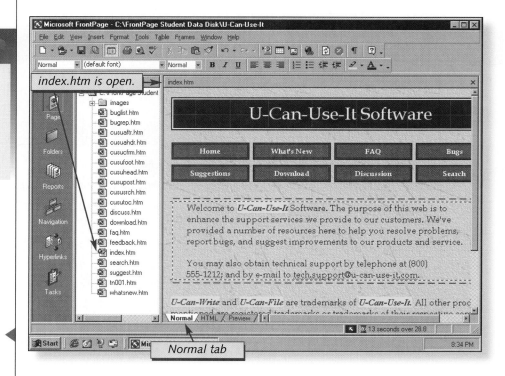

index.htm is open.

Normal tab

Figure 1.6
The Normal tab of the Page view

HANDS On

4. Click the Preview tab.

In the Preview tab, the editing window looks and works much like it will when opened in a Web browser.

5. Click the What's New button within the Web page.

This button brings you to another page within the Web.

6. Click the Normal tab.

The page in the Normal tab appears different than it does in the Preview tab. Notice that in the Normal tab, borders surround the elements on the page.

The Folders View

When in the Folders view, you see details of the contents of your Web. The Folder List shows only folders while the editing window displays the file names, titles, sizes, types, dates, authors, and comments of each of the pages in the Web. Clicking the column headings allows you to sort the pages by category.

Using the Folders View

In this activity, you will see an open Web as it appears in Folders View.

1. Click the Folders icon ▣ **in the Views bar.**

A list of the *U-Can-Use-It* Web folders and files appears. The Folder List shows only folders, while the Web page information appears to the right in columns.

Figure 1.7
The Reports view of a Web

2. Click the Size column header.

The Web pages are sorted with the smallest pages first.

3. Click the Size column header again.

This time the pages appear with the largest pages first.

4. Click the Name column header.

The pages revert to an alphabetic listing.

5. Double-click the *index.htm* Web page.

The page reappears in Page view.

The Reports View

You use the Reports view when you want to check the status and summarize or analyze the pages in your Web. When you click the Reports icon in the Views bar, a toolbar appears in the middle of the screen. From this toolbar you select the kind of information you wish to see.

Using the Reports View

In this activity, you will analyze the contents of a Web using the Reports View in the *U-Can-Use-It* Web.

1. Click the Reports icon 📇 in the Views bar.

The editing window shows a summary of the contents of the Web and the Reporting toolbar floats in the middle of the screen, as shown in Figure 1.7.

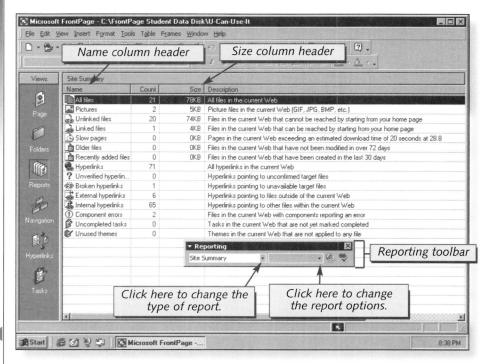

2. Click the **drop-down arrow** in the Reporting toolbar, if necessary, and click **Site Summary** from the list of report options.

3. Move the Reporting toolbar to the bottom of the screen by dragging its title bar.

The default report is called the Site Summary. This report groups the files and objects by 15 categories. From left to right, each category includes a name; the number of objects that belong in the category; the total size of those objects; and a description of what the category means. For example, in Figure 1.7 you can see that there are 21 files (the first line of the report) and that there are two picture files (the second line of the report).

4. Click the **drop-down arrow** in the Reporting toolbar.

A list of report options appears.

5. Click **Slow Pages**.

A download time selection box is activated on the right side of the Reporting toolbar. **Download time** is the amount of time it takes for information to get to your computer from another computer. No pages should take longer than 30 seconds to download when users visit this Web.

6. Click the **drop-down arrow** beside the download time selection box.

A list of download time selections appears. From this list you can define the number of seconds that specifies a slowly loading page.

7. Click **5 seconds**.

Your report shows that three files will take more than five seconds to download. The actual time to download (six seconds for each of the files) appears in the third column of the report.

The download times in the report are based on a 28.8 speed modem—relatively slow by today's standards. You can change the modem speed by clicking the Tools menu, clicking Options, and changing the setting in the Reports View tab next to Assume connection speed of.

8. Double-click the *faq.htm* file.

The *faq.htm* page appears in Page view.

The Navigation View

The Navigation view shows the navigation structure of your Web. The **Web structure** shows the way pages relate to each other in the Web. Table 1.5 describes the types of pages found in a Web structure.

TABLE 1.5	PAGE TYPES IN A WEB STRUCTURE

Page Type	Description
Home or Start page	The first page in a navigation structure, usually given the name *index.htm* or *default.htm*.
Top-level page	The same level as the home page.
Parent page	A page that has a child page below it.
Parent-level pages	The parent page plus pages connected to the parent page on the same level.
Child page	A page directly connected to a parent page above it.
Child-level page	A page directly below another page.
Same-level pages	Pages that are on the same level in the structure and have the same parent page.

The navigation structure is important because it determines the way in which users will move through your Web—generally from parent page to child page and back again or horizontally along the same level.

The Navigation view is useful for more than just the display of the structure. You can use this view to drag pages from the Folder List into the structure, change the relationship between pages, add new pages to the Web, or remove pages from the Web.

Viewing and Printing the Web Structure

In this activity, you will use the Navigation view to display and print the structure of the *U-Can-Use-It* Web.

1. Click the Navigation icon 📁 **in the Views bar.**

The navigation structure of the *U-Can-Use-It* Web appears along with the Navigation toolbar.

2. Move the Navigation toolbar to the bottom of the screen by dragging its title bar.

Your screen should look like Figure 1.8. Note that part of the navigation structure is not visible at the right side of the screen.

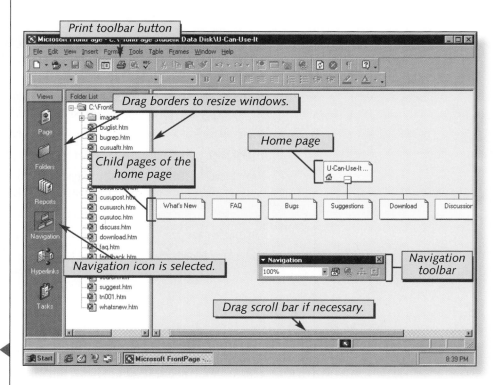

Figure 1.8
The Navigation structure of a Web

Viewing and Printing the Web Structure

1. Open the Web.

2. Click the Navigation icon in the Views bar.

3. Make sure your printer is on and ready.

4. Click the Print button.

3. Drag the horizontal scroll bar to view the entire navigation structure.

You can now see the graphics that extend beyond the right side of the screen.

 *The FrontPage screen is divided into three segments by two vertical borders, as shown in Figure 1.8. In order to resize a window, you can drag these borders to the left or right.*

In this simple structure, there is one parent page (the *U-Can-Use-It* page) identified by the home page icon 🏠 . Each of the other pages is a child page; that is, they are directly below and connected to the home page.

Printing from the Navigation view enables you to discuss modifications to the Web off-line.

 *Make sure the printer connected to your computer is turned on and ready to print. Check with your instructor or lab assistant for further instructions on printing procedures.*

4. Click the **Print toolbar button** 🖶 .

The file is sent to the printer. Shortly you should have a printout of the navigation structure of the *U-Can-Use-It* Web.

The Hyperlinks View

Text or pictures can be hyperlinks. ***Hyperlinks*** are connections that move you to another location when you click them. A hyperlink may move you to another page within the Web, to another page within a different Web, to a new location on the same page, to an e-mail address, a file, or even to another program. When users *surf the Web* they are usually clicking on hyperlinks to jump from one site to another.

Hyperlinks that cause a jump to another page within the same Web are called **internal hyperlinks** because the jump stays within the current Web. **External hyperlinks** cause jumps to other Webs outside the current Web.

You can detect text hyperlinks because they are usually underlined, in a different color, or formatted to appear different than the surrounding text. Objects such as a picture or art graphic can also be hyperlinks. When you move the mouse pointer over a picture hyperlink, the pointer changes shape, usually to the Hyperlink Select pointer.

Using the Hyperlinks View

In this activity, you will use the Hyperlinks view to see the hyperlinks within Web pages in the *U-Can-Use-It* Web.

1. Click the Hyperlinks icon in the Views bar.

The selected page is displayed along with the pages to which it links and which link to it.

2. Click *download.htm* in the Folder List.

The page is displayed as shown in Figure 1.9. You can see that the page *whatsnew.htm* has an arrow leading to the *download.htm* page, indicating that it has a hyperlink to that page. Likewise, you can see that *download.htm* contains two hyperlinks—one to *index.htm* (the home page) and one to a totally different site. The icon indicates an internal hyperlink, while the icon indicates an external hyperlink.

Using the Hyperlinks View

1. Open the Web.

2. Click the Hyperlinks icon in the Views bar.

3. Click the file in the Folder List that you wish to view.

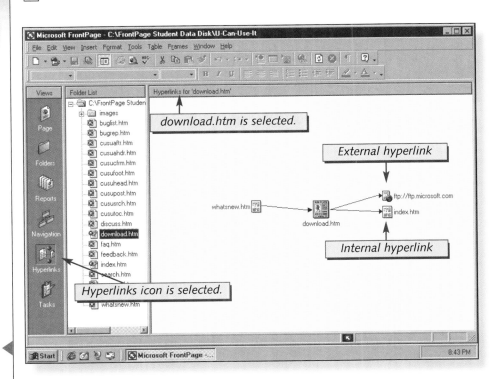

Figure 1.9
The Hyperlinks view of a Web page

The Tasks View

When designing and maintaining a Web, it helps to set up a to-do list, especially when the Web is complex and is being worked on by a team of developers. By defining *tasks* in the FrontPage Tasks view, you record what needs to be done, what pages or objects should be created or modified, how critical the work is, and who is supposed to do it. Within FrontPage, each task you create is assigned to a specific file or page. Within Tasks view, a Start Task button enables you to jump directly to the relevant page so you can begin work. You can define a new task from any view. Once defined, you can see the task details using the Tasks view.

Creating a New Task

In this activity, you will create new tasks that could be used to update a Web. Later, you will delete the tasks.

1. Click the Tasks icon [icon] **in the Views bar.**

A blank screen appears except for a message informing you that there are no tasks in the Web.

2. Click the Reports icon [icon] **in the Views bar.**

3. Click the Reporting toolbar drop-down arrow and click All Files.

A list of all files in the Web appears in the workspace.

4. Right-click the file named *download.htm* in the Name column.

A shortcut menu opens listing the most frequently used options.

5. Click Add Task.

The New Task dialog box is displayed, as shown in Figure 1.10.

Adding a Task to a Page

1. Click the Reports icon in the Views bar.

2. If necessary, choose All Files in the Reporting toolbar.

3. Right-click the page for which you want a new task in the list of files.

4. Click Add Task in the shortcut menu.

5. Type a task name, click a priority, type a description, then click OK.

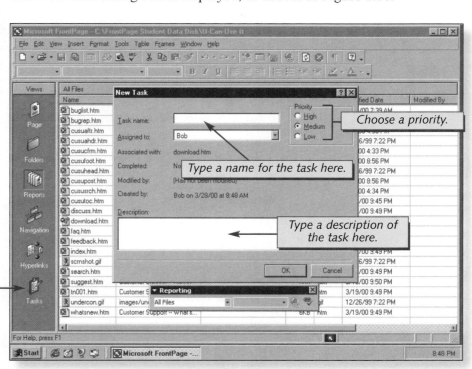

Tasks icon is selected.

Figure 1.10
The New Task dialog box

There are many software tools for building and enhancing a Web site. Check out *www.zdnet.com* for information regarding these tools. Click the <u>Reviews</u> link then the <u>Web Authoring</u> link under the Software heading.

6. Type Modify the page **in the *Task name* text box.**

7. **Click the High control button in the Priority section.**

8. **Click an insertion point in the *Description* text box and type** Add new customer support features.

9. **Click OK.**

10. **Right-click the file named *index.htm*.**

11. **Click Add Task in the shortcut menu.**

The New Task dialog box appears.

12. **Type** Troubleshoot **in the *Task name* text box. Type** Test all hyperlinks **under *Description*.**

13. **Leave the Priority option as medium and click OK.**

14. **Click the Tasks icon 🗒 in the Views bar.**

Your tasks appear in the Tasks window. The status of both tasks is Not Started.

Sorting, Modifying, and Deleting Tasks

Tasks can be modified, started, sorted, completed, or removed using the Tasks view. Double-clicking the column headings while in the Tasks view rearranges the tasks, just as files were sorted when in the Folders view. For example, you can group tasks by status, task, priority, or assigned person. Similarly, you could rearrange the tasks by their modification date.

From the Tasks view you can also begin to work on a designated task. Once you have finished the task, right-clicking the task provides an option to mark the task as complete. After you have marked tasks as complete, you can view your task history.

Starting and Deleting a Task

In this activity, you will see how to start to work on a task and how to mark the task as completed. You will view a task history and delete a task from the Tasks view in the *U-Can-Use-It* Web.

1. **Click the Tasks icon 🗒 in the Views bar, if necessary.**

Your two tasks named Modify the Page and Troubleshoot appear in the Tasks view.

2. **Double-click the Modify the Page task.**

The Task Details dialog box opens. Using this dialog box, you can move directly to the page to begin working on your task.

3. **Click the Start Task button Start Task .**

The Page view of the *download.htm* page appears. As you will learn in later lessons, from here you can make the necessary modifications to the page. When your task is finished, you can mark your task status as completed.

4. **Click the Tasks icon 🗒 in the Views bar.**

5. **Right-click anywhere on the task named Modify the Page.**

Starting a Task

1. Click the Tasks icon.

2. Double-click the task.

3. Click the Start Task button in the Task Details dialog box to jump to the relevant page.

Deleting a Task

1. Click the Tasks icon.

2. Right-click the task.

3. Click Delete in the shortcut menu, then click Yes.

When you click the Print toolbar icon, your Web page is sent immediately to the printer. However, if you click Print from the File menu you can change options, such as the number of copies, before the page is printed.

A shortcut menu appears.

6. Click **Mark as Completed** on the shortcut menu.

The task status changes from Not Started to Completed.

7. Click the **Refresh toolbar button** 🔁.

The task named Modify the Page disappears from the task list since by default the Tasks view only lists current tasks.

8. Right-click on a blank area of the Tasks window.

A shortcut menu appears.

9. Click **Show Task History** in the shortcut menu.

The completed task Modify the Page again appears in the task list.

10. Right-click **Modify the Page** and click **Delete** in the shortcut menu.

A Confirm Delete dialog box appears asking you to confirm your intention to remove the task.

11. Click **Yes**.

The task is deleted from the Tasks view. The task named Troubleshoot remains within the Tasks view.

PRINTING WEB PAGES

You can print any of the views in your FrontPage 2000 Web. Most often, however, you will want to print the actual pages from Page view within the Web. In addition to the text and graphics that comprise Web pages, FrontPage lets you place **headers** and **footers** on the top and bottom of each printed page. A header is text that appears at the top of every page of a document; a footer contains text that appears at the bottom of every page.

There is a difference in the use of the word *page* in reference to a printed document and a Web page. A Web page fills the screen, though you may need to scroll to see the entire page. However, when you print a Web page, the contents may fill more than one piece of paper. Thus a single Web page may result in more than one printed page.

You use headers and footers to identify and number printouts. Typical headers include the name or description of the document. Usually the footer contains a page number. There are no restrictions on what data may appear as a header or a footer. FrontPage 2000 defaults to display the title of the page on the header and the page number on the footer.

Before sending your output to the printer, click Print Preview. Print Preview lets you examine what your Web page will look like before you print. If your Web page does not look right, you can then make changes before wasting paper.

Printing a Web Page

In this activity, you will display and print one Web page from an open Web. Before printing, you will add your name to the footer.

1. Click the **Page view icon** [P] in the Views bar, then double-click *index.htm* in the Folder List to open it in Page view, if necessary.

2. Click **Page Setup** on the File menu.

The Print Page Setup dialog box opens, as shown in Figure 1.11.

Figure 1.11
The Print Page Setup dialog box

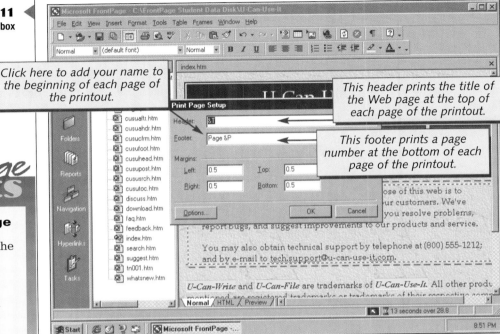

Printing a Web Page

1. Click Page Setup on the File menu.

2. Make changes to the header or footer, then click OK.

3. Make sure your printer is turned on and ready.

4. Click Print Preview on the File menu.

5. Click the Print button in the Print Preview window.

6. Choose the number of copies in the Print dialog box.

7. Click OK.

3. Click an insertion point in front of the *P* in *Page* in the *Footer* text box.

The insertion point flashes at the beginning of the text box.

4. Type your name followed by 3 spaces [Spacebar].

5. Click **OK**.

6. Click **Print Preview** on the File menu.

The page appears exactly as it will print. Note that the footer contains your name. Your name will appear at the bottom of the printed page followed by the page number.

7. Click the **Print button** [Print...] on the Print Preview screen.

The Print dialog box appears. In this dialog box you can select a printer (if you have multiple printers available), change the properties of the printer, choose the range of pages you want to print, and choose the number of copies to print. By default, you will print one copy of the open Web page.

8. Click **OK**.

The keyboard shortcut [Ctrl] + P is a quick way to open the Print dialog box.

Within a few moments, you should be able to retrieve the printout of *index.htm*.

Note   *Make sure your printer is turned on and ready.*

The FrontPage 2000 Help System

In this activity, you will access the Help window for information on features new to FrontPage 2000.

1. Click the Microsoft FrontPage Help button 🛈 on the Standard buttons toolbar.

The Microsoft FrontPage Help window appears.

2. Click the Contents tab, if necessary.

The Microsoft FrontPage Help window displays, as shown in Figure 1.12.

3. Click the plus sign (+) beside the What's New book icon to see the Help pages it contains.

The plus sign turns to a minus sign (-), and the list expands to display a series of Help topics.

4. Click the What's new in Microsoft FrontPage 2000 help page.

5. Click the graphic on the right pane to see the new features.

Figure 1.12
The FrontPage 2000 Help window

A window appears with a list of topics.

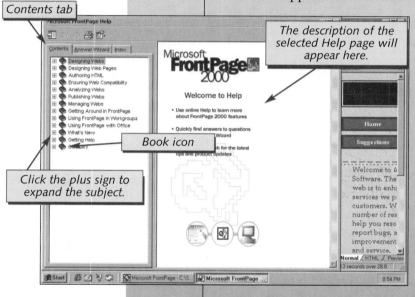

6. Click Getting help on the left side of the window.

The graphic changes to display two new ways to find assistance.

7. Click the Close button ☒ in the Getting help window.

8. Click the plus sign (+) beside the Getting Help book icon to see the Help pages it contains.

The list expands to display additional Help topics.

9. Click Get help about specific commands, buttons, and dialog boxes. Read about how you can find help when working within a dialog box.

10. Click the Close button ☒ in the Help window.

EXITING FRONTPAGE

Before you leave your computer, you should close any open Webs and exit FrontPage 2000. If you have made any changes to an open Web, you will be asked or *prompted* as to whether you want to save your changes. Before you close your Web page, it is also a good idea to check the status of tasks that may be pending within Tasks view.

Closing and Exiting FrontPage

1. Update the status of any current tasks in Tasks view.

2. Click Close Web on the File menu.

3. Click Yes or No if prompted to save changes to each page.

4. Click Exit on the File menu to close FrontPage.

Vermeer Technologies originally developed FrontPage. In 1995 Microsoft Corporation purchased the software. FrontPage 2000 is the third major revision of the program by Microsoft.

Closing a Web and Exiting FrontPage

In this activity, you will close the *U-Can-Use-It* Web and exit the FrontPage program. You also will learn how to save pages in the Web.

1. Click the **Page view icon** 🗐 and double-click *index.htm* in the Folder List, if necessary.

2. Click the **Tasks view icon** 🗐 to check the status of your tasks.

Your task named Troubleshoot appears in the Tasks window. This task is no longer necessary.

3. Position your pointer over the task and right-click.

The shortcut menu appears. It provides the option of editing the task, starting the task, marking the task as completed, or deleting the task.

4. Click **Delete** on the shortcut menu.

The Confirm Delete dialog box appears.

5. Click **Yes**.

The task is deleted.

6. Click the **Page icon** 🗐 in the Views bar to return *index.htm* to Page view.

7. Click an insertion point before the word *Welcome* in the first paragraph, and type Thank you for visiting our site.

8. Click **Close** on the File menu.

A dialog box appears asking if you want to save the changes you just made to the file.

9. Click **No**. (Of course, you would typically choose to save significant changes to your file.)

The Close command on the File menu only closes the current Web page, not the entire Web. Even though the page *index.htm* is now closed, the *U-Can-Use-It* Web is still open, as you can see by the list of pages in the Folder List. In the Folder List, you can still double-click on any file to view it in Page view.

10. Click **Close Web** on the File menu.

Now the entire *U-Can-Use-It* Web is closed.

11. Click **Exit** on the File menu to close FrontPage.

Test your knowledge by answering the following questions. See Appendix D to check your answers.

T F 1. The Page view and Print Preview look exactly the same.

T F 2. Every Web page has underlying HTML code.

T F 3. A Web page is a part of a Web.

T F 4. Internal hyperlinks cause jumps within the Web.

T F 5. The task list can be rearranged by clicking on a column heading.

ON*the*WEB

VIEWING A WEB WITH A BROWSER

Web pages created in FrontPage are designed to be viewed by a Web browser. The two most popular browsers are Internet Explorer and Netscape Navigator. New, improved versions of these browsers are distributed almost annually. To reach the widest audience, Web developers must ensure that their Web sites can be viewed by either browser—ideally, in any of the versions commonly in use.

A Web browser gives you many ways to open Webs. You can enter the Web address or **Uniform Resource Locator (URL)** in the Address toolbar; use the Open command on the File menu; or click on a hyperlink. In this activity, you will open a Web page in your browser through the File menu.

 *The rest of this activity assumes you are using Internet Explorer as your Web browser. If you are using Netscape Navigator or a different browser, the steps will be slightly different.*

1. Click the **Start button** 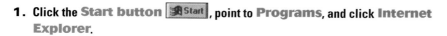, point to **Programs**, and click **Internet Explorer**.

The browser launches. In most cases, you are automatically connected to the Internet and, within a few moments, you should see your start or home page.

 *If you are not sure how to connect to the Internet or you do not know your user name and password, ask your instructor for assistance.*

2. If necessary, click the **Maximize button** 🗖.

3. Click **Open** on the File menu.

The Open dialog box appears.

4. Click **Browse**.

Another dialog box lets you select the directory and page you want to open.

5. Click the **Look in drop-down arrow** and click the drive that holds your Student Data Disk.

6. Double-click the *FrontPage Student Data Disk* folder.

The data disk folders appear.

7. Double-click the *U-Can-Use-It* folder.

The *U-Can-Use-It* folders and Web pages appear.

8. Double-click the *index.htm* page.

The Open dialog box appears containing the file you selected.

9. Click **OK**.

ON*the*WEB

Figure 1.13 shows the familiar *U-Can-Use-It* Web home page. You are now viewing *U-Can-Use-It* within a Web browser just as other Internet users would view it.

Note   *The appearance of your browser may differ slightly from Figure 1.13 depending upon what version of Internet Explorer you are using.*

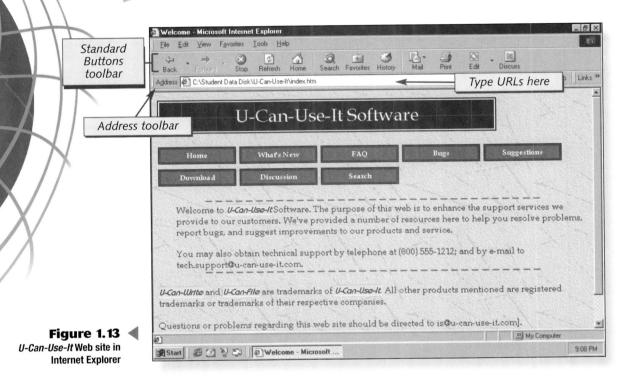

Standard Buttons toolbar

Address toolbar

Type URLs here

Figure 1.13 ◄
U-Can-Use-It Web site in Internet Explorer

Note   *If the Internet Explorer Standard Buttons toolbar or Address toolbar is not showing, click View, point to Toolbars, and click to place a check mark beside the missing toolbar.*

Warning   *You may proceed directly to the exercises for this lesson. If, however, you are finished with your computer session, follow the "shut down" procedures for your lab or school environment.*

Lesson Summary & Exercises

SUMMARY

The explosion in the use of the Internet has changed the way people use the computer. The World Wide Web lets users exchange information whenever it is convenient for them. Many businesses and individuals have their own Web sites. User-friendly software is available to create and maintain Webs. FrontPage 2000 is Microsoft's Web site creation and management software. Lesson 1 described the basics of FrontPage and taught you how to open, view, print, and save Webs. You learned how to create tasks to aid in the organization of Web development. Also, you learned how to use the online Help system to find out the newest features in FrontPage 2000. Finally, you used a Web browser to open Webs, at least one of which was created in FrontPage.

Now that you have completed this lesson, you should be able to do the following:

- Define a Web and name its components. (page 4)
- Use your mouse to point, click, double-click, right-click, select, and drag. (page 4)
- Start FrontPage. (page 5)
- Name the parts of the FrontPage application window. (page 7)
- Open an existing Web. (page 11)
- Display a Web page by double-clicking from the Folder List. (page 11)
- Use the Views bar to examine a Web in Page, Folders, Reports, Navigation, Hyperlinks, and Tasks views. (page 13)
- Switch between the Normal, HTML, and Preview tabs in the Page view. (page 13)
- Sort objects within the Folder List by clicking column headers. (page 14)
- Change report types and their options by selecting from drop-down lists in Reports view. (page 15)
- Name the types of pages by their relationships in the Navigation view. (page 16)
- Print the structure of a Web. (page 17)
- Create and delete a task in the Tasks view. (page 20)
- Mark a task as completed and view a task history. (page 21)
- Print a Web page including a custom footer. (page 22)
- Use Help to find features new to FrontPage 2000. (page 24)
- Close a Web, save changes, and exit FrontPage 2000. (page 24)
- Open a Web in your Web browser through the File menu. (page 26)
- View a Web using your Web browser. (page 26)

Lesson Summary & Exercises

CONCEPTS REVIEW

1 MATCHING

Match each of the terms on the left with the definitions on the right.

TERMS

1. Folders
2. Reports
3. Page
4. Navigation
5. Tasks
6. Hyperlink
7. Normal
8. HTML
9. Preview
10. Print Preview

DEFINITIONS

a. View that checks how pages are linked to other pages and files

b. View that displays the organization of the Web

c. Tab that shows how a Web page will look when opened in a browser

d. View that is used in the design of a Web page

e. View that displays a to-do list of Web maintenance jobs

f. Display that shows what a page will look like before it is printed

g. View that helps you analyze and troubleshoot parts of a Web

h. Tab used to enter and edit objects in a page

i. Tab that shows the page's underlying code

j. View that shows the relationship of pages in a Web

2 COMPLETION

Fill in the missing word or phrase for each of the following statements.

1. The _____ is on the left side of the FrontPage window and controls what you see and how you work on the open Web.

2. A(n) _____ hyperlink causes a jump to another Web.

3. The _____ is the first page of a navigation structure in a Web.

4. Once you have finished a task, you should mark it as _____.

5. Use the _____ option on the File menu to enter a custom footer.

6. _____ is a special language used to encode Web pages.

7. Before producing a printout of a Web page, you should look at it on screen using the _____ feature.

8. A(n) _____ is a program that lets you view pages on the Internet.

9. To check the jumps within a Web page, you should use the _____ view.

10. The _____ is a worldwide network of computers, of which the World Wide Web is one part.

3 SHORT ANSWER

Write a brief answer to each of the following questions.

1. List each of the view icons in the Views bar and in one sentence describe what that view is used for.

2. Describe the way pages relate to each other in the Web structure.

3. Compare and contrast internal versus external hyperlinks.

4. Describe the three tabs in the Page view.

5. List the steps to start editing a page from the Tasks view.

6. Name the three ways to open a Web site using a browser such as Internet Explorer.

7. Describe what is meant by *surfing* the Web.

8. List the steps necessary to open an existing Web from a folder on a disk.

9. How can you display a report of pages in a Web that would take more than one minute to download on a 28.8 speed modem?

10. Describe how to sort Web pages in Folders view from the largest to the smallest.

4 IDENTIFICATION

Label each of the elements in Figure 1.14

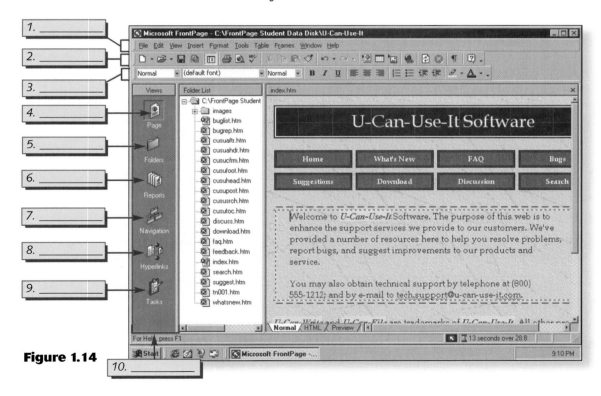

Figure 1.14

Lesson Summary & Exercises

SKILLS REVIEW

Complete each of the Skills Review problems in sequential order to review your skills to start FrontPage; open a Web; switch between views; sort objects; print the Web structure; create and delete a task; use the Help system; and exit FrontPage.

1 Starting FrontPage and Opening a Web

1. Click the **Start button** ![Start].
2. Point to **Programs**, and click **Microsoft FrontPage**.
3. Click the **drop-down arrow** on the Open button ![icon] and click **Open Web**.
4. Click the **Look in drop-down arrow**.
5. Click the drive containing your FrontPage Student Data Disk.
6. Double-click the *FrontPage Student Data Disk* folder.
7. Double-click the *Acme Consultation* Web folder.
8. Click **Open**.

2 Exploring the Page View

1. Double-click *index.htm* in the Folder List.
2. Read the Web page, scrolling to the bottom, if necessary.
3. Click the **HTML tab**.
4. Click the **Preview tab**.
5. Click the **News button** within the *Acme Products* Web page.
6. Click the **Normal tab**.

3 Using the Folders and Reports Views

1. Click the **Folders icon** ![icon] in the Views bar.
2. Click the **Size column header**.
3. Click the **Size column header** again.
4. Click the **Name column header**.
5. Click the **Reports icon** ![icon] in the Views bar.
6. Point to **Toolbars** on the View menu and click **Reporting** if the Reporting toolbar is not visible.
7. Click the **Reporting toolbar drop-down arrow** and click **Slow Pages**.
8. Click the drop-down arrow for the number of seconds and click **5 seconds**.

4 Viewing and Printing in the Navigation View

1. Click the **Navigation icon** ![icon].
2. Click the **Print toolbar button** ![icon].

5 Checking Links in the Hyperlinks View

1. Click the **Hyperlinks icon** 📇.

2. Click *index.htm* in the Folder List.

6 Creating, Starting, and Deleting a Task

1. Click the **Tasks icon** 📇. No tasks are currently listed.

2. Click the **Reports icon** 📇.

3. Click the **Reporting toolbar drop-down arrow** and click **All Files**.

4. Right-click *news.htm* and click **Add Task**.

5. Type Add this week's news in the dialog box next to *Task name*.

6. Type Describe our new products in the *Description* text box and click **OK**.

7. Click the **Tasks icon** 📇. Your screen should look similar to Figure 1.15.

8. Right-click the task and click **Start Task**.

9. Click the **Tasks icon** 📇.

10. Right-click the task, click **Delete**, and click **Yes** on the dialog box.

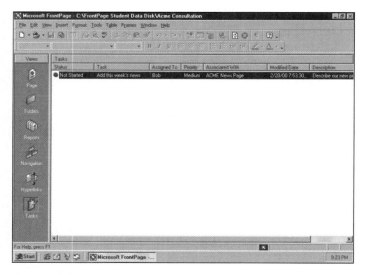

Figure 1.15

7 Printing a Web Page with a Custom Footer

1. Click the **Page view icon** 📇.

2. Double-click *index.htm* in the Folder List.

3. Click **Page Setup** on the File menu.

4. Click an insertion point at the leftmost position in the *Footer* text box.

5. Type your name, enter three spaces, and click **OK**.

6. Click **Print Preview** on the File menu.

7. Click the **Print button** 🔲 on the Print Preview screen, then click **OK** on the Print dialog box.

8 Using Help

1. Press 🔲.

2. Click the **Contents tab**.

3. Click the **plus sign (+)** beside the Glossary book icon.

4. Click the **Glossary help page**.

5. Click the graphic on the right pane.

6. Click the **U** link.

7. Read the glossary entry for URL.

8. Click the **Close button** ⊠ for the Glossary window.

9. Click the **Close button** ⊠ for the Help window.

9 Closing a Web and Exiting FrontPage

1. Click **Close Web** on the File menu to close the current Web.

2. Click **Exit** in the File menu.

3. Click **No** if asked to save changes.

LESSON APPLICATIONS

1 Starting FrontPage, Opening a Web, and Getting Help

Open a Web on your Student Data Disk and get Help.

1. Start FrontPage.

2. Open the Web named *My Web* in the *FrontPage Student Data Disk* folder.

3. Open *index.htm* (the home page) and switch to the Preview tab.

4. Click on each of the links from the home page and read each of the Web pages. (The Favorites page contains external links to remote Web sites. You may return to the home page from a remote site by clicking the Normal tab then the Preview tab.)

5. Open the Help window, and expand the Designing Webs and Hyperlinks book icons.

6. Display the *About hyperlinks* Help page, click the graphic, and read about hyperlinks.

7. Close the Help system windows.

2 Viewing Reports and Creating a Task

Display the slowest loading page and create a task to change it.

1. Switch to Reports view.

2. Display the pages taking more than 20 seconds to load.

3. Create a task for the page.

4. In the dialog box, type Slow page as the Task name, type Try to make page download in under 20 seconds in the *Description* text box, and change the Priority to High. Click OK.

5. Switch to the Tasks view and start the task you just entered. Your screen should look like Figure 1.16.

6. Switch back to the Tasks view and delete the task.

Lesson Summary & Exercises

Figure 1.16

3 Printing a Web Page with a Footer and Exiting FrontPage

Print the Web structure and a Web page with a custom footer.

1. Switch to the Navigation view.

2. Print the Web structure.

3. Double-click the *Interests* page to display it.

4. Create a custom footer with your name at the beginning of the line.

5. Print the Web page.

6. Close the Web and exit FrontPage without saving any changes.

PROJECTS

1 Check It Out

You recently joined a nonprofit organization dedicated to improving computer education in public school systems. The organization has developed a Web site and asks you to give your opinion. The Web named *ComCon2* is on your Student Data Disk. Open the *index.htm* page in your Web browser. Read each of the pages and click the hyperlinks.

Write an analysis of the Web site including the ease of use, the design features you like or don't like, and places in which the text can be improved. Find changes that you would make to at least three of the pages.

2 Get to Work

Your supervisor agrees with the changes you suggested in Project 1. Open the Web in FrontPage and create tasks for the pages you want to change. Decide which of the changes should be done first and assign it a high priority. Choose other priorities for the rest of your tasks.

Use the Reports view to locate pages that take more than 20 seconds to download. Add task(s) to try to reduce the amount of time needed to view the pages. Start each of the tasks you created, then mark them as completed (Hint: right-click on the task in the Tasks view).

Write a report to your supervisor listing the tasks you created. You can also write the changes, as if you made them.

3 Watch Where You're Going

ComCon2 is still not sure that their Web site is properly organized. Some pages seem too long and the way to get from one page to the next could be better. Before making any changes, your supervisor asks you to produce a printout of the site.

Print the navigation structure of the Web. Add a custom header and then print the home page. Check the Site Summary report to see if any problems are listed, such as broken hyperlinks, unlinked files, and component errors.

4 What's My Line?

Each of the members of ComCon2 would like an opportunity to review and revise their biographical information on the members' page. Print the page *members.htm* shown in Figure 1.17. Include a footer with your name, a page number, and the date.

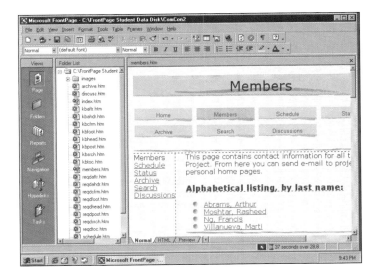

Figure 1.17

Project in Progress

5 Spin Your Own Web

As the owner of a store specializing in collectibles, you have decided it is time to put your store on the Internet. You're not sure if you are ready to start selling your items online, but you would at least like to display your wares to Internet users.

Write your objectives for creating a Web for your store. From what you have seen in the Webs you viewed in this lesson, sketch a Web structure, including a home page and three or more child pages.

LESSON 2

Creating Web Pages from Templates

CONTENTS

OBJECTIVES

After you complete this lesson, you will be able to do the following:

- Design a Web.
- Create a new FrontPage Web based on a template.
- Assign meaningful names to Web pages.
- Add Web pages using templates.
- Use Help to find out how to create your own template.
- Enter text into a Web page.
- Change the appearance of text by changing fonts, font sizes, and type styles.
- Set the alignment of text to the left, right, or center of an area.
- Import text into a Web page from a separate file.
- Get FrontPage assistance using the Office on the Web feature.

In this lesson, you will create a Web site for a student newsletter. You will learn to create Web pages from scratch and add pages to a Web using predesigned formats called templates. Before you start FrontPage, you will see how a Web structure should be planned on paper.

DESIGNING A WEB

All Web sites are designed to serve a purpose. The reasons for the existence of Web sites are varied, but they include:

- Promotion of a company and the sale of its products or services
- Distribution of information in the form of documents, files, or graphic images
- Solicitation of charitable or political contributions
- Establishment of a meeting place for people with common interests
- Presentation of online versions of newspapers, magazines, television stations, or radio channels

Before you start creating a Web with FrontPage 2000, it helps to have a clear idea of what the Web should do. While FrontPage makes changing the design of Web pages fairly simple, it is much easier to begin with the basic structure of your Web already laid out.

Before you start to create your student newsletter Web, it's a good idea to draw a Web structure with the main pages in place. Figure 2.1 is a sketch of a simple Web structure for the newsletter. It includes an events page, a news page, and a gossip page all linked to the home page.

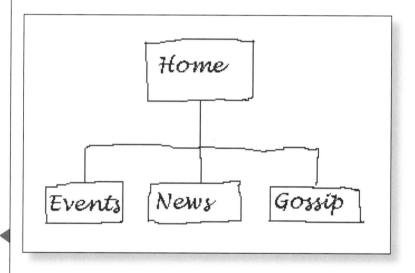

Figure 2.1
Design structure for a Web site

FRONTPAGE TEMPLATES

Webs and Web pages you create in FrontPage 2000 are based on ***templates***. A template is a document that already contains text and design features that you will modify to meet your needs. FrontPage also lets you start new Webs or Web pages from ***wizards***. A wizard asks you to respond to a series of questions. Your answers serve as a basis upon which your new document will be built. You will use a wizard in a later lesson.

When you create a new Web, you can choose to use a template with built-in, preformatted pages; a simple Web with only one page; or even a Web with no pages at all! Likewise, when you add pages to your Web, you can make them as elaborate or as simple as you like.

For an introduction to the Web, visit *www.cohums.ohio-state.edu.* Search the Website using the keywords *Creating Web Pages.* In the search results, click the Creating Web Pages link.

FrontPage Web Creation

When you create a new Web, you must choose a template upon which to base the Web and a location for the Web. If your computer is connected to the Internet and you have established an account, you can save your Web directly to a **Web server**. A Web server publishes documents on the Internet so they can be viewed by others. The Web server accepts requests from browsers and returns appropriate HTML documents.

The Web server is often hosted by an **Internet Service Provider (ISP)** which is a company that provides Web access and various Web-based services (such as e-mail) usually for a monthly fee. Popular ISPs include America Online, Inc. (AOL) and Microsoft Network (MSN).

It is a good practice to save your Web to your local hard drive or local area network and then copy it to a Web server when it is complete. In this way, you always have a copy of the Web in case it is lost or you choose to change Web servers at a later date. Following this procedure also allows you to develop your Web before you set up an account with an ISP and to modify your Web while you are offline.

In Table 2.1, you can see the FrontPage 2000 Web templates upon which you can base your new Web.

TABLE 2.1	FRONTPAGE 2000 WEB TEMPLATES
Name	**Description**
One Page Web	A basic Web site with a single page named *index.htm*—also called a home or welcome page.
Customer Support Web	A multipage Web designed for a company wishing to provide easy access for customers. The text and design are especially useful for a software company.
Empty Web	A Web containing nothing—not even a single page!
Personal Web	A Web upon which an individual or family might display information on hobbies or activities.
Project Web	Lets an organization provide information on its purpose, membership, schedule, status, publications, and so on.

Many Internet Service Providers (ISPs) give their subscribers free space to publish their Web sites.

Creating a New Web from a Template

In this activity, you will create a new Web on your Student Data Disk. This Web will be based on the *One Page Web* template. Later on you will add more pages to the Web.

Creating a New Web from a Template

1. Point to New on the File menu and click Web.

2. Click the icon of the template you want to use.

3. Enter the drive and path to the folder where you want the Web to be saved.

4. Click OK.

1. Click the **Start button** 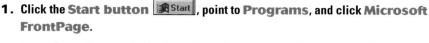, point to **Programs**, and click **Microsoft FrontPage**.

FrontPage launches and displays the Views bar and empty workspace.

2. Click the **Page icon** in the Views bar, if necessary, to activate the toolbar buttons.

3. Click the **Maximize button** , if necessary.

4. Point to **New** on the File menu and click **Web**.

The New dialog box appears, as in Figure 2.2. Here you choose the Web template upon which to base your Web.

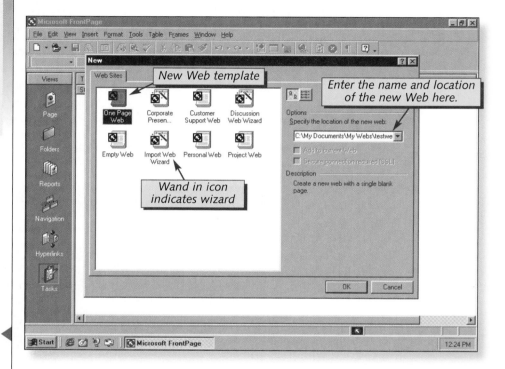

Figure 2.2
New dialog box

The dialog box contains both templates and wizards. The wizards have a wand in their icon; the templates do not.

5. Click the *One Page Web* template icon.

6. Type C:\FrontPage Student Data Disk\Tutorial\School Newsletter in the *Specify the location of the new web* text box.

The new Web will be stored in a subfolder within the *Tutorial* folder of your FrontPage Student Data Disk.

Substitute the drive letter and folder location of your FrontPage Student Data Disk if different than the location indicated in step 6.

7. Click **OK**.

A Creating New Web window displays briefly while the Web is created on your drive. When completed, you see the new Web as in Figure 2.3.

Another Way

To create a new Web, click the New Page drop-down arrow on the Standard Buttons toolbar, click Web, and the New dialog box will appear.

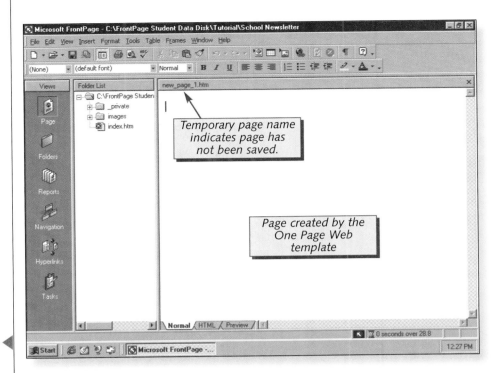

Figure 2.3
Blank *School Newsletter* Web

EDITING A WEB PAGE

Whether you start a new Web or open an existing Web, FrontPage assumes you want to add a new page. If you need to make changes to a Web page, you must **edit** the page. To see which page is currently being edited, check the window header as shown in Figure 2.3. In your new Web, *new_page_1.htm* is the name temporarily assigned to a new page. If you were to add text or otherwise edit this page, it would become part of your Web. If, however, you ignore this page and add or edit another page, the new page is not added to the Web.

All pages in a Web created from a template need to be edited in order to suit your intended purpose. Typical edits may include adding the company, individual, or team name to the home page; assigning a name to the page itself; and typing the text that conveys the content and purpose of the page. As you learned in Lesson 1, you can access any page in a Web to edit it by double-clicking that page in the Folder List. The Folder List contains all of the pages in the Web.

Page Names

Every page has a file name with an *htm* extension that appears in the Folder List (Page view), the Folders view (Name column), and the Hyperlinks view. Every page also has a ***page title*** which is a user-friendly title that you give to a page. The page title appears in the Title column when you are in the Folders view. The page title appears in the title bar of browsers that view your page and also in browser favorites or bookmarks, so it is often necessary to change the title so it reflects the purpose of your page. Changing the page title will not change the file name.

FrontPage
BASICS

Changing the Page Title

1. Click the Page view icon to display the page in Page view.

2. Right-click in the page window and click Page Properties.

3. Type the new page title and click OK.

Changing the Page Title

In this activity, you will change the page title to a user-friendly name that will appear in the Folders view.

1. Double-click *index.htm* in the Folder List and click the **Normal tab**, if necessary.

The *index.htm* or welcome page is now ready for editing, although it looks blank.

2. Click the **HTML tab**, then click the **Normal tab**.

The HTML tab reveals that the page does have some codes in it even though it appears blank in the Normal tab.

3. Right-click in the blank workspace and click **Page Properties** in the shortcut menu.

The Page Properties dialog box appears as in Figure 2.4

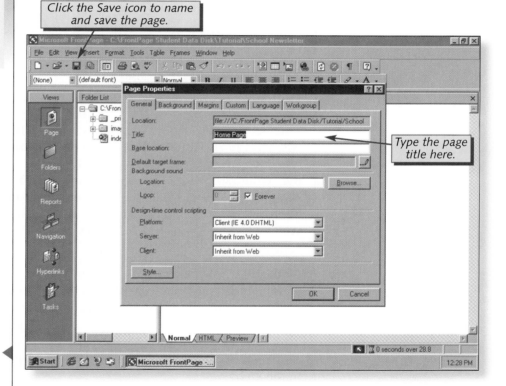

Figure 2.4
The Page Properties dialog box

4. Type State College **in the *Title* text box.**

5. Click **OK**.

The Page Properties dialog box closes. The page needs to be saved before the page title will appear in the Folders view.

6. Click **Save** 🖫 **on the Standard Buttons toolbar.**

7. Click the **Folders icon** 📁 **in the Views bar.**

The folders appear in the workspace. Note the new page title (State College) in the Title column next to the *index.htm* file name listed in the Name column. Changing the page title did not affect the file name.

CREATING A WEB PAGE

You can create a Web and individual Web pages from a template or wizard. When creating pages from a template, try to find the layout that most closely matches your needs. Table 2.2 lists the page templates that ship with FrontPage 2000 as well as their intended purposes.

TABLE 2.2	FRONTPAGE 2000 WEB PAGE TEMPLATES
Name	**Description**
Normal Page	Adds a blank page.
Bibliography	A page that can be used to type references to material used in an article.
Confirmation form	A form that confirms the submission of user feedback.
Feedback form	A page on which visitors to the Web can give you comments.
Form Page Wizard	A Wizard to help you create a form to collect common types of feedback from users.
Frequently Asked Questions	A page in which you supply frequently asked questions and answers on topics related to your Web.
Guest Book	A page in which visitors can leave comments that can be viewed by other visitors.
Narrow Left- and Right-Aligned Body templates	Templates that format pages with a single column on the right or left to allow room for graphic images or other objects.
One-column Body templates	A group of pages with various formats with a single column of text and placeholders for other objects (such as pictures) on the top, bottom, right, or left of the text.
Search Page	Creates a page that can be used to locate information in your Web based on keywords entered by a user.
Table of Contents	Creates a page with links to all pages in your Web in an outline format.
Three-column Body	Page format that has three columns of text as might be found in a newspaper.
Two-column Body templates	A group of pages with various formats with two columns of text and placeholders for other objects on the top, bottom, right, or left of the text.
User Registration	Creates a page where users can register to access a protected Web.
Wide Body with Headings	Creates a page with subheadings and text running across the width of the page.

Adding a Web Page

You can add blank or preformatted Web pages while in any FrontPage view, but this action works best from Page view. When adding a page to a Web, you have to decide where the page belongs within the Web structure. If you have begun with a good design, you should already know where the page should be placed.

Adding a Web Page from a Template

1. Open the Web.

2. Click the Page view icon.

3. Point to New on the File menu and click Page.

4. Double-click the desired template.

Adding Web Pages from Templates

In this activity, you will add Web pages to your *School Newsletter* Web using templates. The Web currently has a blank home page. After this activity, you will have three more pages named *Events*, *News*, and *Gossip*.

1. Click the **Page view icon** .

2. Point to **New** on the File menu and click **Page**.

The New dialog box opens as in Figure 2.5.

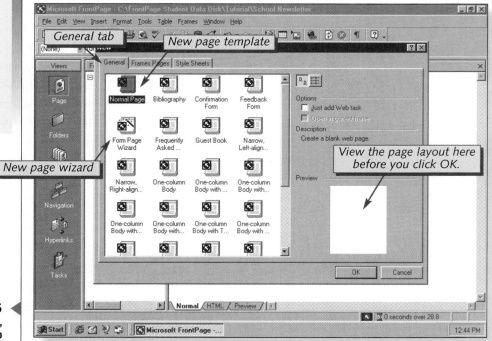

Figure 2.5
The New dialog box,
General tab

3. Click the **General tab**, if necessary.

From the General tab of the New dialog box you can select the template upon which to base your new page.

Click a template to preview it in the Preview section of the New dialog box. Click as many templates as you like to preview them. Click OK to select a template that appears in Preview.

Ctrl + N is the keyboard shortcut for creating a new, blank Web page.

4. Double-click the template *Narrow, Left-aligned Body*.

Within the New dialog box, the longer template names appear to be incomplete. To view the complete name, point to the template graphic and the full name will appear.

A new page is added to your Web with placeholders for a heading, text, and a graphics image, as in Figure 2.6.

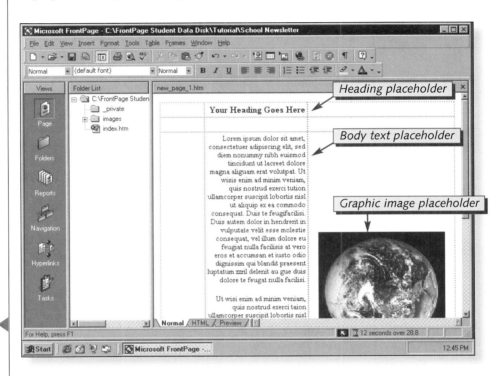

Figure 2.6
Web page based on the *Narrow, Left-aligned Body* template

5. Click the Save button 💾.

The Save As dialog box appears.

6. Type Events as the file name, then click Save 💾 Save.

The Save Embedded Files dialog box appears prompting you to save the graphic image in your file. The graphic image of the earth appears in Picture preview.

7. Click OK.

The files are added to the Folder List.

8. Point to New on the File menu and click Page.

9. Double-click the *Two-column, Staggered Body* template.

10. Click the Save button 💾.

The Save As dialog box appears.

11. Type News as the file name, and click Save 💾 Save.

The files appear in the Folder List.

The Save Embedded Files dialog box appears prompting you to save the graphic images.

12. Click OK.

13. Point to New on the File menu and click Page.

The New dialog box appears.

14. Double-click the *Two-column, Staggered Body* template.

15. Click the Save button 🖫.

The Save As dialog box appears.

16. Type Gossip as the file name and click Save [🖫 Save].

The Save Embedded Files dialog box appears prompting you to save the graphic images.

17. Click OK.

The files appear in the Folder List.

The FrontPage 2000 Answer Wizard

In this activity, you will use the Answer Wizard to find out how you can create your own template in FrontPage 2000.

1. Click Microsoft FrontPage Help on the Help menu.

Figure 2.7
FrontPage 2000 Help Answer Wizard screen

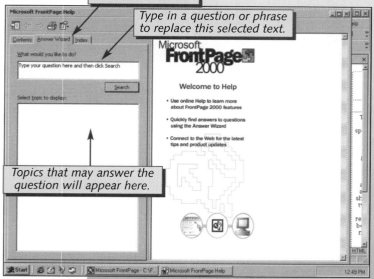

The Microsoft FrontPage Help window appears.

2. Click the Answer Wizard tab.

The Help window appears as shown in Figure 2.7.

3. Highlight the existing text in the *What would you like to do?* text box and type How can I create a template?.

4. Click the Search button.

A list of topics appears in the *Select topic to display* section below the search question. The topic *Create a page template* is highlighted. The corresponding Help page displays to the right.

5. Read the *Create a page template* Help page to learn the steps necessary to create your own template.

6. Click Create a shared template in the *Select topic to display* section and read the Help page to see how you can share your template with people working on the same Web.

7. Click the Close button ⊠ to close the Help window.

ENTERING TEXT

Graphic images, colorful backgrounds, and slick animations may capture the attention of visitors to a Web site; however, words, phrases, and sentences are used to convey most information. Using FrontPage 2000, you can easily control the appearance, size, and placement of text.

There are two basic methods for entering text into a Web page. You can insert the text from a separate file you or someone else has typed (many people prefer to use a word processing program such as Microsoft Word to type text). However, in this lesson you will enter the text by typing directly into the FrontPage 2000 page.

Typing Text into a Web Page

When you point to a text area of a page, you will see the Text Select pointer ⌶ which is the editing pointer with which you can indicate where the characters you type will be inserted. To place text on a Web page, simply click an insertion point where the Text Select pointer appears then begin typing. Several features and techniques have become standard when typing on the computer. Follow these rules and standards, just as when you use a word processing program:

- Press `Enter←` to start a new paragraph or add a blank line.
- Do not press `Enter←` at the end of a line, unless you want to start a new paragraph. Word wrap automatically moves the insertion point down to the beginning of the next line when the text reaches the right margin.
- Type one space character with `Spacebar` to separate words.
- Generally type one space after the end of a sentence.
- Press `Delete` to remove the character to the right of the insertion point; press `Backspace` to remove the character to the left of the insertion point.
- Hold down `⇧ Shift` and type a letter to enter uppercase characters or the symbols at the top of the keys, such as `?` or `@`.
- Press `Caps Lock` to type a series of uppercase characters.

Adding Text to a Web Page

In this activity, you will add text to two pages in your *School Newsletter* Web.

1. **Double-click *index.htm* in the Folder List and click the Normal tab, if necessary.**

The insertion point should be flashing in the workspace on the left side of the blank page.

2. **Type the following text:** Welcome to the unofficial State College Web site. Here you will find out what's really going on in our school. Come back often--we're adding new stuff every day!

Note that the line automatically wraps to the beginning of the next line when you reach the right margin of the page. Your page should resemble Figure 2.8.

Adding Text to a Web Page

1. Display the page in Page view.

2. Click the insertion point where text is to begin.

3. Type the text.

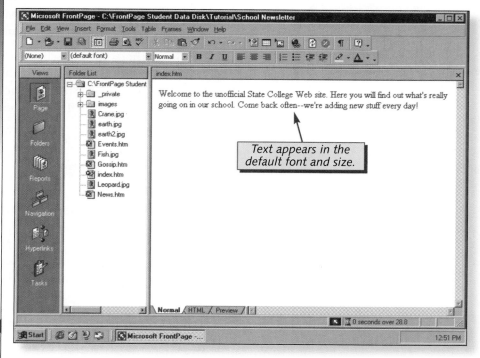

Figure 2.8
Blank Web page with text added

3. Click the **Save button** 💾.

If wavy lines appear beneath misspelled words as you type, FrontPage may be automatically checking your spelling. You may turn off that feature by clicking Page Options on the Tools menu. In the General tab, click to place a check mark next to Hide spelling errors in all documents. To check your spelling, click to remove the check mark next to Hide spelling errors in all documents then click a check mark next to Check spelling as you type.

4. Double-click *Events.htm* in the Folder List.

5. Point just to the left of the *Y* in the *Your Heading Goes Here* box.

The pointer changes to an arrow 🔍.

6. Click to select the line of text *Your Heading Goes Here*.

Your Heading Goes Here appears white on a dark background.

7. Type What's Happening This Week.

The text you type replaces the text you selected.

8. Press `Tab` **six times.**

Each stroke of the `Tab` key moves the pointer to the next square. Every time you move the pointer to a new square, you select the text it contains.

9. Press `Delete`.

The Latin placeholder text is deleted.

10. Type the following. When you are finished, press `Enter◄─┘`.

The SC Cycling Club is sponsoring a free ride Saturday morning, March 20. They'll be gathering at the GT Groceries parking lot (corner of Main and 3rd Streets) at 7:30. The ride should last about two hours, after which refreshments will be available for a nominal fee. For further information contact Sally Jenkins by phone at (434) 555-1212 or e-mail her at s_jenkins@sc.edu.

11. Press `Enter◄─┘`.

Your Web page should look similar to Figure 2.9.

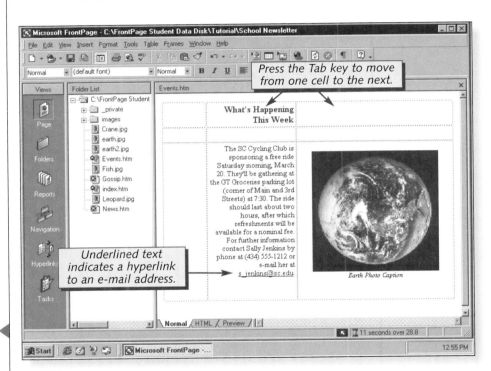

Figure 2.9
Events Web page
with text added

FrontPage recognizes the words at the end of the paragraph as an e-mail address. The underlining below s-jenkins@sc.edu indicates this is a link to an e-mail address.

12. Click the Save button 💾.

FORMATTING TEXT

You can improve the appearance of text on a Web page using word processing-style formatting techniques. FrontPage 2000 includes formatting options that allow you to change the appearance of letters, paragraphs, lists, or lines.

Character Formatting

Character formatting refers to the way letters, numbers, and symbols appear in the page. A *typeface* is a family for type or printed characters that is determined by particular design or style characteristics. A set of characters that appears with a specific typeface, one or more effects, and a specific size is a *font*. Most people use the terms *typeface* and *font* interchangeably. In FrontPage you choose a font, pick the effects, and set the size separately. Thousands of typefaces are available to Windows users although computers rarely have more than 100 typefaces installed. Typefaces can be divided into four basic categories, as shown in Figure 2.10.

SERIF TYPEFACES

Bookman Old Style
Century Schoolbook
Garamond
Times New Roman

SANS SERIF TYPEFACES

Arial
Gill Sans
Lucida Sans
News Gothic

UNUSUAL TYPEFACES

Broadway
COPPERPLATE GOTHIC
Lucida Handwriting
Old English Text

SYMBOL TYPEFACES

Almanac ○·▧▨·◿▴◈☿♏︎♎︎
Monotype Sorts ❑▶︎✳︎✱✚▲✜✓☜
Symbol ωετρψτυιχξβν
Wingdings ▤▥▦▧✤♍︎♌︎♦︎☜☞♁☯

Figure 2.10 ◀
Typeface categories

A *serif typeface* like Times New Roman is adorned with little lines and curves on the tips of each character called *serifs*. The text you are reading now is another example of a serif typeface. In general, serif typefaces are better suited for paragraph text because the serifs help your eyes to flow along each line more smoothly as you read the text.

Sans-serif typefaces like Arial, on the other hand, do not have these lines and curves called serifs. Their appearance is more block-like. Sans-serif typefaces generally work better for headings where reading ease is not as critical.

Unusual typefaces include fonts that are whimsical or elegant. You see these fonts in advertisements, posters, invitations, and certificates. Finally, there are typefaces that do not contain letters or numbers at all—just symbols and icons used to dress up, personalize, or add a professional touch to documents.

Fonts can also be categorized by the way they are horizontally spaced. With *fixed-width fonts*, each character takes up the same amount of space. When you use fixed-width fonts, letters line up in vertical rows and you can precisely control the number of letters that fit on a line. Letters in **_proportional fonts_**, on the other hand, take up only as much space as they need to be legible. Figure 2.11 shows the difference between proportional and fixed-width fonts.

Proportional font
Fixed-width font

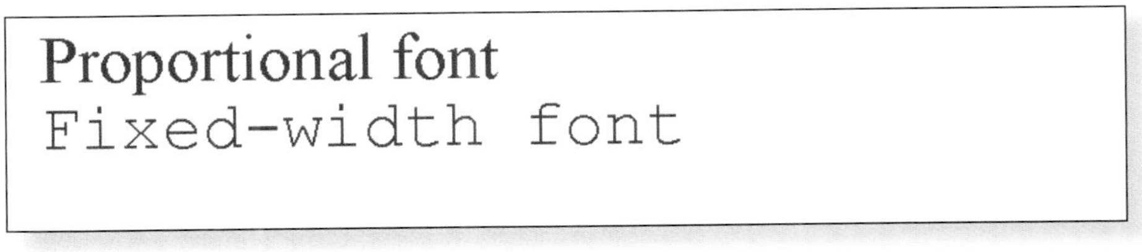

Figure 2.11
Proportional and fixed-width fonts

When you type text on a Web page, the text takes on the **_default_** font. A default is a value or setting that is used automatically unless you change it. FrontPage has two default fonts. FrontPage's default proportional font is Times New Roman. FrontPage's default fixed-width font is Courier New.

When you type text in a page, the text will be in the default font. However, if you change the default font before you begin typing, the font will appear as the one you just chose. If you want to change the font of text you have already typed, you must first select the text then change the font. One way to select text is to click at one end of the text block, hold the mouse button, and drag to the other end. All of the text in the text block will be highlighted. There are a number of other ways to select text, some of which are shown in Table 2.3.

TABLE 2.3	TEXT SELECTION METHODS
To select:	**Do this:**
A word	Double-click the word
Several words	Double-click and drag
A line	Click in the left margin
Several lines	Click in the left margin and drag down
⇧ Shift + →	Select next character to right
⇧ Shift + ←	Select next character to left
⇧ Shift + ↓	Select text to the next line down
⇧ Shift + ↑	Select text to the previous line up
⇧ Shift + End	Select characters to end of line
⇧ Shift + Home	Select characters to beginning of line

HANDS On

Changing Fonts

In this activity, you will change the typeface of text you have already typed.

1. Double-click _index.htm_ in the Folder List and click the **Normal tab**, if necessary.

Changing Typefaces

1. Select the text.

2. Click the Font drop-down arrow.

3. Click the desired font.

The Welcome text appears that you typed in a previous activity.

2. Click an insertion point to the left of the word *Welcome* and drag down and to the right to select the entire paragraph.

The entire paragraph becomes highlighted—the text appears white on a dark background.

3. Click the Font drop-down arrow.

A list of fonts appears as in Figure 2.12. Each of the font names is displayed in its corresponding typeface.

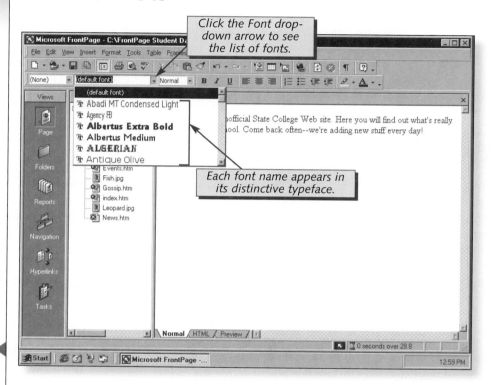

Figure 2.12
Font drop-down list

4. Scroll down to examine the available fonts.

5. Click Lucida Bright or any other serif font available.

The font list closes. The paragraph appears in the font you selected.

6. Click in a blank area of the workspace to deselect the paragraph, then double-click the word *State* and drag to the right to also highlight the next word.

The words *State* and *College* should be highlighted.

If you select the wrong text, click to remove the highlighting and try again. If you accidentally delete or move text, press Ctrl *+ Z to undo your mistake.*

7. Click the Font drop-down arrow, then click Old English Text or any other distinctive font.

8. Click the Save button.

9. Double-click *Events.htm* to open it in Page view.

10. Click and drag to highlight the heading *What's Happening This Week*.

11. Click the Font drop-down arrow and click Century Gothic or other sans serif font.

The heading changes to the new font style.

12. Select the block of text material below the heading to highlight it.

13. Click the Font drop-down arrow and click Lucida Bright (or a similar font).

The text font changes.

14. Click to deselect the text and click the Save button 🖫.

If you chose fonts different than Century Gothic for the Events.htm *heading font or Lucida Bright for the paragraph font, make a note of them. You'll need to use these fonts in a later activity.*

Type Size

The size of a font is measured in **points**. One point is 1/72 of an inch in height. In FrontPage 2000 the default font size is set to Normal rather than a specific point size. This way, you can change the size of all body text by just changing the size of Normal.

In the Font Size drop-down box, a number appears before each point size. For example, the number *3* appears before *12 pt*. In a later lesson you will see how you can change the font size assigned to the number *3*. Changing the font size for *3* will change all text with that size attribute. Thus, if you wanted to enlarge all 12-point text to 13 points, you would only have to change the font size for *3* instead of having to find, select, and modify text on each of the pages within the Web.

Changing the Font Size

In this activity, you will change the size of selected text in your pages in the *School Newsletter* Web.

1. Double-click *index.htm* in the Folder List and click the Normal tab, if necessary.

2. Select the words *State College*, if necessary, in your *index.htm* page.

3. Click the Font Size drop-down arrow.

Available font sizes appear as in Figure 2.13.

4. Click 4 (14 pt).

The Font Size drop-down box closes and *State College* appears in the larger font.

5. Click the Save button 🖫.

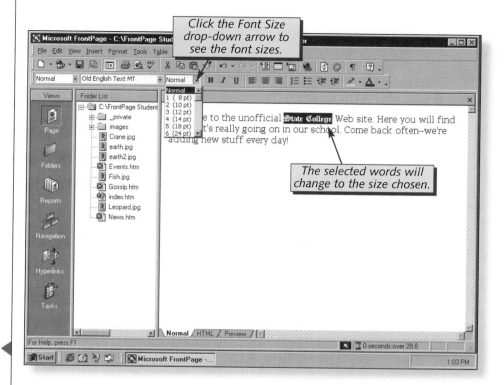

Click the Font Size drop-down arrow to see the font sizes.

The selected words will change to the size chosen.

Figure 2.13
Font Size drop down list

Type Styles

In addition to the typeface and type size, you can change the appearance of characters by applying *effects* or *attributes.* The most common effects used in documents are bold, italic, and underlining. In FrontPage 2000, you can apply these effects to highlighted text by simply clicking one of the buttons on the Formatting toolbar. Less commonly used styles include strike-through, superscripts, subscripts, small caps, and many others.

You can access all character formatting options through the Font dialog box. By choosing the Font option on the Format menu, you can choose the typeface, size, and effects all at once. As an added bonus, you can see how your text will appear before making the change on the page.

HANDS on

Changing the Type Style

In this activity, you will add effects to some of the text in your pages.

1. Double-click *Events.htm* in the Folder List and click the **Normal tab**, if necessary.

2. Select the words *SC Cycling Club* in the first line of the paragraph.

3. Click the **Bold button** [B] on the Formatting toolbar.

The selected text appears in bold.

4. Press [⇧ Shift] + [Tab] to move the insertion point to the empty text box to the left.

5. Click **Font** on the Format menu.

The Font dialog box appears as in Figure 2.14.

Figure 2.14
The Font dialog box

Applying Effects

With the Formatting toolbar:

1. Select the text within your Web page.

2. Click the Bold, Italic, or Underline button.

With the Font dialog box:

1. Select the text within your Web page.

2. Click Font on the Format menu.

3. Click the effects in the Font dialog box.

4. Click OK.

Another Way

The keyboard shortcut for bold is `Ctrl` + B; for italic the shortcut is `Ctrl` + I; and for underline it is `Ctrl` + U.

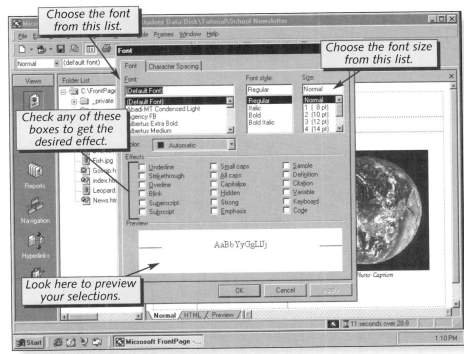

Choose the font from this list.

Choose the font size from this list.

Check any of these boxes to get the desired effect.

Look here to preview your selections.

6. In the Font list, scroll down and click Arial Narrow (or any sans serif font).

The Preview window in the Font dialog box shows the new typeface.

7. In the Size list, scroll down and click 5 (18 pt).

The Preview window reflects the larger size.

8. Click the Emphasis check box in the Effects section.

The Preview window shows how the font looks with that effect applied.

9. Click OK.

The Font dialog box closes; however, since no text was selected, the type on the page does not change.

10. Type Free Ride!.

The new text appears with the options you chose.

11. Click the Save button 🖫.

If you chose a sans-serif font different than Arial Narrow for the Free Ride! *side heading, make a note of it. You will use this font again in the following activity.*

Paragraph Formatting

The appearance of text in the Web page depends on more than character formatting. The placement of the text on the page and the spacing between lines affects the look as well. *Alignment* determines the horizontal and vertical position of text on a page. Figure 2.15 shows how a paragraph of text appears under each of the four alignment options.

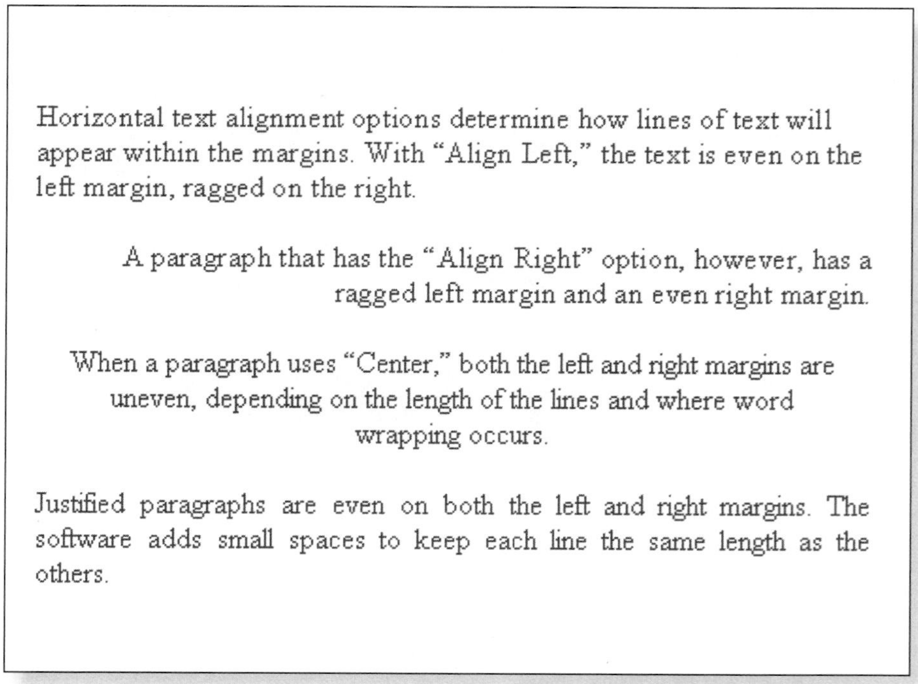

Horizontal text alignment options determine how lines of text will appear within the margins. With "Align Left," the text is even on the left margin, ragged on the right.

A paragraph that has the "Align Right" option, however, has a ragged left margin and an even right margin.

When a paragraph uses "Center," both the left and right margins are uneven, depending on the length of the lines and where word wrapping occurs.

Justified paragraphs are even on both the left and right margins. The software adds small spaces to keep each line the same length as the others.

Figure 2.15
Alignment options

Setting Paragraph Alignment

In this activity, you will type text for the *News* page in the *School Newsletter* Web. You will also set the paragraph alignment for the heading and body text.

1. Double-click *News.htm* in the Folder List and click the Normal tab, if necessary.

The *News.htm* page displays in Page view.

2. Click and drag to select the placeholder text *Your Heading Goes Here*.

The heading appears highlighted.

3. Type SC News.

The characters you type replace the placeholder text.

4. Select *SC News*.

5. Click the Font drop-down arrow and click Century Gothic (or whatever heading font you used for the page heading in *Events.htm* in the previous activity).

6. Click the Font Size drop-down arrow and click the font size 6 (24 pt).

**7. Click the Align Right button 	.**

The text moves to the right side of the text box.

8. Press `Tab` seven times, then press `Delete`.

The placeholder text is highlighted then deleted.

9. Type the following: Sam Waters was elected Student Council President in voting conducted last week. Waters beat Martha Jackson 58% to 42% with 88% of eligible students casting ballots. In his victory speech, Waters proclaimed, "We will see an immediate increase in the number of concerts and other events. That's why I was elected and that's what I'm going to do."

10. Click and drag to highlight the paragraph you just typed.

11. Click the Align Left button ![icon].

Each line of the paragraph now starts at the left margin.

12. Click an insertion point in the blank text box to the right of the box in which you just typed.

13. Click Font on the Format menu.

The Font dialog box appears.

14. Click Arial Narrow (or whatever font you used for the side heading *Free Ride!* on the *Events.htm* page).

15. Click 5 (18pt) to change the font size and click the Emphasis check box in the Effects section.

16. Click OK.

17. Type Election Results.

18. Click the Center button ![icon] **on the Formatting toolbar.**

The heading appears centered within the text box as shown in Figure 2.16.

Hints & Tips

With justified alignment both the left and right margins are even. This option is not on the Formatting toolbar. To find it, choose Paragraph on the Format menu and click Justify on the Alignment drop-down box.

Figure 2.16
Text alignment in the
News Web page

19. Click the Save button ![icon].

Importing a File

1. Position the insertion point where you want to place the imported file.
2. Click File on the Insert menu.
3. Locate the drive and folder that contains the file in the Select File dialog box.
4. Change the *Files of type* to the appropriate file extension.
5. Double-click the file to be imported.

IMPORTING TEXT

You have seen how to enter and format text using the FrontPage text editing features. There is another way, however, to get formatted text into a Web page. **Importing** is the process of bringing a file created by another program into a Web page.

There are many kinds of files you can import. These include text files created by popular word processing programs, worksheets built in spreadsheet programs, and even Web pages from other HTML files.

A file you wish to import might come from a variety of sources. For example, you may have created the file yourself for other purposes, such as a report, an e-mail, or a budget. Or you might choose to use another program, such as Microsoft Word or Corel WordPerfect, to type text since these programs are specifically designed to create and format documents.

Importing a Text File

In this activity, you will add a paragraph to the *Gossip* page in your *School Newsletter* Web by importing text currently stored in a file on your Student Data Disk.

1. Double-click *Gossip.htm* in the Folder List and click the Normal tab, if necessary.

Gossip.htm appears in the workspace.

2. Select *Your Heading Goes Here* and type The Gossip Page.

3. Select *The Gossip Page* and click the Font drop-down arrow.

4. Click Century Gothic (or click the page heading font you chose for *Events.htm*).

5. Click the Font Size drop-down arrow and click 6 (24 pt).

6. Press Tab seven times.

The cell into which you are going to place your imported text is selected.

7. Click File on the Insert menu.

The Select File dialog box appears.

8. Click the Look in drop-down arrow and click the drive containing your FrontPage Student Data Disk.

9. Double-click the *FrontPage Student Data Disk* folder.

10. Double-click the *Tutorial* folder.

11. Click the Files of type drop-down arrow.

12. Scroll, if necessary, and click Word 97-2000 (*.doc).

The file *Gossip One* appears in the Select File dialog box.

13. Double-click *Gossip One*.

The file is imported and the *Gossip.htm* Web page now looks like Figure 2.17.

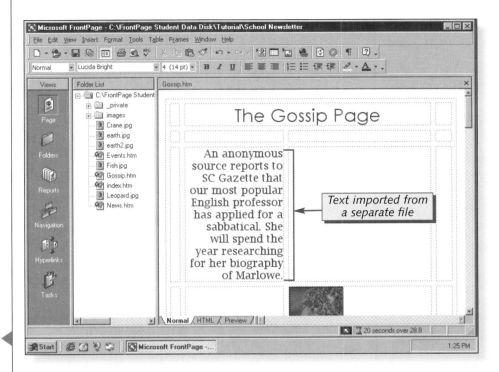

Figure 2.17
Text imported into the
Gossip Web page

If you get a message stating that the format can't be imported, click No and FrontPage should continue to import the file. If you cannot import the text, check with your instructor or lab assistant.

14. Click **Exit** on the File menu.

15. Click **Yes** each time you are prompted to save Web page changes.

Test your knowledge by answering the following questions. See Appendix D to check your answers.

T   F   1. The best way to create a new Web is just to start, then let the design take shape randomly.

T   F   2. The page title is the same as the file name.

T   F   3. Serif fonts have little curves and lines on the tips of the letters.

T   F   4. To change the typeface of text in a Web page, you must first select the text.

T   F   5. Templates are ready-made Web pages that supply the content you need for your web.

ON*the*WEB

FINDING FRONTPAGE HELP ON THE WEB

T oday's software is much too complex for a new user to figure out alone. After taking courses, reading books, and using the program extensively, even experienced users find themselves looking for answers to various questions.

You have learned how to use FrontPage 2000's Help feature to find information and get answers to questions. However, even the best Help system cannot answer all of your questions. One reason is that the Help file is written before the program is released to the public. Some questions and quirks of the software may not be known until many people start using the software. Secondly, programs have to work within an ever-changing computer environment involving new computers, new programs, and new standards. Some questions cannot be foreseen at the time the software is written.

Fortunately, many new applications let you access an online support system over the Internet. At their Web site, companies constantly update their **knowledge base**—large files containing information about the program's features and idiosyncrasies. A separate support section contains the **Frequently Asked Questions (FAQ)**. Since other people are likely to have had the same problems, you may find the answers you seek by first consulting the FAQ.

In this activity, you will explore the Microsoft Office on the Web site to find out the ways in which you can receive support for FrontPage 2000 over the Internet.

   1. **Start FrontPage 2000, if necessary.**

   2. **Click Help on the menu bar and click Office on the Web.**

Your browser launches and, in most cases, you are automatically connected to the Internet. Within a few moments, you should see the Microsoft Office Welcome to FrontPage! Web page.

 *If you are not sure how to connect to the Internet or you do not know your user name and password, ask your instructor for assistance.*

   3. **Click the Maximize button ▣ .**

Your screen should like Figure 2.18 As part of the Microsoft Office Update site, you can find support for all Microsoft Office programs, including previous versions of FrontPage.

   4. **Scroll down and click the FrontPage 2000 Support link in the FrontPage Help Favorites section.**

A separate page appears entitled FAQs & Highlights for FrontPage 2000.

   5. **Click the Maximize button▣ , if necessary.**

   6. **Scroll down the page and click Frequently Asked Questions then click the link See the Frequently Asked Questions for FrontPage 2000.**

The FrontPage for Windows FAQ appears containing an extensive list of hyperlinks to various articles.

ON*the*WEB

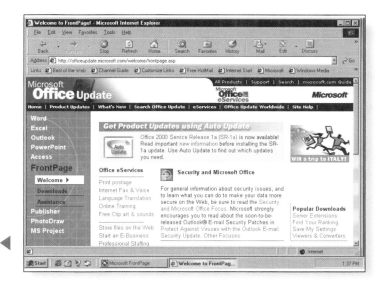

Figure 2.18 ◀
Microsoft FrontPage
welcome page

7. Click a link of interest, read through the article, then click the Close button 🗙.

You return to the Welcome to FrontPage! home page.

8. Scroll up within the Welcome to FrontPage! home page, then click the Assistance link under the FrontPage heading on the left side of the screen.

The FrontPage Assistance page appears containing links to each of the online help sections under the heading Help for FrontPage Users. There is also a list of Additional Resource Links.

9. Click the Tips and Tricks for FrontPage 2000 hyperlink.

The Tips and Tricks page appears.

10. Click the Show all descriptions check box at the top of the screen.

Descriptions for each of the tips appear.

11. Scroll through the Tips and Tricks page, noting the keyboard shortcuts in particular.

12. Close your Web browser.

13. Disconnect from the Internet if your instructor tells you to do so.

You may proceed directly to the exercises for this lesson. If, however, you are finished with your computer session, follow the "shut down" procedures for your lab or school environment.

Lesson Summary & Exercises

SUMMARY

Building your own Web using FrontPage 2000 can be a simple process. There are many preformatted Webs and Web pages upon which you can build. Creating meaningful and attractive Web sites used to be a job for computer professionals; however, FrontPage 2000 empowers anyone to do a good job on their own.

Lesson 2 showed you how to create a new Web and add Web pages based on templates included in the FrontPage 2000 software package. You saw how you could use the online Help system to make your own templates. Once pages were added, you learned to enter and format text. Also, you learned how to import text stored in a separate file into your Web page. Lastly, you found assistance with FrontPage 2000 using Office on the Web, a feature that can provide FAQ answers and tips on keyboard shortcuts.

Now that you have completed this lesson, you should be able to do the following:

- Design a Web. (page 38)
- Understand the purpose for the existence of most Web sites. (page 38)
- Explain the difference between a template and a wizard. (page 38)
- Understand the significance of a Web server. (page 39)
- Explain the role of an Internet Service Provider (ISP). (page 39)
- Create a new FrontPage Web based on a template. (page 39)
- Assign meaningful names to Web pages. (page 41)
- Add Web pages using templates. (page 44)
- Use Help to find out how to create your own template. (page 46)
- Enter text into a Web page. (page 47)
- Change the appearance of text through character formatting, including fonts, font sizes, and type styles. (page 50)
- Explain the difference between a serif and sans-serif typeface. (page 50)
- Describe fixed-width and proportional fonts. (page 51)
- Describe the FrontPage 2000 default fonts and how they function. (page 51)
- Explain how to apply type style effects or attributes. (page 54)
- Set the alignment of text to the left, right, or center of an area. (page 56)
- Import text into a Web page from a separate file. (page 58)
- Get FrontPage assistance using the Office on the Web feature. (page 60)

Lesson Summary & Exercises

CONCEPTS REVIEW

1 MATCHING

Match each of the terms on the left with the definitions on the right.

TERMS

1. Font
2. Importing
3. Wizard
4. Page title
5. Template
6. Proportional
7. Point
8. FAQ
9. Default
10. Sans serif

DEFINITIONS

a. A unit of measurement by which the size of characters is determined.

b. A set of characters with a specific typeface, one or more effects, and a specific size.

c. A Web page that answers commonly asked questions.

d. A process in which a file created by another program is brought into a Web page.

e. Character family in which small lines and curves do not appear on the tips of letters.

f. A program feature in which responses to a series of questions builds a new document.

g. A font type in which letters occupy only as much space as they need to be legible.

h. A user-friendly name that you give to a page within a Web.

i. A value or setting used automatically unless you change it.

j. A document that already contains text and design features that you will modify to suit your needs.

2 COMPLETION

Fill in the missing word or phrase for each of the following statements.

1. A(n) _____ is a company that publishes HTML documents so others can view your Web over the Internet.

2. _____ refers to the way letters, numbers, and symbols appear in the page.

3. Three types of _____ in FrontPage 2000 include left, right, and center.

4. Before you begin to create your Web, you should _____ it by laying out the basic structure.

5. In a _____ font each character occupies the same amount of space.

Lesson Summary & Exercises

6. A(n) _____ accepts requests from browsers and returns appropriate HTML documents over the Web.

7. The editing pointer with which you can select a word or paragraph is the _____ pointer.

8. When adding a new page to a Web, you can choose from a number of _____ that are preformatted pages with placeholders for text and graphics.

9. If you want to add text to a Web page that was created in a separate program and saved in a separate file, you should click File on the _____ menu.

10. To change the appearance of text you have already typed, you must _____ it first.

3 SHORT ANSWER

Write a brief answer to each of the following questions.

1. Describe the steps you must take to create a new Web named *MyWeb* in the *Acme* folder on your C:\ drive.

2. Name the four major categories of typefaces and their characteristics.

3. Name the four types of paragraph alignments.

4. Describe two ways to select a word.

5. What is the difference between a file name and a page title?

6. Name two advantages for using the Font dialog box rather than the character formatting icons on the toolbar.

7. Why do numbers appear before the point sizes in the Font Size drop-down box?

8. Why save your Web on your local hard drive rather than storing it only on a Web server?

9. What's the difference between a template and a wizard?

10. Name two ways to place your insertion pointer into an area on a page.

Lesson Summary & Exercises

4 IDENTIFICATION

Label each of the elements in Figure 2.19.

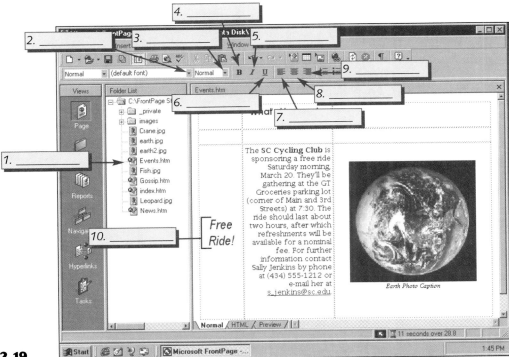

Figure 2.19

SKILLS REVIEW

Complete each of the Skills Review problems in sequential order to review your skills to create and save a new Web using a template; change a page title; add a new Web page using a template; access the FrontPage 2000 Help menu; add text to a Web page; change fonts, font sizes, and styles; set paragraph alignment; and import text.

1 Create and Save a New Web

1. Click **Start** [Start], point to **Programs**, and click **Microsoft FrontPage**.

2. Click **New** on the File menu and click **Web**.

3. Click the *One Page Web* template icon.

4. Type C:\FrontPage Student Data Disk\Skills Review\Acme in the *Specify the location of the new web* text box.

5. Click **OK**.

Lesson Summary & Exercises

2 Change the Page Title and Save the Page

1. Double-click *index.htm* in the Folder List.
2. Right-click the page window and click **Page Properties**.
3. Type Acme Products in the *Title* text box and click **OK**.
4. Click the **Save button** 🖫.
5. Click the **Folders view icon** 📁 to see the page title.

3 Add a New Page to a Web

1. Click the **Page view icon** 📄.
2. Point to **New** on the File menu and click **Page**.
3. Double-click *Narrow, Right-aligned Body*.
4. Click the **Save button** 🖫.
5. Type Products as the file name in the Save As dialog box, then click **Save** 🖫 Save .
6. Click **OK** in the Save Embedded Files dialog box.

4 Using Help

1. Click **Microsoft FrontPage Help** on the Help menu.
2. Click the **Answer Wizard** tab.
3. Type How do I change the space between characters? into the *What would you like to do?* text box.
4. Click **Search**.
5. Click Format text in the *Select topic to display* box.
6. Click <u>Increase or decrease space between characters</u> in the right pane.
7. Read the Help page.
8. Click the **Close button** ☒.

5 Adding Text to a Web Page

1. Double-click *index.htm* in the Folder List.

2. Type the following in the workspace:

We have a lot of exciting new merchandise here at Acme Products. Please explore our Web site to find out how Acme Products can enrich your life.

3. Click the **Save button** 💾.

4. Double-click *Products.htm* in the Folder List.

5. Click and drag to select *Your Heading Goes Here*.

6. Type Acme Leads the Way.

7. Click the **Save button** 💾.

6 Changing Fonts and Font Size

1. Select *Acme Leads the Way*.

2. Click the **Font drop-down arrow**.

3. Click **MS Sans Serif** or another sans-serif typeface.

4. Click the **Font Size drop-down arrow**.

5. Click **5 (18 pt)**, then click to deselect the heading. Your screen should look similar to Figure 2.20.

6. Click the **Save button** 💾.

7 Changing Type Styles

1. Double-click *index.htm* in the Folder List.

2. Select the entire paragraph.

3. On the Format menu, click **Font**.

4. Scroll down in the Font list and click **MS Serif**, or another serif font.

5. In the Size list, click **4 (14 pt)**.

6. Click the **Strong check box** in the Effects section.

7. Click **OK**.

8. Click the **Save button** 💾.

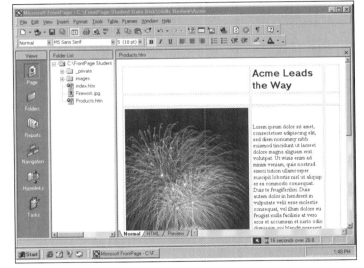

Figure 2.20

8 Setting Paragraph Alignment

1. Double-click *Products.htm* in the Folder List.

2. Select the *Acme Leads the Way* heading.

3. Click the **Center button** ▦.

4. Click the **Save button** 💾.

Lesson Summary & Exercises

9 Importing Text

1. Press `Tab` six times.

2. Click **File** on the Insert menu.

3. Click the **Look in drop-down arrow** in the Select File dialog box.

4. Click the drive containing your FrontPage Student Data Disk.

5. Double-click the *FrontPage Student Data Disk* folder.

6. Double-click the *Skills Review* folder.

7. Click the **Files of type drop-down arrow**.

8. Click **Word 97-2000 (*.doc)**.

9. Double-click *Every day*.

10. Click the **Save button** 💾.

11. Click **Close Web** on the File menu.

LESSON APPLICATIONS

1 Creating and Saving a New Web and Adding New Pages to a Web

Create and save a new Web. Add a new page to a Web based on a template. Change the page title and save the page.

1. Start FrontPage.

2. Create a new Web based on the *Personal Web* template. Save the new Web as *Personal* under the *Lesson Applications* folder of your FrontPage Student Data Disk (C:\FrontPage Student Data Disk\Lesson Applications\Personal).

3. Add a new page to the Web based on the *Two-column, Staggered Body* template, and save the page as *Family*. Save all the graphic images when prompted.

4. In the Page Properties dialog box, change the page title to *Family News*. Save the page.

Figure 2.21

5. Click the Folders icon to view the file name and title of the new page, then click the Page icon. Your screen should look similar to Figure 2.21.

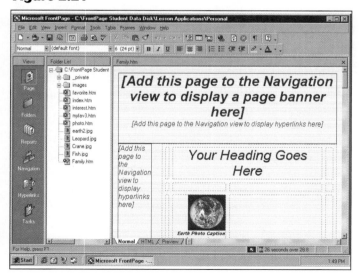

2 Entering Text into a Web Page

Enter text into a Web page and save the page.

1. Select *Your Heading Goes Here* and type What's Going On.

2. Select the paragraph under the earth caption and replace it with the following:

My brother Ron has been doing volunteer work for the Save the River Foundation. He spends every weekend cleaning the river and its banks. The Foundation's goal is to make the river safe for fish and other wildlife--maybe we'll be able to swim there again, as we did when we were kids!

3. Click in the text box to the right and type: My brother, the river rat!

4. Save the page.

3 Formatting Text and Importing Text from a File

Select individual words and change the typeface and font size. Select a paragraph and change type style, font size, and alignment. Import text into a Web from a separate file.

1. Select the words *What's Going On*.

2. Change the typeface to an unusual or whimsical font of your choosing.

3. Change the font size to 36 points.

4. Select the paragraph you typed beneath the earth graphic.

5. Format the paragraph with a 14-point serif font, aligned left.

6. Format *My brother, the river rat!* with a 24-point sans-serif font, centered.

7. Scroll down and click in the text box to the left of the leopard photo. Type Mom and Dad Celebrate 25th and format with the same 24-point sans-serif font, centered, as in step 6.

8. Highlight the leopard photo and placeholder text in the text box to the right of *Mom and Dad Celebrate 25th*. Import the Word document *anniversary.doc* from the *Lesson Applications* folder of your FrontPage Student Data Disk.

9. Format the imported text as described in step 5. Click to deselect the text. Your screen should look similar to Figure 2.22.

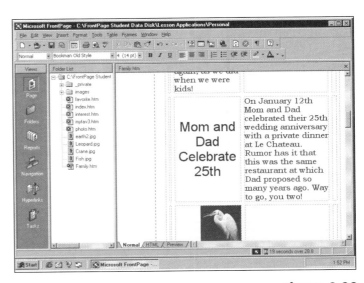

Figure 2.22

PROJECTS

1 Getting and Giving on the Web

The service organization you belong to would like you to spearhead the task of creating a Web site. The Benevolents (the name of the organization) would like to have the site communicate their goals (to aid at-risk youths), their membership, their fundraising events, and their charter.

Using pencil and paper, design a Web structure for the site. Use boxes in your design to represent welcome (*index* or *home*), membership, and fundraising events pages, as well as an *about* box in which you'll describe your organization. You may include additional pages, if you wish. (Since Projects 1–4 are interrelated, read all four projects before beginning Project 1.)

2 Spinning the Web

The executive committee for the Benevolents likes your design for its Web site and has asked you to continue working on the project. Create a Web for the Benevolents from a template of your choosing. Save the Web in the *Projects* folder on your FrontPage Student Data Disk (C:\FrontPage Student Data Disk\Projects\Benevolents). Base your Web on the design you made in Project 1. Add pages as needed to create a welcome page, a membership page, a fundraising events page, and an *about* page. Use templates that will suit the contents of your pages.

3 Author, Author!

You've written some content for the Benevolents Web site and everyone likes it. Write text for each of the Web pages you created in Project 2. Add text to the welcome page, the membership page, and the fundraising page. In the membership page, include a short biography, telephone number, and e-mail address for at least three people. Write a brief history and set of objectives for the *about* page. Enter and type at least one paragraph in a word processor such as Microsoft Word or WordPad. Save the document in the *Projects* folder as a Word file. Import the text into the appropriate page.

4 Making Pages Look "Font-astic"

The Benevolents Web pages now have the content that was agreed upon. To improve the appearance and highlight important items, you should choose three fonts to format the text. Pick two fonts for different sections of body text and another font for the headings. Change font sizes and styles to highlight words. Your Events Web page may resemble Figure 2.23 when it is complete.

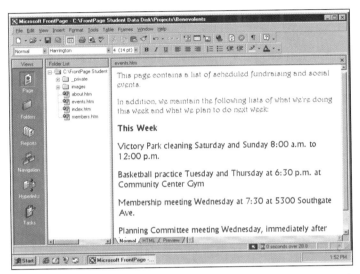

Figure 2.23

Project in Progress

5 Web Collectibles

Build a Web site for your collectibles store. Base the pages on the Web structure you designed in Lesson 1. Modify the structure, if necessary, so that the site includes a home page, one or more products pages, and a page with information about your store (telephone number, address, parking, store hours, and so on). Format the text to reflect the image you want.

Navigating a Web

CONTENTS

OBJECTIVES

After you complete this lesson, you will be able to do the following:

- Create a navigation structure for your Web.
- Add shared borders to all pages in your Web.
- Display a page banner at the top of every page.
- Type contact information so it will appear on the bottom of every page.
- Create and use a navigation bar so visitors can move through the Web site easily.
- Set a transition effect that occurs when moving from one page to another.
- Preview a Web in a browser.
- Create, verify, and edit hyperlinks that jump to another page, to an Office document, to an e-mail message, to a bookmark, or to another Web.

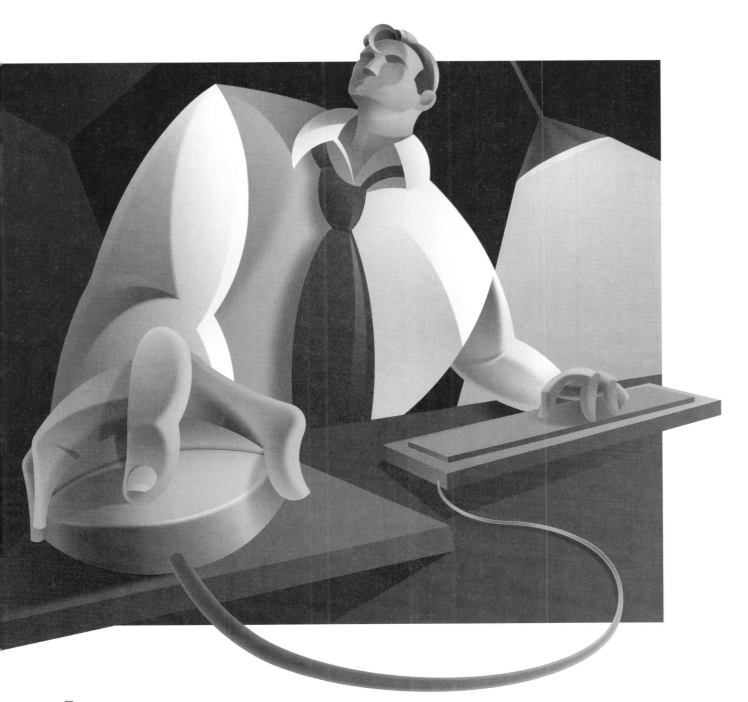

To be effective, a Web site must be well organized and users must be able to easily access the information they need. In this lesson, you will organize the Web you created in Lesson 2, insert hyperlinks, and control the way the user will move from one page to another.

ORGANIZING WEB PAGES

When you build a Web page by page, you must determine the relationship that should exist between the pages. You must indicate the parent pages, child pages, and the pages that share the same level.

When you design a Web, as you did in the previous lesson, you create the Web structure. Viewing your Web in the Navigation view, you can move your Web pages so that they match your intended structure. As a reminder, Figure 3.1 illustrates the design for the School Newsletter Web you created in Lesson 2.

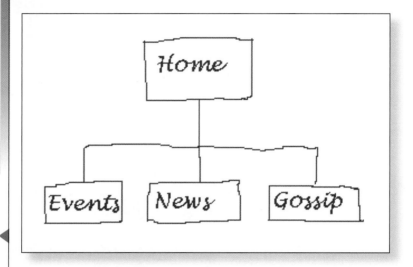

Figure 3.1
School Newsletter Web structure

Understanding the Navigation Structure

An unstructured Web consists of a home page and one or more unconnected pages. To create a navigation structure within Navigation view, you can drag pages from the Folder List and position them at appropriate levels under the home page. Dragging an unconnected page to a position beneath the home page, for example, will make the home page the parent page.

Within Navigation view, the pages appear in the workspace as page graphics (simply a box containing a page name). The page names within these graphics are called **page labels**. Page labels are important since they are the names used within navigation bars within your Web pages, so each label should effectively identify the content of the page. A navigation bar is a set of internal links on a page used to navigate to other pages in your Web. You will learn more about navigation bars later in this lesson.

To better understand how page labels and page titles affect your Web, you may want to review the information about page titles in Lesson 2. Table 3.1 summarizes the differences between page labels and page titles.

TABLE 3.1	PAGE NAMES IN FRONTPAGE 2000		
	Name Location:	**Name Appears In:**	**To Change:**
Page title	Folders view, Title column	Browser title bar and favorites or bookmarks (The terms *favorites* in Internet Explorer and *bookmarks* in Netscape Navigator refer to saved Web links that allow you to return quickly to favorite sites.)	In Folders view, click the file, right-click, then click Properties. Change the title in the Properties dialog box. Changing the page title does not affect the page label in Navigation view.
Page label	Navigation view page graphics	Navigation bars and page banners	In Navigation view, click the page graphic, right-click, click Rename, and type the label. In Page view, click the Save button. Changing the page label does not change the page title.

Creating a Navigation Structure

1. Click the Navigation view icon.

2. Drag a page from the Folder List to place it at the appropriate location in the Navigation window.

3. Right-click the page graphic, click Rename, and type a new page label, if necessary.

Creating the Navigation Structure

In this activity, you will create a navigation structure for the *School Newsletter* Web you created in Lesson 2.

1. Launch Microsoft FrontPage 2000.

2. Click Open Web on the File menu.

The Open Web dialog box appears.

3. Click the Look in drop-down arrow and locate and open the *School Newsletter* Web in the *Tutorial* folder on your FrontPage Student Data Disk.

4. Click the Navigation view icon 🗒.

By default, FrontPage displays your home page as a page graphic in the Navigation window. *Home Page* is the default page label for the file *index.htm*. This is the starting point for your Web navigation structure. You will now change the page label *Home Page* to make it consistent with the page title you assigned to this page in Lesson 2.

5. Right-click on the Home Page graphic and click Rename on the shortcut menu.

The words *Home Page* appear highlighted.

6. Type State College.

The new page label *State College* appears within the page graphic. Your screen should look like Figure 3.2.

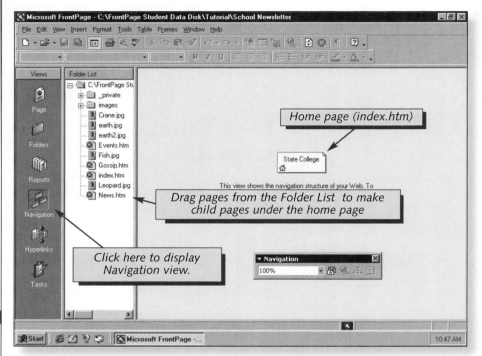

Figure 3.2
The Navigation view of the
School Newsletter Web

7. Click *Events.htm* in the Folder List and drag it into the Navigation window to place it beneath the *State College* page.

As you position *Events.htm*, a line appears linking the *State College* home page to the Events page. The page title *Your heading goes here* (abbreviated) appears within the *Events.htm* page graphic. You did not assign a page title to *Events.htm* in Lesson 2, so the default placeholder title *Your heading goes here* (visible in the Title column in Folders view) appears within the page graphic.

8. Right-click Your heading . . . in the *Events.htm* page graphic, and click Rename in the shortcut menu.

The name appears highlighted.

9. Type Events.

10. Drag *News.htm* just to the right of *Events*.

11. Right-click the *News.htm* page graphic, click Rename, and type News.

12. Drag *Gossip.htm* just to the right of *News*.

13. Right-click the *Gossip.htm* page graphic, click Rename, and type Gossip.

14. Click in the blank area of the workspace to dehighlight the text.

Your Navigation view will look like Figure 3.3.

Netiquette is a term that describes the rules of acceptable behavior for users of the Internet. For more information, browse to find the rules of netiquette home page at *www.albion.com.*

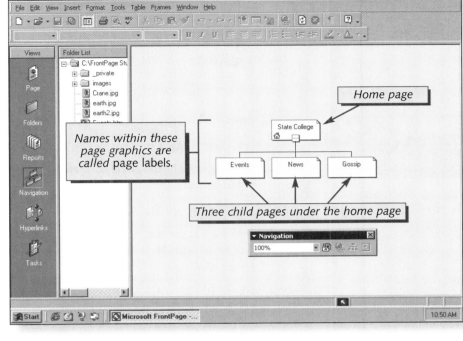

Figure 3.3
Completed navigation structure

USING COMMON PAGE ELEMENTS

In Lesson 2, you chose particular fonts and sizes to give the pages in your Web a consistent look. As you refine your Web, often you will want to add the same text or graphic elements to every page. For example, these elements may consist of a company logo, a copyright notice, an e-mail address, or a Web title. Additionally, you might want to add hyperlinks that users can click to navigate through the pages of your Web.

Using Shared Borders

Shared borders are areas on the edges of a Web page into which you can place Web elements that will appear on other pages in the Web. Shared borders can be placed on the top, left, right, or bottom of the Web page. When placed at the top or bottom, the border is similar to a header or footer, the text that appears on every page of a document.

Typically, the top border is used to display the title of the page or a logo. The bottom border is often used for copyright notices or the e-mail address of the organization or person responsible for maintaining the Web.

The main advantage to using shared borders is that you can change content in one place and automatically update all pages in a Web. If you wish, you can turn off shared borders for selected pages: Click Shared Borders on the Format menu then click Current Page to modify individual page settings.

Adding Shared Borders to All Pages

In this activity, you will add shared borders to the top, left, and bottom of your Web pages. In later activities, you will add a page banner, hyperlinks, and contact information.

1. Double-click *index.htm* and click the Normal tab, if necessary.

The Web page *index.htm* appears in Page view.

2. Right-click in a blank area of the *index.htm* window, then click Shared Borders in the shortcut menu.

The Shared Borders dialog box appears.

3. Click the All pages option button, then click the Top, Left, and Bottom check boxes. Make sure that the two *Include navigation buttons* check boxes are *not* checked.

The Shared Borders dialog box appears as shown in Figure 3.4. The preview window shows where the borders will appear on the page.

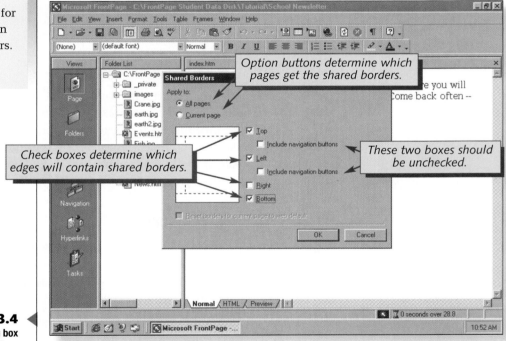

Adding Shared Borders to All Pages

1. Right-click the page window, then click Shared Borders on the shortcut menu.

2. Click the *All pages* option button.

3. Click the check boxes for the parts of the page on which you want borders.

4. Click OK.

Figure 3.4
The Shared Borders dialog box with selected options

4. Click OK.

The borders (a dashed line) appear on the top, left, and bottom of the home page, as in Figure 3.5. There are comments in each border that serve as placeholders for the text or Web elements you will add later.

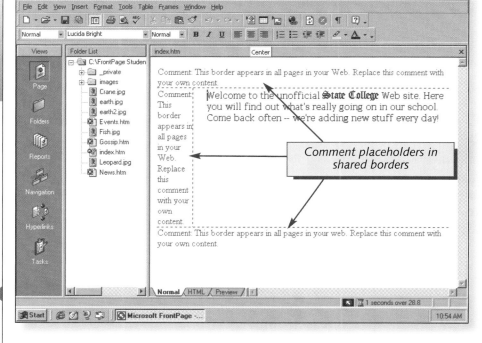

Comment placeholders in shared borders

Figure 3.5
Shared borders with comment placeholders

---

5. Double-click *Events.htm* in the Folder List.

The borders appear in this page as well.

6. Click the Preview tab.

No borders appear within the Preview tab. Until you replace the comment placeholders with your own text or graphic image, the borders will remain empty in the Preview tab.

7. Click the Normal tab.

You return to *Events.htm* displaying shared borders.

Adding Page Banners

The top shared border is a good place to display the name of the page. When placed at this location, the page name is called the ***page banner***. The page banner may be either formatted text or a graphic image. The page label is used as the name of the page—you may change the page label in Navigation view if you want to change the contents of the page banner.

Page banners can appear as either formatted text or as a picture. When you choose to have the page banner displayed as a picture, the appearance will depend on the theme that is in effect. You will learn how to assign a theme to a Web in a later lesson.

Page banners will not be displayed in pages that are not included in the navigation structure.

Adding a Page Banner to the Top Border

1. Click the comments placeholder.

2. Click Page Banner on the Insert menu.

3. Click the Text option button, then click OK.

4. Select and format the text as desired.

Adding a Page Banner to the Top Border

In this activity, you will add a page banner to the top shared border of your Web.

1. Double-click *index.htm* in the Folder List of your *School Newsletter* Web.

The page *index.htm* appears in Page view in the Normal tab.

2. Move the pointer to the comment placeholder in the top shared border.

The pointer changes to the shape of a hand holding a piece of paper.

3. Click the comment placeholder.

The comment placeholder is selected.

4. Click Page Banner on the Insert menu.

Note — *If you don't see the Page Banner option on the Insert menu, point to the arrow at the bottom of the menu and additional options will appear.*

The Page Banner Properties dialog box appears as in Figure 3.6. The page banner text—*State College*—is already completed (by default, this is the page label from Navigation view).

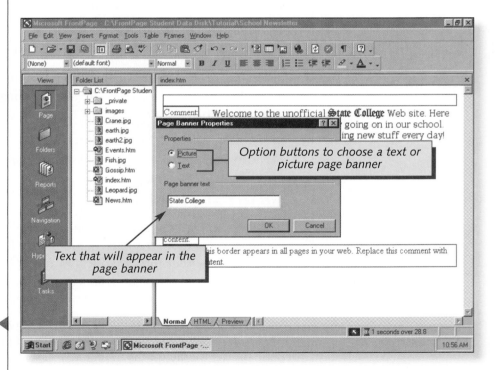

Figure 3.6
The Page Banner
Properties dialog box

5. Click the Text option button.

6. Click OK.

The page banner text is now in the top border of the page banner. The appearance of the page banner is rather unattractive since it has not yet been formatted.

7. Click the page banner text.

The words *State College* become highlighted.

8. Click the Font drop-down arrow, and click Old English (or click the same font you chose for *State College* in the paragraph below the banner).

The font changes to the new style.

9. Click the Font Size drop-down arrow and click 7 (36) pt.

The font changes to the larger size.

10. Click the Center button 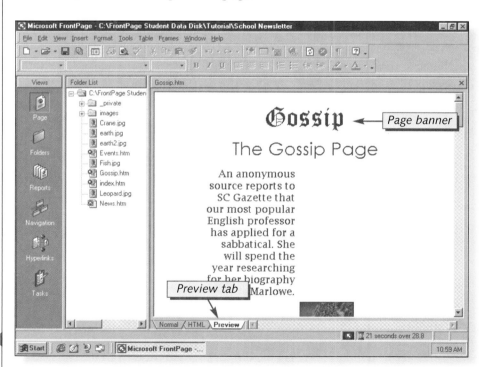 on the Formatting toolbar.

The banner text becomes centered.

11. Click the Preview tab.

The page *index.htm* appears without the borders. The page banner now dominates the top of the page in the font, font size, and alignment you have chosen.

12. Double-click *Gossip.htm* in the Folder List, then click the Preview tab.

The page banner *Gossip* appears in the *Gossip.htm* page, as shown in Figure 3.7. The font, font size, and alignment are the same as those you chose for *index.htm*, the *State College* home page.

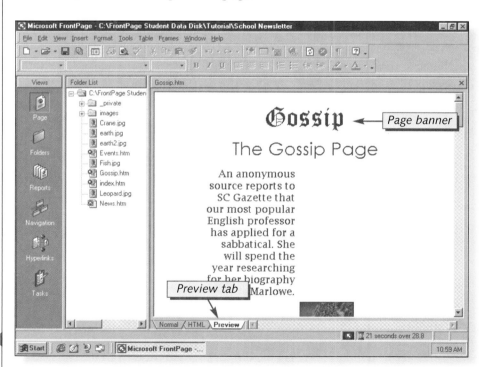

Figure 3.7
Web page with formatted page banner

13. Click the Normal tab.

The *Gossip.htm* page reappears with placeholder text within shared borders.

Adding Text within a Shared Border

You can place text within a shared border. On the bottom shared border, many Web sites display the e-mail address of the *webmaster*—the person responsible for the maintenance of the Web. Including the e-mail address of the webmaster in the bottom shared border provides a way for visitors to make contact from any page within the Web site. Later in this lesson, you will learn how to turn the e-mail address into a hyperlink, enabling visitors to compose and send a message by clicking on the link.

Adding Contact Information within a Shared Border

In this activity, you will add contact information to the bottom shared border. Within this text, you will include an e-mail address that visitors can use to send a message to the webmaster.

1. **Double-click *index.htm* in the Folder List of your *School Newsletter* Web.**

2. **Click the Normal tab.**

3. **Click the comment placeholder in the bottom shared border.**

4. **Type** Please send your complaints, comments, or suggestions to our Webmaster at webmaster@sc.edu.

5. **Double-click *News.htm* in the Folder List.**

6. **Click the Preview tab.**

7. **Scroll to the bottom of the page.**

The text you typed into the border appears at the bottom of this page, as in Figure 3.8.

Typing Text within a Shared Border

1. Click the comments placeholder in the shared border.

2. Type the text you wish to add.

3. Format the text as desired.

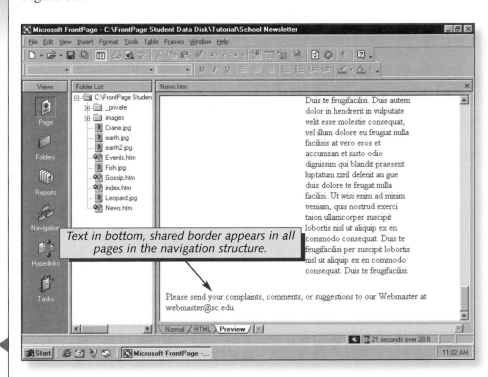

Text in bottom, shared border appears in all pages in the navigation structure.

Figure 3.8
Text in a shared border

USING NAVIGATION BARS

Once your Web has a navigation structure, you must give users the means by which they can move from one page to another. Rather than requiring you to insert internal hyperlinks into each page, FrontPage makes the process nearly automatic.

A **navigation bar** is a set of internal hyperlinks that users click to get to the pages within a Web. The navigation bar can be composed of buttons or formatted text. You need not have a hyperlink to every page in the Web. You may choose to include only links to the home page and the page's child pages. Or, you may wish to link only pages of the same level. You can set up separate navigation bars for any page, or make a navigation bar that will appear on every page.

Navigation bars can be placed in any shared border. You can add a navigation bar to the top or left shared border at the same time that you create the border. Later on, you can change the rules that govern which hyperlinks should be added to the navigation bar.

Adding a Navigation Bar to a Shared Border

Once you have a shared border, you can add a navigation bar at any time. The navigation bar appears as underlined page labels of your Web pages.

HANDS On

Adding a Navigation Bar

In this activity, you will add a navigation bar to the left shared border. You will include hyperlinks to all child pages under the home page (*Events*, *News*, and *Gossip*) as well as the home page itself.

1. **Double-click *index.htm* in the Folder List of your *School Newsletter* Web.**

2. **Click in the left shared border.**

The placeholder text is highlighted.

3. **Click Navigation Bar on the Insert menu.**

The Navigation Bar Properties dialog box appears as shown in Figure 3.9. This dialog box lets you connect various pages with hyperlinks in the navigation bar.

Note *If you move a page or add a page to your Web, FrontPage will automatically maintain your navigational hyperlinks.*

Figure 3.9 ◄
The Navigation Bar Properties
dialog box

Adding a Navigation Bar

1. Select the shared border that is to contain the navigation bar.

2. Click Navigation Bar on the Insert menu.

3. Click the option button that determines the pages to contain the links and the pages they should link to.

4. Click the Home page check box to include a link to the home page.

5. Click option buttons for the orientation and appearance you want.

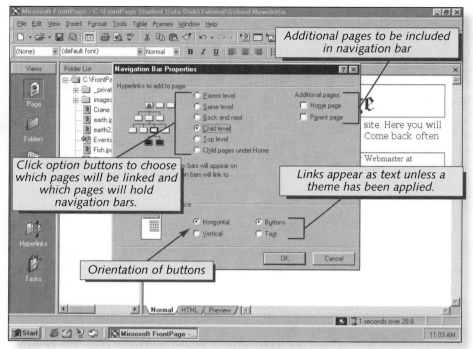

Additional pages to be included in navigation bar

Click option buttons to choose which pages will be linked and which pages will hold navigation bars.

Links appear as text unless a theme has been applied.

Orientation of buttons

4. Click the Child pages under Home option button.

This option will cause hyperlinks to appear to each of the main sections of the Web.

5. Click the Home page check box in the Additional Pages section.

This option will let the user jump back to the home page from any page within the Web.

6. Click the Vertical and Text option buttons in the Orientation and appearance section.

Your hyperlinks will only appear as buttons if you apply a theme to the Web, which you will do in a later lesson.

7. Click OK.

8. Click the Preview tab.

Your navigation bar appears as shown in Figure 3.10.

To delete a navigation bar from a shared border, click the navigation bar and press [Delete] while in Page view. The navigation bar will be removed from all pages that have the shared border.

To make your Web site usable by people with disabilities, check the guidelines and techniques available at *www.w3.org/WAI/*.

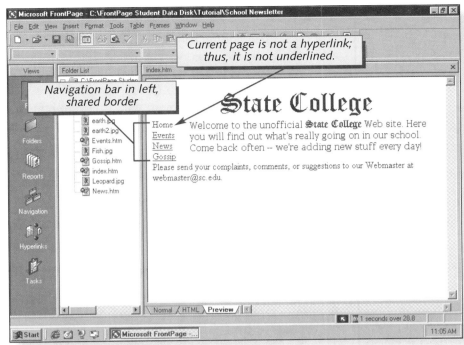

Figure 3.10
Web page with navigation bars in Preview mode

9. **Click the Save button** .

10. **Click any of the hyperlinks to move through the pages of your Web.**

Note
To test your hyperlinks in the Normal tab you can hold Ctrl and click each link. However, it is easier to click the hyperlinks within the Preview tab. Note that your hyperlinks change color after you click them. This color change lets the user know that the link has been clicked.

USING TRANSITION EFFECTS

FrontPage 2000 includes a number of ***transition effects*** that make your Web site more attractive and exciting to visitors. You will learn how to apply these effects to your Web. In this lesson, you will add transition effects to the *School Newsletter* Web.

Transition effects give your Web a slide-show appearance. As the visitor goes from one page to another the transition effect determines how a Web or page first appears in the browser.

There are many transition effects. An example of a transition effect is having a page fade in or out or open like window blinds. The effect can take place quickly or slowly—you set the duration to determine how fast the transition happens. Finally, you can choose when the transition takes place—when the page opens, when the page exits, when the site is entered, or when the site exits.

Applying Page Transitions

When adding transition effects to your Web, you should not overdo it. If you apply a different effect to every page, the overall impression to the visitor is one of chaos and confusion. Assuming that's not the look you want, choosing one transition effect for your Web or section of a Web is best. You should feel free to experiment with different effects and durations. It's easy to view the transitions by switching to the Preview tab.

Adding a Page Transition

In this activity, you will add a transition effect to the home page. The effect will occur slowly as the visitor leaves the page.

1. **Double-click *index.htm* in the Folder List of your *School Newsletter* Web.**

2. **Click the Normal tab.**

3. **Click Page Transition on the Format menu.**

The Page Transitions dialog box opens, as in Figure 3.11. The box includes controls for the event, the duration, and the transition effect.

Adding a Page Transition

1. Double-click the page in the Folder List, then click the Normal tab.

2. Click Page Transition on the Format menu.

3. Click when the effect should occur on the Event drop-down list.

4. Type the number of seconds in the Duration box.

5. Click an option in the Transition effect list.

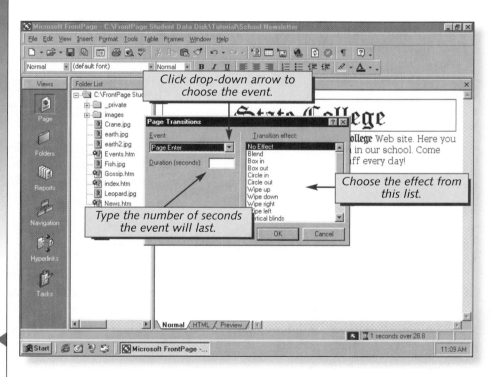

Figure 3.11
The Page Transitions dialog box

4. **Click the Event drop-down arrow, then click Page Exit.**

The effect will occur when the visitor clicks a link to leave the home page.

5. Click in the **Duration box**, then type 5.

The transition will take five seconds to complete.

6. Scroll down the Transition effect list, click **Random dissolve**, then click **OK**.

7. Click the **Save button** .

8. Click the **Preview tab**.

9. Click the **Events** hyperlink in the navigation bar.

Over a period of five seconds, the home page "twinkles away" and the *Events* page emerges. The same effect will occur whenever you click a link to exit the home page. The effect will not occur, however, when you move from one child page to another or back to the home page from a child page.

Note   *Cancel a page transition effect in the Page Transitions dialog box by clicking the event you previously chose for the page then clicking No Effect in the Transition effect list.*

Previewing a Web in a Browser

It is important to preview your Web to ensure that it looks as you intended and the hyperlinks function properly. As you have seen, the Preview tab makes it easy to check your links and preview the page. However, it is also a good idea to view your Web as a visitor would see it; that is, within a browser. One way to do this is to close your Web, saving pages if necessary. Then open your Web in your browser (such as Internet Explorer). If you want to view the Web within a second browser (such as Netscape Navigator) on the same computer, you should close the first browser and repeat the procedure for the second browser.

However, a better way to preview your Web is to use the Preview in Browser feature in FrontPage 2000. Using this method, you can launch your Web in your browser directly from FrontPage. If you open your Web in more than one browser, you have the advantage of seeing your Web as different browsers will see it. This is important since not all browsers display pages in exactly the same way.

Previewing in a Browser

In this activity, you will open the *School Newsletter* Web in your Web browser. If you have a second browser installed on your computer, you can also open the Web in that browser.

1. Click **Preview in Browser** on the File menu.

The Preview in Browser box should appear as in Figure 3.12. If more than one browser appears in the Browser window, you can repeat these steps to see the Web in each browser that you have.

Previewing in a Browser

1. Open the Web in FrontPage 2000.

2. Click Preview in Browser on the File menu.

3. Click the browser.

4. Click Preview.

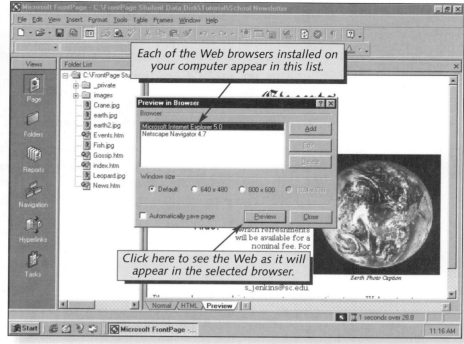

Each of the Web browsers installed on your computer appear in this list.

Click here to see the Web as it will appear in the selected browser.

Figure 3.12
The Preview in Browser dialog box

2. Click the browser in which you want to view your Web.

3. Click **Preview** [Preview].

4. If you see a message reminding you that you haven't saved your changes, click **Yes** to save them.

Your browser opens and the home page loads, as shown in Figure 3.13.

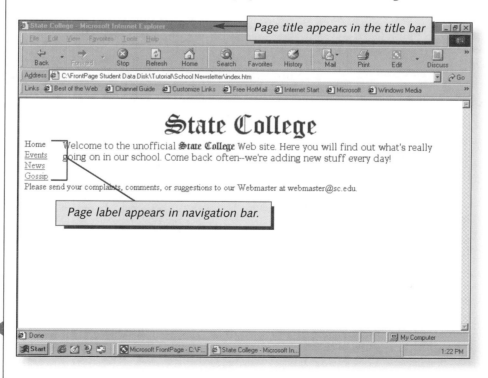

Page title appears in the title bar

Page label appears in navigation bar.

Figure 3.13
School Newsletter Web as seen in Internet Explorer

 As you have learned, the page title you assigned to your page (see the Title column in Folders view) appears in the title bar of your browser. The page label you assigned to your page in Navigation view appears in the Navigation bar. An exception to this is that regardless of the page label you assigned to your home page in Navigation view, _Home_ always appears by default in the Navigation bar.

5. Click the links in the navigation bar to explore the Web site. Note that your transition effect when leaving your home page is much more pronounced when viewed full-screen within a browser.

 Page transitions may not work in browsers other than Internet Explorer.

6. Click the **Close button** ⊠ to return to FrontPage.

7. Repeat steps 2 through 6 for each browser in the list within the Preview in Browser dialog box.

 If you receive a message asking to change your default browser, click No.

If you have Netscape Navigator in your list, your Web will appear as shown in Figure 3.14.

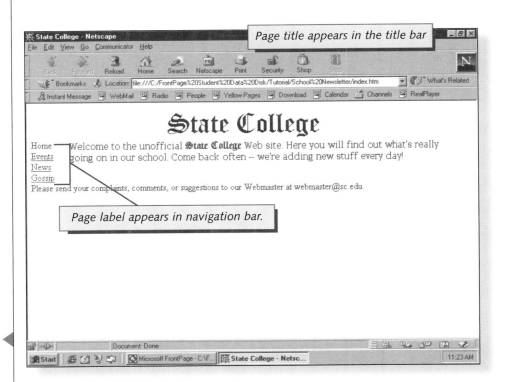

Figure 3.14
School Newsletter Web as seen
in Netscape Navigator

UNDERSTANDING HYPERLINKS

Hyperlinks are what make the Web such a unique medium. Books or tape must be accessed sequentially—from one page or scene to the next. But within a Web a single click of the mouse gives the user the power to skip elsewhere within a page, to another page, or to another Web. Hyperlinks can even launch another program, send an e-mail message, download a file, or conduct an online meeting.

A hyperlink does what the Web designer tells it to do. You added hyperlinks to your Web when you put the navigation bar in the shared left border. FrontPage 2000 automatically created a hyperlink to each page in the navigation structure. Hyperlinks can appear as formatted text, a button or other graphic, or one of several locations within a graphic.

Regardless of their appearance, hyperlinks share several common features— they are located in a particular place on the Web page; they cause an action to take place when clicked; and the action tied to a hyperlink depends upon the file, page, or location assigned as the destination URL. ***URL*** stands for ***Uniform Resource Locator***, which is a string of characters that defines the Internet address of a Web site or file on the World Wide Web, as well as the ***protocol***, or rules, that control how that information is accessed. An example of a URL is given in Figure 3.15 along with the identification of its parts.

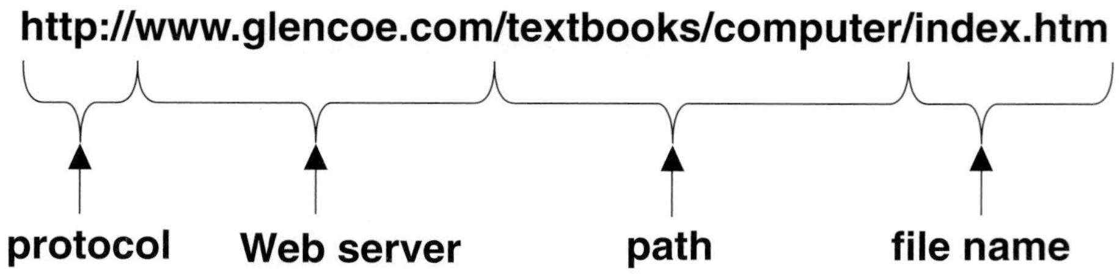

http://www.glencoe.com/textbooks/computer/index.htm

Figure 3.15
Parts of a URL

protocol   Web server   path   file name

There are only a few protocols you are likely to encounter. They are summarized in Table 3.2.

A ***Web server***, or host, is a computer that holds Web pages and files. Special software interprets *http* protocol giving visitors access to its Webs. The ***path*** is the hierarchy of drives and folders that locates a file on a disk. Most of the Internet access you conduct when you "surf the Web" uses *http* protocol.

TABLE 3.2	PROTOCOLS	
Protocol	**Stands for:**	**Functions**
http	Hypertext Transfer Protocol	The protocol that lets Web browsers get information stored on Web servers.
ftp	File Transfer Protocol	The protocol that controls the transfer of files between computers.
Gopher	Gopher	The protocol that presents a menuing interface containing links to documents, programs, or other gopher menus.
nntp	Network News Transfer Protocol	The Internet protocol that allows you to read and post messages over the USENET News system.
telnet	Telnet	The Internet standard protocol to log on to a remote computer.
file	File	The protocol that controls the access of files on your personal hard drive or network.
mailto	E-mail message	The Internet protocol that lets the visitor send an e-mail message by clicking on a hyperlink.

When a site wishes to make files available to users, an *ftp* site makes the process of ***downloading*** (copying files to your computer from another computer) and ***uploading*** (copying files from your computer to another computer) almost as simple as manipulating files on your own hard drive or local area network.

Gopher is a protocol for accessing menus of downloadable documents, programs, and other gopher menus. Telnet is used to log on to a remote computer and have your computer act more or less as a terminal on a network. There are two basic methods for exchanging messages over the Internet: direct mail using e-mail and posting and reading messages over the USENET news system.

File is not really a protocol—rather, it lets you load data from your own disk drive or on your local area network (LAN) into your Web browser. Likewise, *mailto* provides a way to open and address an e-mail message.

Using Relative and Absolute URLs

When you enter a URL, the requested page or file must be found and displayed quickly. If the file or page is moved or renamed, all of the hyperlinks must be updated as well. In addition, companies and individuals change Web servers for a variety of reasons relating to cost, size, and service. In a large Web the process of checking and revising hyperlinks can be long and tedious. One way to make the maintenance of Webs and their hyperlinks much easier is to avoid the use of **absolute URLs**. With an absolute URL, each part of the URL must be typed including the protocol, the server, each folder within the path, and the file name.

If you use a **relative URL** your hyperlinks remain valid even when the Web is moved to a new Web server. When entering a relative URL you omit some or all of the path. The hyperlink is then assumed to be in the same location as the page that contains the hyperlink. For example, assume your page URL is *http://www.myweb.com/main/index.htm*. If this page has a hyperlink with a URL of *contents.htm*, the page is assumed to be on the same server in the *main* folder. If the URL was */departments/product.htm* the page is assumed to be on the same server in the *departments* subfolder of the *main* folder. Using the relative URL method, only the home page has to have an absolute URL. If all of the links are relative and the Web is moved, only the URL of the home page is different.

Creating a Hyperlink to Another Page in the Web

There are several ways to create a hyperlink to another page in your Web. If you want the hyperlink to look like formatted text (colored and underlined text, by default), type the text, select it, click the Hyperlink button ⬜, and complete the Create Hyperlink dialog box. If you want the name of the page to be the hyperlink, put the insertion point where you want the hyperlink to be, click the Hyperlink button ⬜, then click the page to which you want to link.

Creating a Hyperlink to Another Page

In this activity, you will add a hyperlink that jumps to another page within your Web.

1. Click the **Page view icon** 🔲, double-click *index.htm* in the Folder List, and click the **Normal tab**, if necessary.

The page *index.htm* displays in Page view.

2. Select the text *what's really going* on within the *index.htm* page.

The four words are highlighted.

3. Click the **Hyperlink button** ⬜.

The Create Hyperlink dialog box appears, as in Figure 3.16.

Creating a Hyperlink to Another Page

1. Select the text to serve as the hyperlink.

2. Click the Hyperlink button.

3. Click the page in the Create Hyperlink dialog box and click OK.

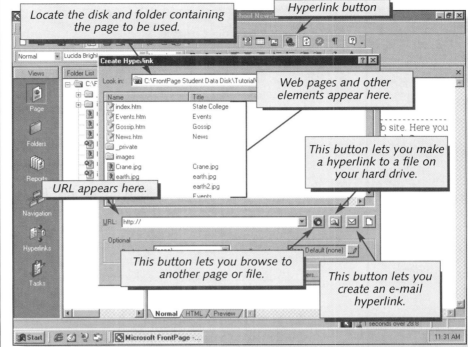

Locate the disk and folder containing the page to be used.

Hyperlink button

Web pages and other elements appear here.

This button lets you make a hyperlink to a file on your hard drive.

URL appears here.

This button lets you browse to another page or file.

This button lets you create an e-mail hyperlink.

Figure 3.16
The Create Hyperlink dialog box

Another Way

You can right-click on the selected text, then click Hyperlink to get to the Hyperlink dialog box.

4. Click *Events.htm* in the list of files.

The page's file name is automatically entered into the *URL* text box at the bottom of the Create Hyperlink dialog box.

5. Click OK.

You return to *index.htm* in FrontPage.

6. Click in the text area to deselect the highlighted words.

The four words appear in color and underlined, indicating that they form a hyperlink.

Verifying Hyperlinks in a Web

When creating or editing a hyperlink, you should follow it to make sure the hyperlink takes you to the right location. You can click the Preview tab or preview in your browser to check that the hyperlinks work. You can also check your hyperlinks in the Normal page view by holding down Ctrl while clicking the link. The process of checking your hyperlinks is called *verifying* or *following* your hyperlinks.

Verifying a Hyperlink

In this activity, you will follow the hyperlink you just created to make sure it works.

1. Double-click *index.htm* in the Folder List and click the Normal tab, if necessary.

2. Point to the what's really going on hyperlink.

1. In the Normal page view, press Ctrl and click the hyperlink.

2. Make sure the correct page, file, or location is displayed.

Creating a Hyperlink to an Office Document

1. Click the position to insert the hyperlink.

2. Click the Hyperlink button.

3. Click the Make a hyperlink to a file on your computer button.

4. Browse to the file, click the file, and click OK.

A message reading *Use Ctrl+Click to follow a hyperlink* appears over the text.

3. Press the Control key Ctrl.

The pointer changes into the Hyperlink Select pointer 👆.

4. Click the **what's really going on** **hyperlink.**

You jump to the *Events* page. You have verified that your hyperlink works exactly as you intended.

Opening an Office Document in a Web Browser

In Lesson 2, you learned to import text into a Web page through the Insert menu. You could use the same technique to place a spreadsheet into a Web page. However, such a document does not always give visitors the information they need. For example, if the data in the original document changes, the document you placed in the Web page will not change and will become outdated. Secondly, the document may take up valuable space in the Web.

A more effective way to present data from a document is to create a hyperlink to it. In this manner, when visitors click the hyperlink they will see the most recent version of the document. By inserting a hyperlink, the document takes up almost no space in the Web.

Creating a Hyperlink to an Office Document

In this activity, you will add a hyperlink that opens a Microsoft Word document into your *School Newsletter* Web.

1. Double-click *Events.htm* **in the Folder List and click the** **Normal tab**, **if necessary.**

2. Click an insertion point at the bottom of the page after s jenkins@sc.edu, **press the** Spacebar, **then type** For a detailed itinerary, click here.

3. Click the **Hyperlink button** 🌐.

The Create Hyperlink dialog box appears.

4. Click the **Make a hyperlink to a file on your computer button** 🔍.

The Select File dialog box opens.

5. Locate the *itinerary.doc* **file in the** *Tutorial* **folder of the FrontPage Student Data Disk.**

6. Double-click *itinerary.doc*.

 *Your computer may not list the extensions for known file types. In such a case, you will see the file as* itinerary *without the .doc extension.*

The Select File dialog box closes and the hyperlink appears in the page as the file name in color and underlined. The *../* in front of the file name is part of the relative URL. It indicates that the file is in the same parent folder as the *School Newsletter* Web; that is, the *Tutorial* folder.

7. Click the **Save button** 💾.

8. Click **Preview in Browser** on the File menu.

9. Click your browser, then click the **Preview button** [Preview].

The *School Newsletter* Web opens in your Web browser.

10. Click **../itinerary.doc**, the new hyperlink.

The document appears in the browser as in Figure 3.17.

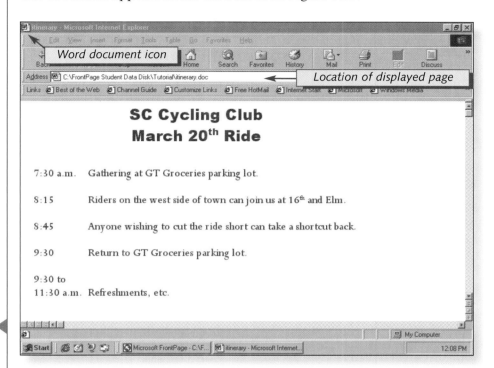

Figure 3.17
Microsoft Word document
opened by hyperlink

11. Click **Close** on the File menu to exit your browser and return to FrontPage.

Using E-mail Links

Electronic mail (e-mail) is the primary means of sending messages over the Internet. E-mail lets Internet users send and receive messages when it is most convenient for them. By including an e-mail hyperlink in a Web page, visitors can click the link and be presented with an open window of their e-mail editor with the recipient's e-mail address already completed. E-mail addresses are of the format *username@mailserver*. Sample e-mail addresses include: *bob@mymail.com* or *mary_kim@herisp.net*.

Many of the latest application software products (such as Microsoft Office and Corel Office Suite) tightly integrate their programs with Web browsers and other Internet functions. When you type text in URL or e-mail address format, these programs create a hyperlink automatically.

The e-mail window that opens when the visitor clicks the hyperlink (or when you verify it) depends on the default e-mail editor that is selected for your computer. In this tutorial, Microsoft Outlook Express 5 is configured as the default e-mail editor. Though your computer may be set up to use another e-mail editor, the steps in the following activity should be very similar.

Hints & Tips

If you don't want a program such as Microsoft Word to automatically create a hyperlink, you should undo the formatting, select the link and edit the format, or change the program's options that automatically format hyperlinks.

If you want to set Outlook Express 5 as your default e-mail program, launch Outlook Express. Click Options on the Tools menu and click the General tab. In the Default Messaging Programs section, click Make Default next to This application is NOT the default Mail handler.

HANDS On

Creating an E-mail Link

1. Click to create an insertion point for the hyperlink.

2. Click the Hyperlink button.

3. Click the Make a hyperlink that sends e-mail button.

4. Type the e-mail address and click OK.

Hints & Tips

If you want to remove a hyperlink altogether, you can delete the e-mail address that's formatted as a hyperlink directly within the page. If you want to keep the text, delete the URL in the Edit Hyperlink dialog box.

Creating an E-mail Link

In this activity, you will add a hyperlink that gives visitors the opportunity to send an electronic mail (e-mail) message to a predetermined recipient.

1. **Double-click *Events.htm* in the Folder List and click the Normal tab, if necessary.**

2. **Select the words webmaster@sc.edu in the bottom, shared border.**

3. **Click the Hyperlink button 🖼.**

The Create Hyperlink dialog box opens.

4. **Click the Make a hyperlink that sends E-mail button ✉.**

The Create E-mail Hyperlink dialog box appears.

5. **Type yourname@null.com in the *Type an E-mail address* text box (substitute your own first name for "yourname").**

6. **Click OK to close the Create E-mail Hyperlink dialog box.**

7. **Click OK to close the Create Hyperlink dialog box.**

You return to *Events.htm*.

8. **Click away from the selected e-mail address.**

The e-mail address is no longer highlighted. The address now appears underlined and in color as a hyperlink.

9. **Click the Preview tab then scroll down the page and click webmaster@sc.edu, the new hyperlink.**

Your e-mail program launches and a New Message window appears.

10. **Click the Maximize button ☐, if necessary.**

In the New Message e-mail window, you may enter a brief subject in the *Subject* text box, enter the text of your message in the workspace, and click Send to send your message. As you can see, the *To* text box contains the e-mail address you typed in the Create E-mail Hyperlink dialog box.

11. **Click the Close button ☒ on the New Message window.**

12. **Click No if you are asked to save changes.**

Editing a Hyperlink in a Web

Even when you use relative URLs, situations occur when you must manually edit a hyperlink or remove it. Fortunately, the procedure for editing a hyperlink is almost the same as creating one. Edit a hyperlink by highlighting the hyperlink, clicking the Hyperlink button , and editing the URL within the Edit Hyperlink dialog box. If you want to remove the hyperlink completely, just delete the URL from the Edit Hyperlink dialog box.

Editing a Hyperlink

In this activity, you will change the URL of a hyperlink in your Web.

1. **Double-click *Events.htm* in the Folder List and click the Normal tab, if necessary.**

2. **Click and drag to highlight the e-mail hyperlink s_jenkins@sc.edu.**

3. **Click the Hyperlink button.**

The Edit Hyperlink dialog box appears as in Figure 3.18 with *mailto:s_jenkins@sc.edu* highlighted in the *URL* text box.

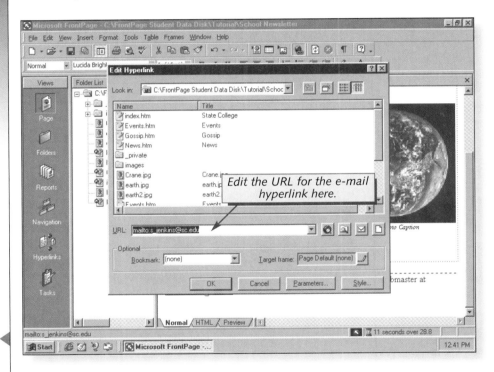

Editing a Hyperlink

1. Click and drag to highlight the hyperlink.

2. Click the Hyperlink button.

3. Change the URL to edit it, or delete the URL to remove it.

4. Click OK.

4. **Type mailto: then your e-mail address or, if you don't have one, type an e-mail address provided by your instructor.**

5. **Click OK.**

The Edit Hyperlink dialog box closes and you return to *Events.htm* within FrontPage.

6. **Click s_jenkins@sc.edu within the Preview tab of *Events.htm* to verify your hyperlink.**

Your e-mail program launches a New Message window.

7. **Compose and send a message, if you used a functioning e-mail address in step 4.**

8. **Save the changes you made to *Events.htm*.**

The world's first e-mail was sent by Ray Tomlinson of ARPANET (the precursor of the Internet). It said, "Testing 1-2-3." His second message told all users how to send e-mail using the *username@mailserver* format.

Changing the Color of Hyperlinks

In this activity, you will use the FrontPage Help system to find out how to change the appearance of hyperlinks.

1. Click **Microsoft FrontPage Help** on the Help menu.

2. Click the **Index tab**.

3. Type hyperlink in the *Type keywords* text box.

4. Click the **Search button** Search.

The Help system provides search results as topics in the bottom left pane and corresponding topic information in the right pane of the Help window.

5. Scroll down in the *Choose a topic* list box and click **Set hyperlink colors**.

The Help window should appear as shown in Figure 3.19.

Figure 3.19

Help window, Index tab

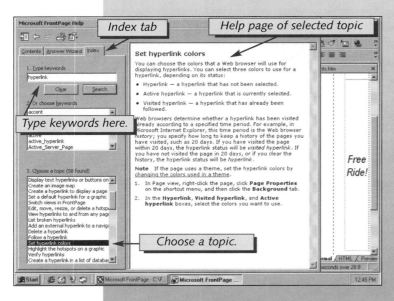

6. Read how to change the colors of three catagories of hyperlinks—those hyperlinks that have not yet been selected; those hyperlinks that are active (currently selected); and those hyperlinks that have already been visited or followed.

7. Click the **Close button** ☒ to close the Help window.

You return to the *School Newsletter* Web.

The term *bookmark* is also used to describe a program function of the Netscape Navigator browser that enables users to save favorite Web sites so they can quickly return to them.

Using Bookmarks

Bookmarks are place markers to a location or selected text within a Web page. Once you have placed a bookmark in a page, you can create a hyperlink that jumps to it. The bookmark can be on the same page or on another page—relative or absolute URLs determine the page. If the bookmark is just a location on the page, you will see a bookmark icon ⚐. If the bookmark is created from selected text, the text will appear with a dashed underline.

You can also use bookmarks to jump to sections within a page during the design and editing of a Web. Give each section a bookmark, and then use the Bookmark dialog box to go to the section you need to edit.

HANDS On

FrontPage BASICS

Creating a Bookmark

1. Click an insertion point (to bookmark a location) or select the text (to bookmark text), as appropriate.

2. Click Bookmark on the Insert menu.

3. Type a name for the bookmark and click OK.

Creating a Bookmark

In this activity, you will add a location bookmark that will let you jump to the top of a page. In the next activity, you will add the hyperlinks that use this bookmark.

1. Double-click *Gossip.htm* in the Folder List and click the Normal tab, if necessary.

2. Click an insertion point to the left of the letter *T* in the heading *The Gossip Page*.

3. Click Bookmark on the Insert menu.

The Bookmark dialog box appears as in Figure 3.20. In this dialog box, you create a new bookmark by typing a bookmark name; jump to an existing bookmark by selecting it and clicking *Goto*; or delete a bookmark by selecting it and clicking Clear.

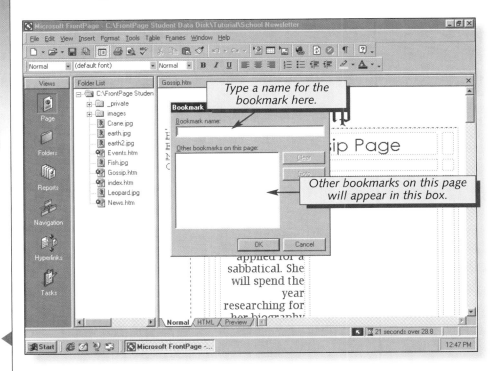

Type a name for the bookmark here.

Other bookmarks on this page will appear in this box.

Figure 3.20
The Bookmark dialog box

4. Type top in the *Bookmark name* text box, then click OK.

The Bookmark dialog box closes and the bookmark flag 🚩 appears next to *The Gossip Page* heading. For the bookmark to be functional, you must use a *Goto* command to jump to the bookmark while editing the page or create a hyperlink to allow Web visitors to jump there.

5. Click the Save button 💾.

Creating a Hyperlink to a Bookmark

To create a hyperlink that jumps to a bookmark, you use the Hyperlink button ![icon]. If the bookmark is on another page, you must first select the page. Then you use the Bookmark drop-down list to find the name of the bookmark to be used. In the URL box, a pound symbol (#) will precede the bookmark name—that symbol indicates a link to a bookmark.

Adding a Hyperlink to a Bookmark

In this activity, you will add hyperlinks that jump to the top of the Web page from each of the sections within the page. You will use the bookmark that you created in the previous activity.

1. **Double-click** *Gossip.htm* **in the Folder List and click the** **Normal tab**, **if necessary.**

2. **Click anywhere within the paragraph that begins** *An anonymous source . . . .*

3. **Press** Ctrl + ↓.

This keyboard shortcut jumps the insertion point to the end of the paragraph.

4. **Press** Enter⏎ **to move to a new line.**

5. **Click the** **Font Size drop-down arrow and click** **2 (10 pt).**

6. **Type** back to top, **then click and drag to select back to top.**

7. **Click the** **Hyperlink button** ![icon].

The Create Hyperlink dialog box appears.

8. **Click the** **Bookmark drop-down arrow**, **then click** **top** (the name of your bookmark).

The bookmark appears in the *URL* text box as shown in Figure 3.21.

Adding a Hyperlink to a Bookmark

1. Select the text that will become the hyperlink.

2. Click the Hyperlink button.

3. In the Create Hyperlink dialog box, click the name of your bookmark then click OK.

4. Click your hyperlink to verify it.

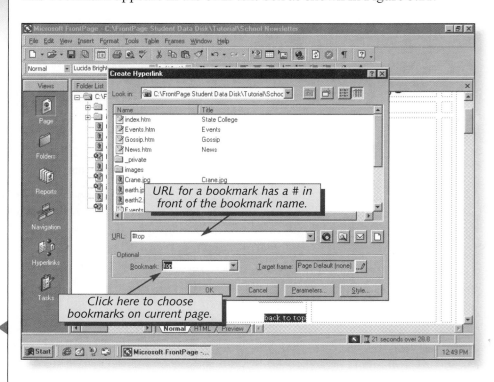

Figure 3.21
A bookmark used as the target of a hyperlink

9. Click OK.

The Create Hyperlink dialog box closes and you return to *Gossip.htm* in the *School Newsletter* Web.

10. Click in a blank area of the workspace.

The text <u>back to top</u> now appears as a hyperlink.

11. Press [Ctrl] and click **back to top**.

You jump to the top of the page, and the bookmark flag 🚩 appears highlighted.

12. Copy and paste the hyperlink <u>back to top</u> on a new line at the end of each of the other paragraphs on the page.

13. Click the Save button 💾.

14. Close the Web and exit FrontPage.

Test your knowledge by answering the following questions. See Appendix D to check your answers.

T F 1. Protocols are rules for proper user behavior while on the Internet.

T F 2. You must select text before you can create a hyperlink.

T F 3. When you enter text in a shared border, the text can appear on every page.

T F 4. If you drag a page under the home page in Navigation view, it will be a child of the home page.

T F 5. An e-mail hyperlink will send a message automatically when clicked.

ON*the*WEB

LINKING TO ANOTHER WEB

Web pages often contain links to other Webs that are in some way related. For example, the links may lead to Webs on the same subject. They may be sites that the webmaster likes or feels that other visitors would enjoy. The link may be to an ftp site that helps you download a related file. Creating hyperlinks to other Webs saves visitors the trouble of manually recording complicated URLs. These links enable users to *browse* or *surf* the Web.

1. **Launch Microsoft FrontPage and open** *index.htm* **within the** *School Newsletter* **Web in Page view in the Normal tab.**

2. **Click an insertion point after** *every day!,* **the last words in the main paragraph, then press** Enter⏎ **.**

The insertion point moves to a new line.

3. **Type** Please support our sponsor U-Can-Use-It Software.

Your page should look like Figure 3.22.

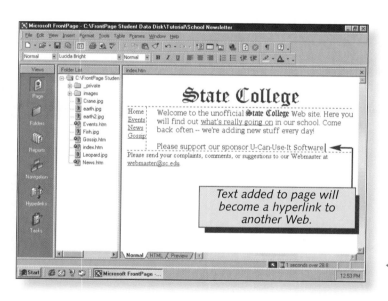

◀ **Figure 3.22**
Text added to the School Newsletter home page

4. **Click and drag to select the words** *U-Can-Use-It Software.*

5. **Click the Hyperlink button** 🖼️.

The Create Hyperlink dialog box appears.

6. **Click the Use your Web Browser to select a page or file button** 🔘.

Your Web browser opens and you connect to the Internet. At this point, you can browse to any Web site to make that your hyperlink.

From this point you can easily create an external link to a Web page through your browser. Navigate to the Web site in your browser, then minimize your browser window. The URL of the Web site will appear in the Edit Hyperlink dialog box; click OK. Verify the link in the Preview tab.

7. Click **Open** on the File menu.

The Open dialog box appears. Here you can either enter a file to open or click to browse to the file.

8. Click the **Browse button** [Browse...].

9. Click the **Look in drop-down arrow**, then navigate to the folder containing your FrontPage Student Data Disk.

10. Double-click the *U-Can-Use-It* folder.

11. Scroll as necessary, then double-click *index*.

12. Click **OK**.

The *U-Can-Use-It Software* home page opens in your Web browser.

13. Click the **Edit button** [Edit] on the toolbar of your browser.

The Create Hyperlink dialog box appears containing the URL of the *U-Can-Use-It* Web page.

14. Click **OK**.

Your browser window is minimized and you return to *index.htm* in the *School Newsletter* Web.

The text U-Can-Use-It Software (still highlighted) is now a hyperlink to the *U-Can-Use-It* Web page.

15. Click the browser icon on your taskbar (below your Web page) to maximize your browser window, then click **Close** [X] to close your Web browser.

You return to *index.htm* in the *School Newsletter* Web.

16. Click the **Preview tab**.

17. Click the **U-Can-Use-It Software** hyperlink.

Your page transition effect fades the *index.htm* page in the *School Newsletter* Web from the screen and the *index.htm* page in the *U-Can-Use-It* Web appears. Note that the Folder List still shows the pages in the *School Newsletter* Web.

18. Close the Web, saving changes to the Web pages when prompted, and exit FrontPage.

You may proceed directly to the exercises for this lesson. If, however, you are finished with your computer session, follow the "shut down" procedures for your school or lab environment.

Lesson Summary & Exercises

SUMMARY

Just as important as the contents of a Web site is the means by which visitors navigate to the information. In this lesson you learned how to organize your Web's structure, identify pages with a page banner, add contact information, and establish a navigation bar within shared page borders. Once you learned how to create a navigation bar, you created a transition effect to enhance the appearance of your Web.

You learned that adding hyperlinks to your Web provides a means by which visitors can jump from one page to another; open Office documents in a Web browser; open a new message window to send e-mail; and jump to bookmarked locations in a page. Using FrontPage 2000 Help, you learned where to find information to change the colors of hyperlinks. Finally, you created a hyperlink to enable visitors to jump from your Web to another Web.

Now that you have completed this lesson, you should be able to do the following:

- Create a navigation structure for your Web in Navigation view. (page 75)
- Add shared borders to all pages in a Web. (page 77)
- Display a page banner at the top of every page in a Web. (page 80)
- Type contact information in a shared bottom border so it will appear on the bottom of every page. (page 82)
- Add a navigation bar to a shared border. (page 83)
- Apply a transition effect. (page 86)
- Preview a Web in a browser. (page 87)
- Understand the significance of relative and absolute URLs. (page 92)
- Create a hyperlink to another page in a Web. (page 92)
- Verify navigation bar hyperlinks in a browser and in Page view through the Normal and Preview tabs. (page 93)
- Create a hyperlink to a document so it can be accessed in a browser. (page 94)
- Create and use e-mail hyperlinks. (page 96)
- Edit and change the color of a hyperlink. (page 97)
- Create bookmarks and set a hyperlink to a bookmark to navigate within a page. (page 99)

Lesson Summary & Exercises

CONCEPTS REVIEW

1 MATCHING

Match each of the terms on the left with the definitions on the right.

TERMS

1. protocol
2. bookmark
3. relative URL
4. verifying
5. shared borders
6. transition effects
7. downloading
8. page banner
9. navigation bar
10. e-mail

DEFINITIONS

a. The act of following a hyperlink to make sure it works

b. A location within a page to which you can hyperlink

c. One of the primary means of sending messages over the Internet

d. A set of rules that govern how computers communicate with each other

e. Graphic element or text that appears in the top shared border

f. The process of copying files from another computer

g. An address to a Web page written to make it easy to maintain a Web site that has to be moved

h. A set of internal hyperlinks that jump to other pages in the Web

i. An event that may occur during the opening or closing of a Web page

j. Areas of a page that may contain common elements for other pages in the Web

2 COMPLETION

Fill in the missing word or phrase for each of the following statements.

1. To make a Web page the child of another page, you should drag the page while in the _____ view.

2. To control how long a transition effect takes place, change the _____ in the Page Transitions dialog box.

3. The format of an e-mail address is **username@** _____.

4. When the URL for a hyperlink starts with a pound sign (#), the link will jump to a(n) _____.

5. A(n) _____ placed in a shared border, gives every page a set of hyperlinks to other pages.

6. A(n) _____ URL remains valid even when the Web is moved to a new location.

7. A(n) _____ is a computer that runs special software giving users access to Web pages and files.

8. The page names that appear within the page graphics in Navigation view are called _____.

9. _____ are areas on the edges of a Web page in which you can place elements that will appear on other pages in the Web.

10. _____ is the Internet protocol that lets Web browsers get information stored on Web servers.

3 SHORT ANSWER

Write a brief answer to each of the following questions.

1. Describe the difference between absolute and relative URLs.

2. List three Internet protocols. Give one use for each.

3. What kinds of page elements can be placed in a shared border? Name at least three.

4. Describe what happens when a visitor clicks an e-mail hyperlink.

5. What are the three options to select when creating a page transition? What does each do?

6. Briefly describe the steps to create a hyperlink to another page in the same Web.

7. Assume you are starting with a Web with no navigation structure. Explain the steps necessary to add a navigation bar to all pages in your Web.

8. What must you do if you want to create a jump to a specific location on a page?

9. Name two methods for verifying a hyperlink.

10. What is the difference between uploading and downloading?

4 IDENTIFICATION

Label each of the elements in Figure 3.23.

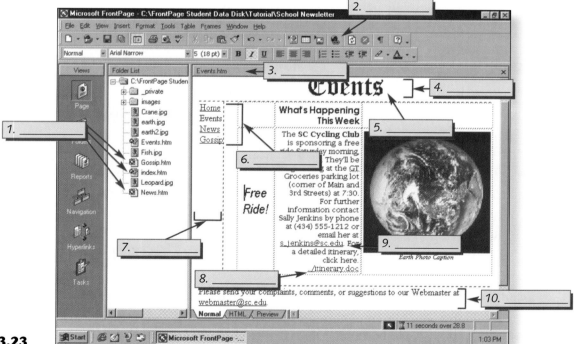

Figure 3.23

Lesson Summary & Exercises

SKILLS REVIEW

Complete each of the Skills Review problems in sequential order to review your skills to create a navigation structure; add shared borders to all pages; add a page banner, text, and a navigation bar to shared borders; add a transition effect and preview your Web in a browser; and create, edit, and verify hyperlinks to another page in a Web, to an Office document, to an e-mail window, and to bookmarks.

1 Creating a Navigation Structure

1. Launch Microsoft FrontPage 2000.
2. Click **Open Web** on the File menu.
3. Locate and open the *Acme* Web in the *Skills Review* folder on your FrontPage Student Data Disk.
4. Click the **Navigation view icon**.
5. Drag *Products.htm* to make it a child page under the Acme Products home page graphic.
6. Right-click in the new child page graphic and type Products.

2 Adding Shared Borders to All Pages

1. Double-click *index.htm* in the Folder List to display it in Page view in the Normal tab.
2. Right-click on the page, then click **Shared Borders** on the shortcut menu.
3. Click the **All pages option button** in the Shared Borders dialog box.
4. Click the **Top**, **Left**, and **Bottom check boxes**.
5. Uncheck the **Include navigation buttons boxes**, if necessary, and click **OK**.

3 Adding a Page Banner and Text to the Shared Borders

1. Click the comment placeholder in the top shared border to highlight it.
2. Click **Page Banner** on the Insert menu.
3. Click the **Text option button** in the Page Banner Properties dialog box, then click **OK**.
4. Click the page banner to highlight it, then click the **Font drop-down arrow** and click **Arial Rounded** or a headline font of your choosing.
5. Click the **Font Size drop-down arrow**, click **6 (24 pt)**, and click the **Center button**.
6. Click the comment placeholder in the bottom shared border.
7. Type Let us know how we can best serve you.
8. Click the **Align Right button**.

4 Adding a Navigation Bar

1. Click the comment placeholder in the left shared border to highlight it.
2. Click **Navigation Bar** on the Insert menu.

3. Click the **Child pages under Home option button** in the Navigation Bar Properites dialog box.

4. Click the **Home page check box**.

5. Click the **Vertical** and **Text option buttons**, then click **OK**.

6. Click the **Save button** 🖫.

5 Adding a Page Transition and Previewing Your Web in a Browser

1. Click **Page Transition** on the Format menu.

2. Click the **Event drop-down arrow** in the Page Transitions dialog box, then click **Page Exit**.

3. Type 4 in the Duration box.

4. Click **Circle out** in the Transition effect list.

5. Click **OK**, then click the **Save button** 🖫.

6. Click **Preview in Browser** on the File menu.

7. Click your browser in the Preview in Browser dialog box, then click the **Preview button**.

8. Click **Yes** if asked to save changes, then click the **Maximize button** ⬜ when the Web launches in your browser, if necessary.

9. Click the **Products** link in the navigation bar to observe the transition effect. Your screen should resemble Figure 3.24.

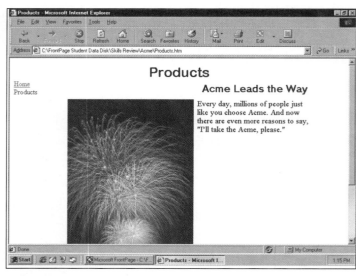

Figure 3.24

10. Click the **Close button** ⊠ on your browser to return to FrontPage.

6 Creating and Verifying a Hyperlink to Another Page in the Web

1. Double-click *index.htm* in the Folder List to view it in Page view in the Normal tab.

2. Select the word *merchandise* in the paragraph.

3. Click the **Hyperlink button** 🖼.

4. Click the page *Products.htm* in the Create Hyperlink dialog box, then click **OK**.

5. Click the **Save button** 🖫.

6. Click to deselect the hyperlink.

7. Press `Ctrl` and click **merchandise** to verify the hyperlink.

Lesson Summary & Exercises

7 Creating a Hyperlink to an Office Document

1. Click an insertion point at the end of the paragraph in *Products.htm*.
2. Press ⌨Enter⏎ to move to a new line, then type Click here to see what our customers think of Acme products.
3. Select the sentence you just typed.
4. Click the **Hyperlink button** 🌐.
5. Click the **Make a hyperlink to a file on your computer button** 🔍.
6. Navigate to the *Skills Review* folder on the FrontPage Student Data Disk.
7. Double-click the *endorsements.doc* file.
8. Click the **Save button** 💾.
9. Click **Preview in Browser** on the File menu.
10. Click your browser in the Preview in Browser dialog box, and click the **Preview button**.
11. Click to verify the link **Click here to see what our customers think of Acme products**.
12. Click **Close** on the browser's File menu.

8 Creating and Editing an E-mail Link

1. In the bottom shared border select *Let us know how we can best serve you*.
2. Click the **Hyperlink button** 🌐.
3. Click the **Make a hyperlink that sends E-mail button** ✉ in the Create Hyperlink dialog box.
4. Type yourname@null.com in the Create E-mail Hyperlink box.
5. Click **OK** to close the Create E-mail Hyperlink box, then click **OK** to close the Edit Hyperlink dialog box.
6. Click the **Hyperlink button** 🌐.
7. Select *yourname@null.com*, and type your e-mail address or an e-mail address provided by your instructor.
8. Click **OK**.
9. Click the **Save button** 💾.
10. Click the **Preview tab**, scroll down, then click the link **Let us know how we can best serve you**.
11. Click the **Close button** ✕ in the New Message window of your e-mail program.

9 Use Help to Learn about Repairing Broken Hyperlinks

1. Click **Microsoft FrontPage Help** on the Help menu.
2. Click the **Index tab**.
3. Type hyperlink in the *Type keywords* text box.

Lesson Summary & Exercises

4. Click the **Search button**.

5. Click **Repair Broken Hyperlinks** in the *Choose a topic* list.

6. Read the Help page.

7. Click the **Close button** ☒ on the Help window.

10 Creating a Bookmark and Linking to the Bookmark

1. Double-click *Products.htm* in the Folder List, if necessary. Make sure you are in Page view in the Normal tab.

2. Click an insertion point in the text box to the left of *Acme Leads the Way* (below the *Products* heading).

3. Click **Bookmark** on the Insert menu.

4. Type top as the Bookmark name in the Bookmark dialog box, then click **OK**.

5. Click in the paragraph of text next to the photo, then click Ctrl + ↓ twice.

6. Press Enter↵ eight times.

7. Click the **Font Size drop-down arrow** and click **3 (12 pt)**.

8. Type Top of page and then select it.

9. Click the **Hyperlink button** 🖼.

10. Click **top** in the **Bookmark drop-down list**, then click **OK**.

11. Click the **Save button** 💾.

12. Press Ctrl then click the new hyperlink to verify it.

13. Click **Close Web** on the File menu.

LESSON APPLICATIONS

1 Setting the Navigation Structure and Shared Border Elements

Create the navigation structure in Navigation view, change shared borders, and add text to a shared border.

1. Start Microsoft FrontPage 2000, if necessary, and open the *Personal* Web in the *Lesson Applications* folder on your FrontPage Student Data Disk.

2. In the Navigation view, make *Family.htm* the second child page from the left under *Home Page*. Make *myfav3.htm* a child page under *Favorites*.

3. Change the shared borders for all pages by removing the left border and adding a bottom border.

4. Type the following bottom border: Write me and let me know what you think of my site.

5. Save your changes.

Lesson Summary & Exercises

2 Adding Navigation Bars and Page Transitions

Change the navigation bar, apply page transitions, and verify the navigation bar links in a browser.

1. Add a navigation bar to the top border. Within *index.htm*, right-click *Edit the Properties for this Navigation bar . . .* and click Navigation Bar Properties on the shortcut menu.

2. In your navigation bar, include child pages under the home page and the home page itself. Orientation should be Horizontal and appearance should be Text. Your *index* page should look like Figure 3.25.

3. Choose a page transition to occur when you enter the home page and an opposite effect when you exit the home page (for example, wipe left and wipe right or vertical blinds and horizontal blinds).

4. Use the Preview in Browser option to verify your navigation bar and to observe your page transitions.

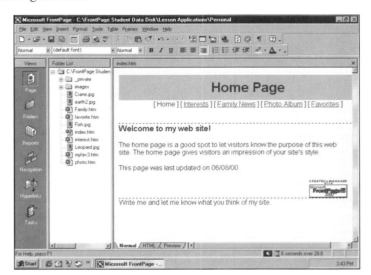

Figure 3.25

3 Creating, Editing, and Verifying Hyperlinks and Bookmarks

Add and verify hyperlinks to open another Web page, a document, and an e-mail message window. Edit a hyperlink to an external Web site. Add bookmarks and create hyperlinks to the bookmarks.

1. Add and verify a text hyperlink on the *Photo Album* page that opens the *Interests* page. The hyperlink should appear above the bottom, shared border.

2. Add and verify a text hyperlink on the *Photo Album* page that opens the document *About these pictures.doc* in the *Lesson Applications* folder on your FrontPage Student Data Disk. This hyperlink should appear just below the hyperlink to the *Interests* page from step 1, above the bottom shared border.

3. Add and verify a text hyperlink that opens a new message window with your e-mail address as the recipient. Use the existing text in the bottom, shared border of the *Personal* Web to create the link.

4. Edit a hyperlink on the *myfav3.htm* page to link to your favorite Web site. (Hint: Highlight the comment text *You will want to replace the hyperlink . . .*, right-click on the text, and click Hyperlink on the shortcut menu.) Enter the URL of your favorite site or use the appropriate button to surf to your favorite site to create the hyperlink. Add an appropriate heading above the link to introduce it.

5. Create bookmarks in the top two sections of the *Family* page. Then create hyperlinks at the bottom of the *Family* page (above the shared border) allowing visitors to jump to each section.

6. Save changes to all Web pages and exit FrontPage 2000.

Lesson Summary & Exercises

PROJECTS

1 Weaving Through the Web

Your design of a Web site for the Benevolents charitable organization has progressed beyond the content phase. To make the site functional and accessible, you must create its navigation structure and add shared borders, including a page banner, contact information at the bottom of each page, and a navigation bar across the top border. Also, remember to add page transitions to the Web. Figure 3.26 is an example of what your home page might resemble after completing the above tasks.

Figure 3.26

2 Missing Links

As you navigate your *Benevolents* Web, you can see the need for hyperlinks. Add bookmarks within selected pages and hyperlink to them; add hyperlinks, as appropriate, from one page to another page; and add e-mail hyperlinks where necessary (provide at least one of each of these). Verify your hyperlinks in the Preview mode after you save them. When you have added all hyperlinks, use the Preview in Browser feature to follow all links in your browser.

3 From Here to There (and Back Again)

Once the Benevolents Web committee sees how useful hyperlinks can be, they decide that the site should include links to the local Parks & Recreation department that has youth activities; to other organizations aiding troubled youths; and to newspaper, magazine, and journal articles on the subject. Surf the Web in your browser looking for the URLs of Web sites that would be useful or interesting to visitors to your site. Then create a new *Links* page and add external hyperlinks to these Web sites. You may either add this page to your navigation structure so it will appear on the navigation bar, or you may create a hyperlink to it from one of the other pages in your Web.

4 Reading, Writing, and Arithmetic

The Benevolents has an entire library of documents and worksheets showing their financial status, reports on success stories, and so on. None of these documents are stored on disk. Write at least 2 short (1–2) page documents using Microsoft Word, WordPad, or Microsoft Excel, and save these documents in the *Projects* folder of your FrontPage Student Data Disk. (If you don't have access to these programs, use the word processing or spreadsheet programs you have and save the documents in the corresponding Microsoft Office format.) Create hyperlinks from the *Benevolents* Web to these documents. You can include the hyperlinks on one of the existing Web pages or create a new page for these links.

Project in Progress

5 Collectibles Web Navigation Features

Review the navigation structure of the *Collectibles* Web site. Based upon the concepts you learned in this lesson, rearrange the Web navigation structure in Navigation view, if necessary. This is your opportunity to add or delete pages, change page labels, and fine tune the organization of your Web. After you have refined the navigation structure, use the techniques learned in this lesson to add the following features to the *Collectibles* Web site. After you have added these features, make sure to verify all hyperlinks.

- Page banner
- Navigation bar
- Contact information
- Page transitions
- Hyperlinks to other pages
- Hyperlinks to Office documents you created
- Hyperlinks to e-mail
- Hyperlinks to bookmarks
- Hyperlinks to external Web sites

LESSON 4

Applying Themes and Polishing the Web

CONTENTS

OBJECTIVES

After you complete this lesson, you will be able to do the following:

- Apply a theme to a Web using default settings.
- Apply selected elements from a theme to a Web.
- Modify the colors, graphics, and text of a theme before applying it to a Web.
- Apply a style to text.
- Use the Format Painter to copy character and paragraph formatting from one place in your Web to another.
- Spell check your body text as you type, one page at a time, or throughout the entire Web.
- Use Find and Replace to locate and replace text.
- Add a search form to your Web by creating a new page based on the *Search Page* template.
- Modify the search form by changing text in buttons and the display of search results.
- Use search engines to find Web sites and help them find your site.

In this lesson you will apply built-in themes and customize those themes to give all pages in your Web a striking and consistent look. You will use the Format Painter to give the same consistency to character and paragraph formatting in all your Web pages. The spell check and the Find and Replace features help ensure that the content of your Web is accurate. Finally, you will add a search form to your Web, giving visitors a simple method for locating the information they need when your Web is published.

FrontPage
in the workplace

APPLYING THEMES

Putting your pages together into a Web is a relatively easy task. Giving these pages a consistent, meaningful look is essential toward capturing the attention of visitors to your Web site. After all, there are millions of Web sites from which to choose—a confusing, hard-to-read page won't even be fully downloaded before users click to another site.

You have already learned how to give a Web site a consistent look by choosing similar fonts, templates, and shared borders for all pages in the Web. If you add a *theme* to your Web, the look of the Web will be more interesting while retaining this consistency. A theme is a set of coordinated colors, fonts, and other design elements that improve the appearance of a Web.

A theme maintains a similar look for all pages to which it is applied. As you will see, your choice of a theme can make a dramatic difference in the mood or overall look that your page conveys.

Applying a Built-in Theme

Microsoft FrontPage 2000 has fifty professionally designed themes you can employ. Each theme consists of color, graphics, and text options. About a dozen of the themes are available with a standard installation of the program—the others can be easily installed from the Microsoft Office 2000 CD.

When you add a theme to your Web, you choose the options in the Themes dialog box. The dialog box is divided into three sections, as follows:

■ The theme options area. On the left side of the dialog box, this section lets you select the theme to apply, the elements to include, and the pages to which the theme should be applied.

■ The theme modification area. The Modify button at the bottom of the dialog box allows you to change the theme's colors, graphics, and fonts. Clicking the Modify button displays additional buttons through which you can make these selections.

■ The Sample of Theme window. The majority of the dialog box is filled with this preview showing how your choices will affect the appearance of each of the elements in the theme.

HANDS On

Applying a Theme to a Web

In this activity, you will apply a theme to your *School Newsletter* Web pages using the default settings for the theme.

1. Click **Start** 🏁 **Start**, point to **Programs**, and click **Microsoft FrontPage**.

2. Click **Open Web** on the **File menu**.

The Open Web dialog box appears.

Applying a Theme to a Web

1. Click Theme on the Format menu.

2. Preview the themes, then click to choose a theme.

3. Click to apply the theme to all pages or selected pages.

4. Click the appropriate check boxes to include the theme elements.

5. Click OK.

3. Locate and open the *School Newsletter* Web in the *Tutorial* folder on your FrontPage Student Data Disk.

4. Double-click *index.htm* in the Folder List and display it in Page view in the Normal tab.

5. Click Theme on the Format menu.

The Themes dialog box appears as shown in Figure 4.1.

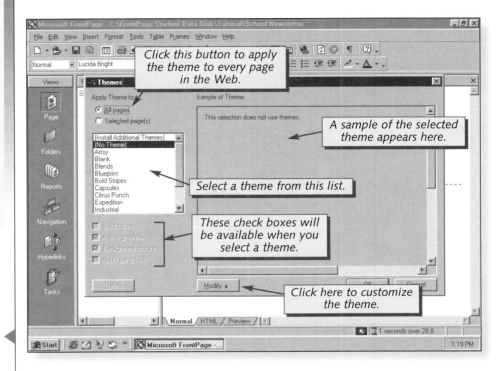

Figure 4.1
The Themes dialog box

When using the Internet for research, make sure to list the date you viewed the Web pages you may include in your bibliography. The contents of the Internet are in a constant state of change and today's Web page may be unavailable tomorrow.

6. Click the All pages option button, if necessary.

7. Scroll down the themes list, then click Romanesque.

The Romanesque theme appears in the Sample of Theme window.

8. Click the Active graphics and Background picture check boxes, if necessary. (Vivid colors and Apply using CSS should not be checked.)

9. Click OK.

A dialog box appears asking you to confirm your intention to apply the theme.

10. Click Yes.

Within a few seconds, you will see some subtle and some not so subtle changes to your page, as shown in Figure 4.2. The most obvious change is the background image that appears behind your text. You may be surprised to find that your page elements (navigation buttons, page banner, and fonts) have not changed at all.

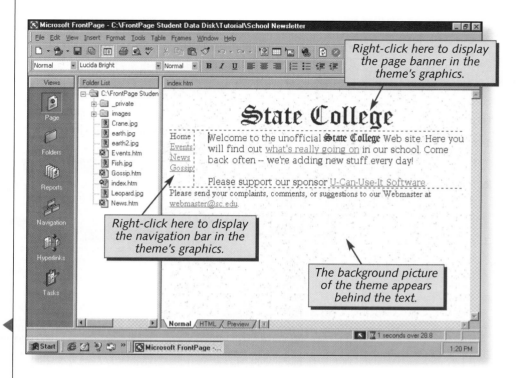

Figure 4.2
School Newsletter **Web page**
with a Theme

When you apply a theme, the theme fonts usually override the default fonts. However, in this instance the fonts did not change since you already made custom font selections to override the default. The FrontPage theme respects the font selections you already made. Your page banner and buttons didn't change because they were set to display text.

11. **Right-click the page banner, then click** **Page Banner Properties** **on the shortcut menu.**

The Page Banner Properties dialog box appears containing the State College banner text.

12. **Click the** **Picture option button**, **then click** **OK**.

Your page banner displays in a different font within the Romanesque graphic.

13. **Right-click the navigation bar, then click** **Navigation Bar Properties** **in the shortcut menu.**

The Navigation Bar Properties dialog box appears.

14. **Click the** **Buttons option button** **in the Orientation and Appearance section, then click** **OK**.

You return to *index.htm* which now displays navigation buttons.

15. **Click on a blank area of the page to dehighlight the navigation bar.**

The navigation bar buttons appear within the same style graphic as the page
banner, as shown in Figure 4.3.

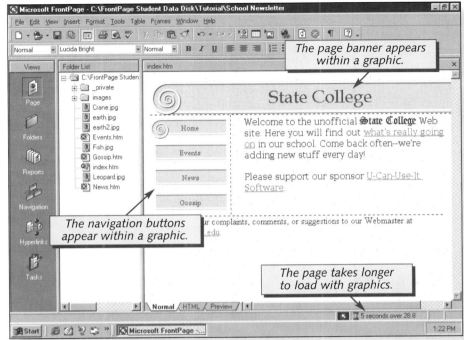

Figure 4.3
Web page with graphical
buttons and banner

16. Click the Save button 🖫.

CREATING CUSTOM THEMES

If none of the fifty built-in themes suits your needs, you can create your
own. You begin by selecting one of the supplied themes, modifying the elements and options as you prefer, and saving the theme under a new name.
When you create a custom theme you choose the colors, graphics, and text
attributes for each Web element.

Modifying Theme Colors

Clicking the Modify button [Modify ±] in the Themes dialog box displays the
Colors, Graphics, and Text buttons. From this point you can make selections
to modify your theme. The Colors button [Colors...] presents three tabs
through which you can change colors—Color Schemes, Color Wheel, and
Custom.

■ The Color Schemes tab lets you choose a group of colors to use in your Web. Just as an inte-
rior decorator chooses a set of colors for the walls, furniture, and carpeting in a house, Web
designers limit color choices to about four or five colors that go well together depending on
the mood, emotion, attitude, or effect they are trying to achieve. Note that you can change or
use any color you wish—the color scheme sets the default for the page elements such as
the color of the background, the banner, the text, and the hyperlinks.

- The Color Wheel tab gives you a much wider selection of colors from which to choose. While there are many color schemes, there are an almost unlimited number of colors available through the color wheel. The color wheel provides a continuous spectrum of colors from which you can create your own color scheme.

- The Custom tab lets you set the color of individual elements such as hyperlinks, text, backgrounds, and so on. You pick the type of item you want to change and then use a variety of tools to pick the exact color you want that item to have.

One additional option continually appears regardless of the color tab you select; that is, Normal or Vivid colors. The Vivid colors option button provides a richer and brighter set of colors in your theme.

Setting colors for your custom theme can involve all three color tabs in the Modify Theme dialog box. A good approach is to start with a built-in color scheme that's close to the one you want. Then use the color wheel to adjust that scheme. Finally, use the Custom tab to individually modify the colors of each item.

Creating a Color Scheme

In this activity, you will create your own color scheme and apply it to your *School Newsletter* Web pages.

1. Double-click *index.htm* in the Folder List and click the Normal tab, if necessary.

2. Click Theme on the Format menu.

3. Click the Modify button [Modify ▾] **, then click the Colors button** [Colors...].

The Modify Theme dialog box appears as in Figure 4.4.

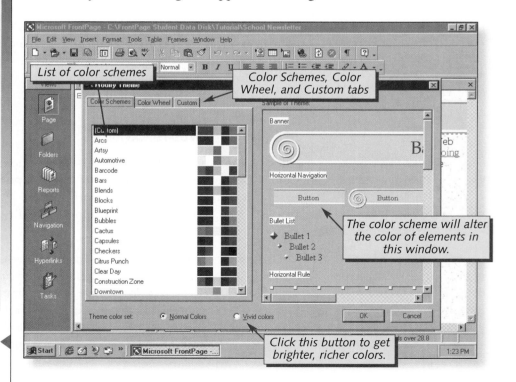

Figure 4.4
The Modify Theme dialog box

4. Scroll down within the Color Schemes tab, then click Travel.

The Sample of Theme window shows a dark blue background for the page.

5. Click the Color Wheel tab.

The dialog box now appears as in Figure 4.5

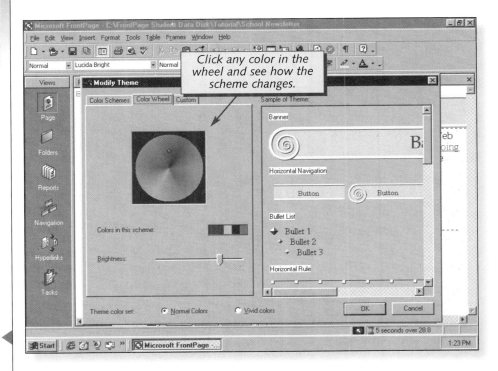

Figure 4.5
The color wheel

6. Click in the middle of the red area of the color wheel.

Most of the text in the Sample of Theme window turns red while the background and the button colors stay the same.

7. Click the Custom tab.

The Custom tab consists of two drop-down boxes: Item and Color.

8. Click Background in the Item drop-down list.

9. Click the Color drop-down arrow.

A set of color choices appears.

10. Click the Blue color box.

 *Position the pointer over the color box and the color name will appear.*

The background changes to a bright blue.

11. Click OK.

You return to the main window of the Themes dialog box. The blue background does not appear because the background picture is hiding it.

12. **Click the** Background picture check box **in the lower left of the Themes dialog box to remove the check mark.**

A dialog box asks if you want to save your changes to the Romanesque theme.

13. **Click** Yes.

The dialog box informs you that you cannot change the theme; however, you can give your modifications a new name.

When you change a preset theme, you must save your changes as a new theme. You cannot overwrite the original theme, so you must simply save it under a new name.

14. **Type** Newsletter, **then click** OK.

15. **Click** OK **in the Themes dialog box to apply the new color theme to your Web.**

After a few seconds, the new color theme changes your background and text colors of the Web page. Figure 4.6 illustrates how your new theme alters the appearance of your Web page.

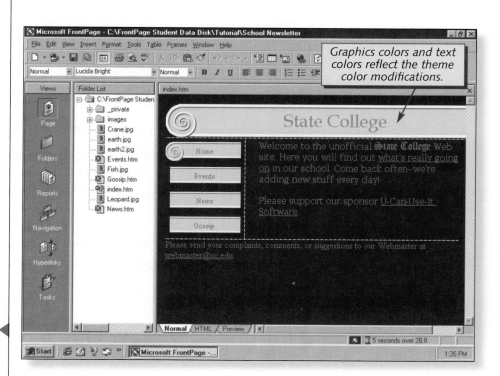

Figure 4.6
Web page with new
theme applied

Using Theme Graphics

In the previous activity you saw how the Romanesque theme included a background picture. You cleared this picture so you could see the background color that you selected as part of your color scheme. You are not limited to the background pictures that are a part of each theme—you can use almost any graphics image as your page background. Similarly, you can change the graphic images used for navigation and other buttons, the page banner, and the horizontal lines, also known as *horizontal rules*. And, if the graphic contains text, you can alter the font, size, and alignment of the characters.

Each theme can use two sets of graphics—normal and active. The ***active graphic*** elements can be made to change their appearance (such as their shape, color, or font) when you point to them, click them, or double-click them. When you apply your theme graphics, you choose which set of graphics the pages should use. The active graphics are composed of three different graphic images—one image when first viewed; a second image when clicked on; and a third image when pointed to (pointing to an image is also called ***hovering***).

Graphic images come in a variety of file formats, depending upon the program or method used to save the image onto disk. Microsoft FrontPage 2000 uses images stored in all of the popular formats. When the image is saved with the Web page, however, it is saved in the GIF, JPG, or PNG format. (In a later lesson, you will learn more about acquiring graphic images and inserting them into your Web.)

Modifying Theme Graphics

In this activity, you will change some of the graphic elements in your theme and apply the changes to your *School Newsletter* Web pages.

1. Double-click *index.htm* in the Folder List and click the **Normal tab**, if necessary.

2. Click **Theme** on the Format menu.

The Themes dialog box appears.

3. Click the **Modify button** Modify ± .

The Colors, Graphics, and Text buttons appear.

4. Click the **Graphics button** Graphics... .

The Modify Theme dialog box appears as shown in Figure 4.7. This dialog box includes an Item drop-down list, Picture and Font tabs, and a Sample of Theme window. A Theme graphic set area with normal and active graphics option buttons appears at the bottom of the dialog box. The Background Picture and the Picture tab are selected by default. The options within the Theme graphic set and the Font tab are dimmed since these options are not needed when selecting a background picture.

Figure 4.7
Modify Theme dialog box
for setting graphics

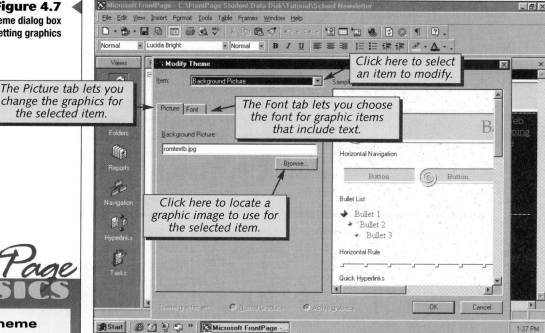

The Picture tab lets you change the graphics for the selected item.

Click here to select an item to modify.

The Font tab lets you choose the font for graphic items that include text.

Click here to locate a graphic image to use for the selected item.

FrontPage BASICS

Modifying Theme Graphics

1. Click Theme on the Format menu.

2. Click the Modify button, then click the Graphics button.

3. Click the graphic item you wish to modify within the Item list.

4. Click the normal or active graphics set.

5. Click the Picture tab and choose a graphic image file.

6. Click the Font tab and choose the text attributes.

7. Click to close the Modify Theme dialog box.

8. Click to place a check mark in the Background picture check box.

9. Click Save then click OK to close the Themes dialog box.

5. Click the Browse button Browse.

The Select Picture dialog box opens. Through this dialog box you can locate a graphic image to use as the background of your Web pages.

6. Click the Select a file on your computer button

The Select File dialog box appears.

7. Navigate to the *Tutorial* folder on your FrontPage Student Data Disk.

8. Double-click the image file *newsback.jpg*.

The new background image appears in the Sample of Themes window.

9. Click the Item drop-down arrow, then click Banner.

10. Click the Font tab.

The dialog box displays a list of font choices and characteristics to use in the page banner.

11. Scroll through the Font list and click Old English or another distinctive font for your banner.

The banner font changes in the Sample of Theme window.

12. Click the Size drop-down arrow, then click 7 (36 pt).

13. Click OK.

14. Click to place a check mark in the Background picture check box.

A dialog box appears asking you to save your changes to the custom theme.

15. Click Yes, click the Vivid colors check box, then click OK.

Your Web page now has the background image and page banner attributes similar to Figure 4.8.

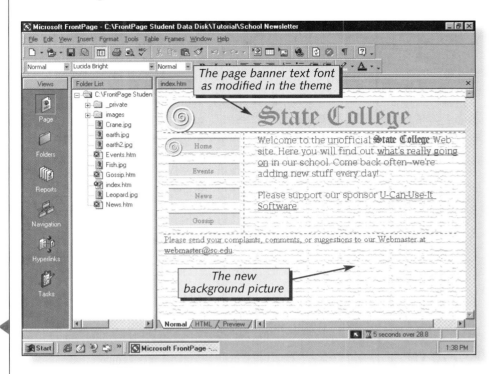

The page banner text font as modified in the theme

The new background picture

Figure 4.8
Web page with new background and page banner

Working with Theme Text

When you created your first Web page, the text took on the default font, default size, and default color assigned to new pages by FrontPage 2000. When you apply a theme to the page, the defaults for each of these attributes change. You fine-tune these attributes by modifying the theme's text.

As you already learned, the selection of fonts should be done thoughtfully to enhance the page and avoid confusing the site visitor. Another factor must be taken into account when choosing fonts—not every computer contains the same set of fonts. Indeed, there are thousands of different fonts and an almost infinite number of combinations of fonts on any given computer. Some fonts are relatively common. Times New Roman, Arial, and Courier, for example, are available on most computers.

When your Web browser opens a Web page, the specified font will be used, if it is available. If not, a substitute font will be chosen. Sometimes the substitute font will be a close cousin to the correct font; other times the font will be so different that the page is nearly impossible to read. Fortunately, FrontPage 2000 has anticipated this problem and given Web designers a means by which to minimize it. Rather than selecting a single font, you can enter a list of fonts separated by commas. When the visitor's browser opens the page, the first available font in the list will be used.

Styles are huge time savers
since they allow you to
apply any number of
character and paragraph
formats with a single
command.

Themes do not just set one font and format for all text in your document—rather, they choose different fonts and formats for the headings, the body text, lists, and other text elements. The character and paragraph formatting applied to text elements are called *styles*. When you choose a theme, your Web page uses the styles built-in to the theme. Then you can modify those styles to suit your own needs. You can also create your own styles and apply them to any text you desire.

Styles help you keep your pages consistent—especially when you decide to make a change to the text in your Web. For example, if you've used a style to format all of the body text in your Web and you need to enlarge the font size, you just have to modify the style and all of the text using that style will change automatically. Later in this lesson, you will learn how to create, apply, and modify styles.

Modifying Theme Text

In this activity, you will change the attributes of the fonts used in your *School Newsletter* Web pages.

1. Double-click *index.htm* in the Folder List and click the **Normal tab**, if necessary.

2. Click **Theme** on the Format menu.

3. Click the **Modify button** [Modify *], then click the **Text button** [Text].

The Modify Theme dialog box appears with a drop-down list of items to change, a list of fonts from which to choose, and a Sample of Theme window, as in Figure 4.9.

4. Click the **Item drop-down arrow** and click **Body**, if necessary.

Modifying Theme Text

1. Click Theme on the Format menu.

2. Click the Modify button, then click the Text button.

3. Click the text item you wish to change in the Item list.

4. Click the font and click OK.

5. Click Save to save changes to the theme.

6. Click OK to close the Themes dialog box.

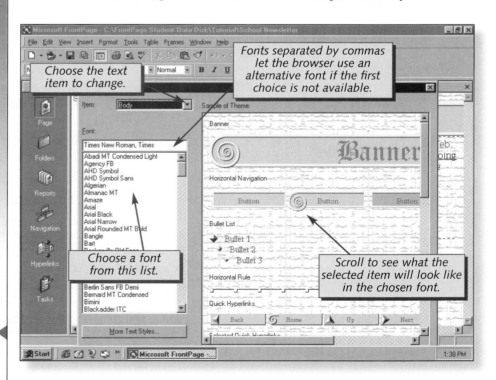

Figure 4.9
The Modify Theme dialog box
for changing text

Did you know?

In 1999 the management of the Internet domain name system (DNS) became the responsibility of the private, nonprofit organization ICANN (Internet Corporation for Assigned Names and Numbers), previously handled by the Internet Network Information Center or InterNIC (pronounced "inter nick").

5. Scroll down the Sample of Theme window until *Heading 1 Style* appears at the top.

6. Click **Arial** in the Font list.

The Regular Text Sample and the hyperlinks text samples change to Arial in the Sample of Theme window.

7. Click the **Item drop-down arrow**, then click **Heading 1**.

8. Click **Gill Sans MT** or a distinctive headline font of your choice.

The font changes for the Heading 1 Style text item in the Sample of Theme window.

9. Click **OK** to close the Modify Theme dialog box.

10. Click **Save** then click **OK** in the Themes dialog box.

The dialog box closes and you return to the *School Newsletter* Web.

Applying Styles to Text

When you change text items in a theme, you may find no noticeable changes in the Web page's text. Only those items that use the default style will be changed. In your *School Newsletter* home page, each of the paragraphs has been formatted explicitly. To apply styles to your text, you must first select the text, tell FrontPage to use the default font, and choose the style from the Style drop-down list on the Formatting toolbar.

HANDS On

FrontPage BASICS

Applying a Style

1. Select the text to which a style should be applied.

2. Click *(default font)* on the Font drop-down list.

3. Click the appropriate style on the Style drop-down list.

4. Click Save to save your changes.

Applying a Style

In this activity, you will apply a style to body text within the *School Newsletter* Web.

1. Double-click *index.htm* in the Folder List and click the **Normal tab**, if necessary.

2. Select the two paragraphs of text directly under the State College banner within the *index.htm* page.

3. Click **Normal** in the Style drop-down list on the Formatting toolbar, if necessary.

4. Click the **Font drop-down arrow**.

5. Click **(default font)** at the top of the list.

The font changes to Arial, the font you selected for the body text in your theme.

6. Double-click *News.htm* in the Folder List.

7. Select *SC News* near the top of the page.

8. Click the **Font drop-down arrow** then click **(default font)**.

9. Click the **Style drop-down arrow** and click **Heading 1**.

The selected heading now appears in the Gill Sans MT font or whatever font you chose when you modified the Heading 1 text in the *Newsletter* theme.

10. Click the **Save button** 🖫.

USING THE FORMAT PAINTER

Formatting text is hardly an exact science—it may take a lot of experimentation to get the look you want. As long as you stick to applying styles and themes, you can maintain consistent formatting by changing the style or theme. However, to experiment with formatting using styles and themes, you must work with sample text in a dialog box. Changing fonts and attributes directly on the page can give you the immediate feedback many users demand. The trade off seems to be consistency and ease of maintenance versus the ability to see your formatting choices in place and right away.

Formatting Text with the Format Painter

Fortunately there is a way to combine the strengths of both methods. The *Format Painter* takes the character or paragraph formatting from one place and copies the formatting to another place. The formatting that is copied depends upon the text you select and/or use as a model. If the text is formatted with a style, the Format Painter will apply that style. If the text has been formatted without a style, the Format Painter will use the character and paragraph formatting in effect. If you select characters before using the Format Painter, the character formats are applied. If you select a paragraph (or just move your insertion pointer into a paragraph), the paragraph formats are applied.

Copying Formats with the Format Painter

In this activity you will use the Format Painter to apply character and paragraph formatting from one page to another.

1. **Double-click *News.htm* in the Folder List and click the Normal tab, if necessary.**

2. **Select the body text beginning with *Sam Waters was elected . . .* and ending with *. . . what I'm going to do."***

This is the text that was given the Normal style and assigned the default font in the previous activity.

3. **Click the Format Painter button 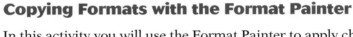.**

4. **Double-click *Events.htm* in the Folder List, and click the Normal tab, if necessary.**

The Format Painter command stays in effect until you click or select text to be formatted. That is, you can scroll or navigate elsewhere in the page or to another page until you locate the text you want to "format paint."

5. **Move the pointer into the page—it takes the shape of a paintbrush.**

6. **Select the text beginning with *The SC Cycling Club . . .* and ending with *. . . /itinerary.doc.***

When you release the mouse button, the text takes on the same style and font as in *News.htm*.

7. **Click the Save button.**

8. **With the body text still selected, click the Format Painter button.**

9. Double-click *Gossip.htm* in the Folder List and click the **Normal tab**, if necessary.

10. Select the text beginning with *An anonymous source . . .* and ending with *. . . of Marlowe.*

11. Click in a blank area of the workspace to dehighlight the text.

This text appears in exactly the same font and style as the body text in the other pages. Now that all the pages use the default style and font, any changes to the text in the theme will affect the body text throughout the Web.

12. Click the **Save button** 💾.

If you want to paint a number of sections of text with the same format, double-click the Format Painter icon. You can select any sections of text you want and the Format Painter will stay in effect. To turn off the Format Painter, click the icon again or press Esc.

SPELL CHECKING A WEB

Nothing makes a page look less professional than improper spelling, incorrect punctuation, and text that has not been proofread. Though FrontPage 2000 lacks the grammar checking capabilities of a word processor like Microsoft Word, spell checking is available and simple to use.

FrontPage 2000 has several different ways for you to check spelling in a Web page. The methods are listed in Table 4.1.

TABLE 4.1	SPELL CHECKING METHODS
Method	**Description**
Check Spelling as you type	Unless this feature is turned off (Tools, Page Options, General tab), potentially misspelled words will appear underlined with a wavy red line as you type.
In Page View	Click the Spelling button to spell check text on the displayed page.
In Folders View	Click the Spelling button to spell check text on selected pages or the entire Web. Optionally, you can create a task for each page that contains potential spelling errors.

Regardless of the method you use, the spelling checker will notify you of each word in the text that is not in the Microsoft Office dictionary. The spelling checker recognizes these as potential spelling errors—they are

potential errors because not all words are in the dictionary. Proper names, slang, and technical jargon are some of the categories of words that may show up as spelling errors even if they are properly spelled.

> *Using the Spelling Checker is not a substitute for proofreading your text. It will not highlight words that are ungrammatical or out of context as long as they are spelled correctly.*

Comparing those words in your document with those in the dictionary is only half of what the spelling checker does. Whenever possible, the spelling checker suggests correctly spelled words to replace the incorrect word. You can also make your own spelling changes to a selected word. If the word is spelled right, you can tell the spelling checker to ignore it. Finally, if the word is not in the dictionary, is correctly spelled, and is used frequently in your document, it makes sense to add the word to the dictionary.

Check Spelling as You Type

The spelling checker provides the option of matching each word—as you type it—with words in the dictionary. With this option turned on, each word you type that doesn't match the dictionary is underlined in red. Right-clicking on the word provides options to correct, ignore, or add the word to the dictionary.

Some users prefer to turn this option off while they are working, since they find that the wavy underlines are distracting. They would rather type the text first then check the spelling for the entire page later—a choice supported by FrontPage and other Office programs.

Spell Checking as You Type

In this activity, you will make sure FrontPage is set to check the spelling of words as they are typed. Then you will check the spelling of the entire Web page.

1. **Double-click the page *Gossip.htm* in the Folder List and click the Normal tab, if necessary.**

2. **Click Page Options on the Tools menu.**

The Page Options dialog box appears.

3. **In the General tab, click to place a check mark next to *Check spelling as you type*, then click OK.**

The dialog box closes and you return to *Gossip.htm*.

4. **Scroll to the bottom of the first paragraph.**

The last word in the first paragraph of body text—*Marlowe*—is underlined in red. As with many proper nouns, the name *Marlowe* is not in the dictionary.

If you are using a special dictionary or if someone has added the name Marlowe *to the dictionary, the name will not be underlined in red.*

Spell Checking as You Type

1. Click Page Options on the Tools menu.

2. Click the General tab.

3. Click to check the *Check spelling as you type* box check box and click OK.

4. Right-click on words in your document with wavy underlines.

5. Click to replace or ignore the word or add the word to the dictionary.

5. Right-click *Marlowe*.

A shortcut menu appears as in Figure 4.10. At the top of the menu is a list of alternate spellings with which you can replace the underlined text. Clicking Ignore All will tell the spelling checker to ignore all occurrences of the word. Clicking Add will add this word to the dictionary.

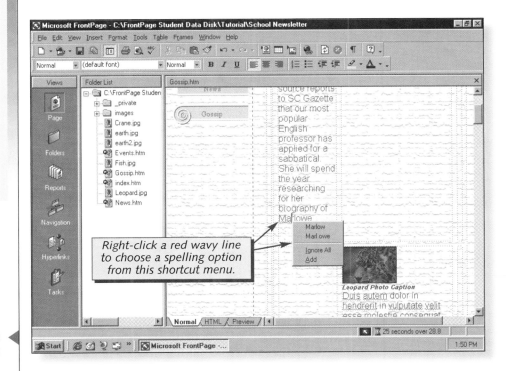

Right-click a red wavy line to choose a spelling option from this shortcut menu.

Figure 4.10
The spell check shortcut menu

6. Click Ignore All.

The underlining is removed from the word. Subsequent uses of *Marlowe* in this Web will not be marked. It would have made sense to add the word to the dictionary if you knew it was used often in other Webs.

Check Spelling on a Page

The Spelling button ![abc] also activates the spelling checker. Again, the spelling checker compares each word of text against the list of words in the dictionary. However, when initiated by the Spelling button ![abc], the spelling checker skips from word to word and displays each possible misspelled word in the Spelling dialog box. The Spelling dialog box contains the same basic options as the spelling shortcut menu, with a few minor variations. Table 4.2 describes the function of each button in the Spelling dialog box.

TABLE 4.2	SPELLING DIALOG BOX BUTTONS
Button	**Function**
Ignore	This occurrence of the word is accepted and red underlining is removed. Subsequent spell checks will find the word misspelled, however.
Ignore All	This and every other occurrence of the word is accepted and red underlining is removed. Subsequent spell checks will find the word misspelled, however.
Change	Substitutes the word in the *Change To* box for the misspelled word.
Change All	Substitutes the word in the *Change To* box for the misspelled word wherever it appears in the page.
Add	Places the word into the dictionary. From then on, the word will be accepted as correctly spelled.
Suggest	If the correct spelling is not listed, click a word in the Suggestions list to activate this button and to display another list of suggestions.

The spelling checker only checks the spelling of text material that can be edited in Page view in the Normal tab. Words within graphical elements, such as the page banner and navigation bar, will not be checked for spelling errors.

You can check the spelling on a page through the Spelling button regardless of whether you have checked the *Check spelling as you type* option in the Page Options dialog box. The users who turn off the *Check spelling as you type* option usually prefer to spell check the entire page at once rather than as they work on the document.

Spell Checking the Current Page

In this activity, you will enter text with some intentional misspellings. Then you will use the spell checking feature to fix the misspellings.

1. Double-click *Gossip.htm* in the Folder List and click the **Normal tab**, if necessary.

2. Scroll down to the <u>back to top</u> hyperlink at the bottom of the first section of text that ends with . . . *biography of Marlowe*.

3. Click the leopard photo and press Delete .

Spell Checking the Current Page

1. Display the page in Page view in the Normal tab.

2. Click the Spelling button on the Standard Buttons toolbar.

3. Click the correctly spelled word in the Suggestions list, then click the Change or Change All button to change to the suggested spelling.

4. Click the Ignore or Ignore All button to ignore the spelling and continue the spell check.

5. Click the Add button to add the word to the dictionary.

Another Way

Press F7 to run the speller whether in Page or Folders View.

4. **Select the leopard photo caption placeholder text and all the Latin placeholder text above the next** <u>back to top</u> **hyperlink, and press** Delete.

5. **Type the following text:** According to an <u>admenistrative</u> memo we <u>recieved</u>, next year's fall <u>semmester</u> will begin a week <u>earlyer</u> than usual. The last day of the spring <u>semmester</u> will not be changed.

The underlined words are misspelled intentionally. Do not underline them, but type them exactly as shown.

6. **Press** Enter↵**, and then press** Tab **three times.**

The crane photo and next section of placeholder text is selected.

7. **Press** ⇧ Shift **+** Ctrl **+** End **(hold down the Shift and Control keys and press the End key).**

The balance of the material on the page is selected, including the fish photo and the placeholder text.

8. **Press** Delete.

The material is deleted.

9. **Click the Spelling button** ABC✓.

The first misspelling (*admenistrative*) appears within the Spelling dialog box as shown in Figure 4.11. The correct spelling appears in the *Change To* box and is the only choice given in the Suggestions list.

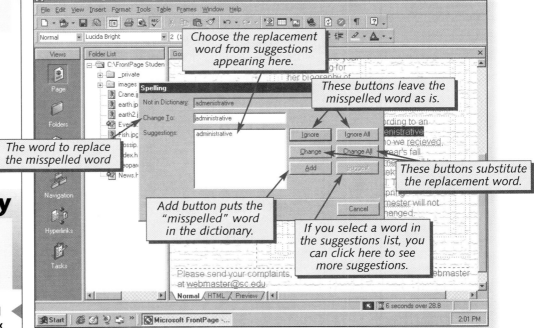

Figure 4.11
The Spelling dialog box

HANDS On

10. Click Change.

The word *administrative* is corrected and the misspelled word *received* is detected. This time, two suggestions are listed, but the proper choice is given in the *Change To* box.

11. Click Change.

The next word that appears in the Spelling dialog box is *semmester*.

12. Click Change All.

Change All corrects both occurrences of the misspelled word to *semester*. The spelling checker now stops at the word *earlyer*.

13. Click Change.

A dialog box appears informing you that the spelling check is complete.

14. Click OK.

Your Web page *Gossip.htm* is now spell checked.

15. Click the Save button 🖫.

Check Spelling of the Entire Web

Before a Web is published, you should check the spelling of all Web pages. It is easy for misspellings to get into pages when many people collaborate on the Web or when text is imported from a variety of sources.

To spell check all pages, you must be in the Folders view. When you click the Spelling button [ABC✓] you have the choice to check the pages you have selected or the entire Web. You can also choose to create an entry in the Tasks list for each page found to have one or more misspellings. From the Tasks view, you can either fix the errors yourself or you can assign the job to someone else if you are working in a Web development team.

 *FrontPage will check spelling only for text elements that can be edited in Page view in the Normal tab.*

Spell Checking All Pages in a Web

In this activity, you will switch to the Folders view and check the spelling for all pages in the Web. You will then use the Tasks view to fix the misspellings.

1. Click the Folders view icon 📁 **in the *School Newsletter* Web.**

2. Click the Spelling button [ABC✓].

A dialog box appears as shown in Figure 4.12.

Hints & Tips

You can spell check several pages at once by selecting the pages in the Contents window of the Folders view. Hold `⇧ Shift` to select consecutive pages or hold `Ctrl` to select nonconsecutive pages before clicking the Spelling button.

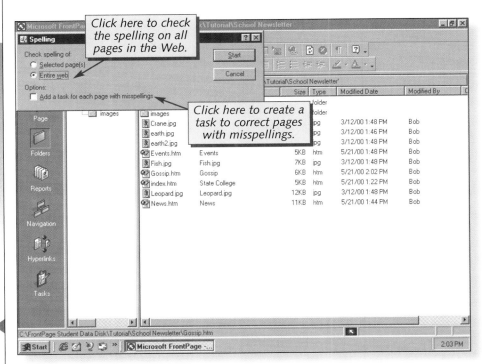

Figure 4.12
Spelling dialog box in Folders view

Spell Checking All Pages

1. Click the Folders view icon to display the Web in Folders view.

2. Click the Spelling icon.

3. Click the Entire web option button.

4. Click the *Add a task for each page with misspellings* box.

---

3. Click the Entire web option button, if necessary.

4. Click to place a check mark in the *Add a task for each page with misspellings* check box.

5. Click Start.

Within a few seconds, three tasks appear in the Spelling dialog box. You could double-click a task in this dialog box to fix the spelling errors or you can work with them in the Tasks view.

6. Click Cancel.

7. Click the Tasks icon in the Views bar.

The three tasks appear in Tasks view. (The Web page names appear under the *Associated With* heading.) The misspellings in the *News* page (the first task) are due to the Latin placeholder text.

8. Click the *News* task to highlight it, if necessary, then press Delete.

9. Click Yes in the Confirm Delete dialog box.

The *News* task is removed from the list.

10. Double-click the task for the *Events* page.

The Task Details dialog box displays the words that need to be fixed in this page, as shown in Figure 4.13.

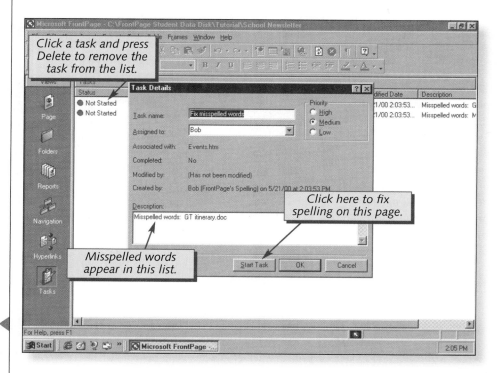

Figure 4.13
Task Details dialog box
with misspelled word

11. Click Start Task.

The Spelling dialog box displays the *Events* page and highlights the letters *GT*. These letters are part of a proper name, however, and do not need to be changed.

12. Click Ignore.

The spelling checker stops on <u>itinerary.doc</u>, the document name in a hyperlink.

13. Click Ignore.

The Spelling dialog box closes. A dialog box announces that the spelling check is complete.

14. Click OK.

15. Click the Save button 🖫 **.**

A dialog box reminds you that this page was opened in order to complete a task.

16. Click Yes to mark the task as completed.

17. Click the Tasks icon 🗒 **.**

18. Double-click the *Gossip* page in the Tasks list and click Start Task in the Task Details dialog box.

The Spelling dialog box highlights the word *Marlowe* as a misspelled word within the *Gossip* page.

19. Click Ignore, then click OK to confirm the spell check is complete.

20. Click the Tasks icon 🗒 **.**

21. Right-click the task for the *Gossip* page, then click Mark as Completed on the shortcut menu.

USING GLOBAL FIND AND REPLACE

The maintenance of Webs frequently involves locating and changing text. FrontPage has two commands that make it easy to find and, if necessary, change text automatically—Find and Replace.

Finding Text Quickly

In a large Web, searching for a word or phrase manually would involve opening each page and carefully scrolling through it to examine each line. It is easy to miss the word or phrase you are looking for. Most application programs have a feature that makes searching much easier. The **Find** command on the Edit menu displays the Find dialog box, as shown in Figure 4.14.

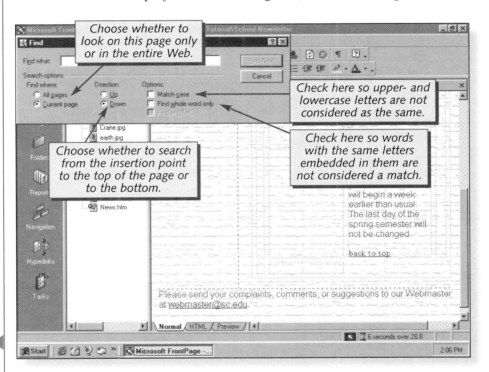

Figure 4.14
The Find dialog box

In the *Find what* text box, type the text you are looking for. Click the Find Next button. The first occurrence of the word or phrase will appear highlighted in the document while the Find dialog box remains open. Click the Find Next button again to find the next occurrence of the text. Click the Cancel button to close the dialog box and end the search.

Option buttons in the *Find where* section of the dialog box give you the choice of searching all pages in the Web or only in the current page. If you are searching the current page, use the option buttons in the *Direction* section to control whether the search begins from the insertion point up to the top of the page or from the insertion point down toward the bottom. These options in the *Direction* section don't affect the search if you are searching all pages in the Web.

The Find dialog box provides two check box options to help refine your search: *Match case* and *Find whole word only*. When *Match case* is not checked, it will find text in both uppercase or lowercase; when it is checked, it will find the text in upper and/or lowercase just as you type it (thus, if you search for *to*, you will not find the word *To*). When *Find whole word only* is not checked, your text will be found even if it's embedded within another word (thus, searching for the word *to* will find the letters *to* in the word *together*). A third check box in this section of the Find dialog box extends the search to the HTML code.

You can click the Find in HTML check box (in the Find dialog box) to locate text in HTML code. This will let you search for text that is not visible on the page, such as a page title or a string of characters in HTML. Click the All Pages option button to activate the Find in HTML check box.

When a match is found, the search results list containing each page with a match appears in the dialog box along with the number of times the word was found in each page. At this point you can double-click the page to select the first occurrence of the word or add the page to the Task list where it can be worked on at a later date.

HANDS On

Searching for Text in All Pages of a Web

In this activity, you will search all pages of the *School Newsletter* Web for a specific word.

1. **Double-click *index.htm* in the Folder List and click the Normal tab**, if necessary.
2. **Click Find on the Edit menu.**

The Find dialog box appears.

Another Way

Press Ctrl + F as the keyboard shortcut for Find.

3. **Type Waters in the *Find what* text box.**
4. **Click the All pages option button.**

FrontPage will search all pages of your Web. The option buttons in the Direction section are intended for the search in a current page and do not affect the search of all pages in a Web.

5. **Click to check the Match case and Find whole word only check boxes.**

Only whole words with an exact match to the uppercase and lowercase characters in the word *Waters* will be found.

6. **Click the Find in Web button.**

The search results appear in the Find dialog box (Figure 4.15) indicating that three occurrences of the word *Waters* were found in the *News.htm* page.

Figure 4.15
Find dialog box with
search results

FrontPage BASICS

Searching for Text in All Pages of a Web

1. Click Find on the Edit menu.

2. Enter the text you wish to find in the *Find what* text box.

3. Click the All pages option button.

4. Click to check the *Match case* or *Find whole word only* check boxes, if appropriate.

5. Click the Find in Web button.

6. Double-click a page in the search results list to make changes in the page or click the Add Task button to work with the pages later.

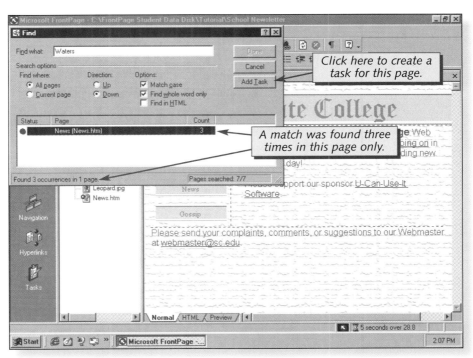

Click here to create a task for this page.

A match was found three times in this page only.

7. Double-click *News.htm* in the search results.

The *News.htm* page is displayed and the first occurrence of Waters appears highlighted. The Find dialog box now contains a Find Next and a Back to Web button. Find Next will highlight each occurrence of *Waters* within the current page; the Back to Web button allows you to return to your search of the entire Web.

8. Click the Find Next button.

The next occurrence of *Waters* is highlighted within *News.htm*.

9. Click the Find Next button twice.

The next occurrence is highlighted, and then a *Finished checking documents* message box informs you that all documents (pages in your Web) have been checked.

10. Click OK to close the current document (*News.htm*).

11. Click Cancel in the Find dialog box.

You return to the *index.htm* page.

Replacing Text

Frequently, you will want to search for text in order to replace it. For example, employee information might change. If Mr. Smith's job is taken over by Ms. Jones, you may have to find instances of "Mr. Smith" and change them to "Ms. Jones" on all Web pages.

The **Replace** command on the Edit menu displays the Replace dialog box, as shown in Figure 4.16.

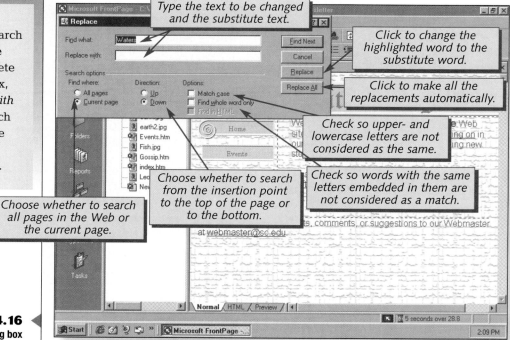

Figure 4.16
The Replace dialog box

As in the Find dialog box, type the text you wish to search for in the *Find what* text box. Then type the replacement text in the *Replace with* text box. The Search options section is identical to the Find dialog box. The *Find where* option buttons let you choose whether to search all pages in the Web or just the current page. The *Direction* option buttons allow you to search an individual page up or down from the insertion point. *Match case* and *Find whole word only* work the same as in the Find dialog box to allow you to match the specific case of your text and avoid searching for your text embedded within other words. Two new command buttons appear in the Replace dialog box. The Replace button lets you replace each individual occurrence of the text as you find each match. The Replace All button will replace every occurrence of the text automatically.

Activating the All pages option activates the Find in Web button so you can begin your search of the entire Web. After FrontPage finds an occurrence of the text, you can open a page from the results list and make replacements. When you open the page you will have the following choices:

1. **Click Find Next to search for the next occurrence without making the replacement.**

2. **Click Back to Web to return to your search of the entire Web.**

3. **Click Replace to make the designated replacement.**

4. **Click Replace All to replace all occurrences of the text you are searching for on the page.**

Hints & Tips

Be cautious before using the Replace All button. For example, if you replace the name "Brown" with "Smith" you might wind up with a "smith desk" or a person with "smith eyes."

Replacing Text in All Pages of a Web

1. Click Replace on the Edit menu.

2. Enter text in the *Find what* and *Replace with* text boxes.

3. Click the All pages option button.

4. Click to check the *Match case* or *Find whole word only* boxes, if appropriate.

5. Click Find in Web.

6. Double-click a page in the search results list to make changes in the page.

7. Click Find Next to go on to the next occurrence without making the replacement.

8. Click Replace or Replace All to make the replacement.

The keyboard shortcut for Replace is Ctrl + H.

In dialog boxes you can usually move the insertion point to the next location by pressing the Tab key.

Replacing Text in All Pages of a Web

In this activity, you will use Replace to search all pages in the *School Newsletter* Web for the abbreviation *SC* and replace it with the words *State College*.

1. **Double-click *index.htm* in the Folder List and click the Normal tab, if necessary.**

2. **Click Replace on the Edit menu.**

The Replace dialog box appears. If you have continued working directly from the previous activity, the text you entered in the Find dialog box appears highlighted in the *Find what* text box.

3. **Type SC in the *Find what* text box, and then press Tab.**

The insertion point moves to the *Replace with* text box.

4. **Type State College in the *Replace with* text box.**

5. **Click the All pages option button.**

6. **Click to check the Match case and Find whole word only boxes.**

The dialog box is now set to find all instances of *SC* and replace them with *State College*.

7. **Click Find in Web.**

The search results appear. One occurrence of *SC* is found in each of three pages in the Web—*News*, *Events*, and *Gossip*.

8. **Double-click *News.htm*.**

The match *SC* appears highlighted in the *News.htm* page.

9. **Click Replace.**

SC News changes to *State College News* in the *News.htm* page. A *Continue with the next document?* dialog box prompts you to save changes and close the document (*News.htm*) or move on to the next document.

10. **Click Next Document.**

The *Events* page opens with *SC* in *SC Cycling Club* highlighted.

11. **Click Find Next to skip the replacement on this page.**

The *Continue with the next document?* dialog box reappears.

12. **Click Next Document.**

The page *Gossip.htm* appears with another occurrence of *SC* highlighted.

13. **Click Find Next.**

A *Finished checking documents* message box appears.

14. **Click OK to close the current document (*Gossip.htm*).**

The Replace dialog box again displays the search results; however, in the Status column the dialog box now tells you that all three pages have been edited.

15. **Click Cancel.**

You return to *index.htm*.

CREATING A SEARCH FORM

You now have experience using the search tools that FrontPage supplies to developers of Web sites. By now you may be wondering what kind of search tools are available to visitors. As you can imagine, there may be hundreds of links throughout a large Web site. You can give visitors the ability to find the right page quickly by creating a *search form*.

You can create a search form by using the *Search page* template when you create a new Web page. Within the search page is the search form. The form has a text box for users to enter keywords and buttons to begin searching or to clear the box in order to begin a new search. There are instructions on the search page concerning how to perform ***Boolean searches.*** Boolean searches are used to narrow or refine your search, especially when you have two or more keywords. Boolean searches use the words *AND, OR,* and *NOT* to determine how the search engine should evaluate the keywords.

For example, if you want information on baseball bats and enter the keywords *baseball OR bats* in a search engine, you might be surprised to find some Web pages about bats (the mammal) listed in the search results. To get information about baseball bats, you should enter *baseball AND bats*. With these keywords only Web pages with both words will be listed as matches. Likewise, if you are seeking information about bats (the mammal), you may enter *bats NOT baseball* to limit the search results.

Creating a Search Form in Page View

Adding a new page to your Web is simple as long as you are in the Page view. When you right-click in the Folder List background without selecting a folder, the New Page option appears on a shortcut menu. By choosing the *Search Page* template, you can add a page complete with a search form, instructions, and Web search capabilities to your Web.

The search form will only work when you publish the Web to a Web server that is running Microsoft FrontPage Server Extensions. Consult your system administrator to determine the status of your Web server. Keep in mind that you will not be able to use your search form while it is only on your hard drive.

Adding a Search Form to a Web

In this activity, you will create a search form based on the *Search Page* template. Then you will save the page, adding it to your *School Newsletter* Web.

1. Double-click *index.htm* in the Folder List and click the **Normal tab**, if necessary.

2. Right-click the Folder List background.

Adding a Search Form

1. Right-click the Folder List background while in Page view.

2. Click New Page on the shortcut menu.

3. Double-click the *Search Page* template.

4. Click Save on the File menu.

5. Enter a file name and page title in the Save As dialog box, then click Save.

Figure 4.17 ◀
Search form based on template

3. Click New Page on the shortcut menu.

The New dialog box opens in the General tab containing templates upon which to base the new page.

4. Scroll down if necessary and double-click *Search Page*.

The search page opens using the custom theme you created for this Web, as shown in Figure 4.17. The page banner and navigation bar will be filled out when you add the page to the navigation structure.

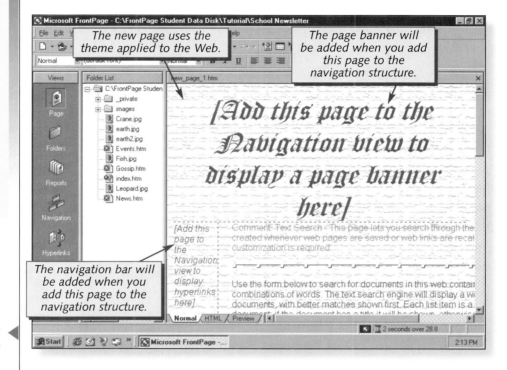

5. Click the Save button 💾.

The Save As dialog box opens. The first words of the body text (*use the form below . . .*) are the defaults for the page title and file name.

6. Type Search as the file name.

7. Click the Change button to the right of the *Page title* text box.

The Set Page Title dialog box appears.

8. Type Search Form, and then click OK.

9. Click Save.

The page is added to the *School Newsletter* Web as the last item in the Folder List.

Adding the Search Page to the Navigation Structure

Before your Web page can display a page banner and a navigation bar, it must be added to the navigation structure; that is, you must designate at which level the page belongs. You have already seen how pages can be related to each other as parent and child. This search page could be added as a child to the home page. However since its function is not to give information about the school, the search page would be best added as another top level page. The problem with this is that the navigation bar has no option for displaying hyperlinks to top level pages other than the home page. A solution is to either create a simple hyperlink to the search page or to include a link to it in another navigation bar within a shared border.

Navigating to the Search Page

In this activity, you will add the search page to the navigation structure of your *School Newsletter* Web and then add a new navigation bar to a shared border.

1. Click the Navigation view icon 🔲 **.**

The Web page graphics representing your Web structure appear in the workspace.

2. Drag *Search.htm* from the Folder List to the right of the *State College* page.

The search page is now at the top level of the navigation structure, although not a parent or child of any other page, as seen in Figure 4.18.

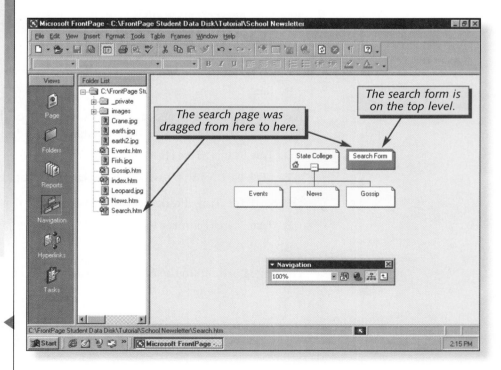

Adding the Search Page

1. Click the Navigation icon.

2. Drag the search page from the Folder List to the right or left of the home page.

3. Click the Page icon.

4. Click in a shared border, then click Navigation bar on the Insert menu.

5. Click the top level option button and uncheck the Home page box.

6. Click OK.

Figure 4.18
Search page added to navigation structure

3. **Click the Page view icon** 📄.

The page *Search.htm* appears in Page view.

4. **Click an insertion point after webmaster@sc.edu at the end of the comments in the bottom, shared border.**

5. **Press** Enter⏎ **to start a new line, then type** To find information quickly, click here **followed by a space.**

6. **Click Navigation Bar on the Insert menu.**

The Navigation Bar Properties dialog box appears.

7. **Click the Top level option button, uncheck the Home page box, and click the Horizontal and Buttons option buttons, if necessary.**

8. **Click OK.**

The new navigation bar appears in the bottom, shared border as shown in Figure 4.19.

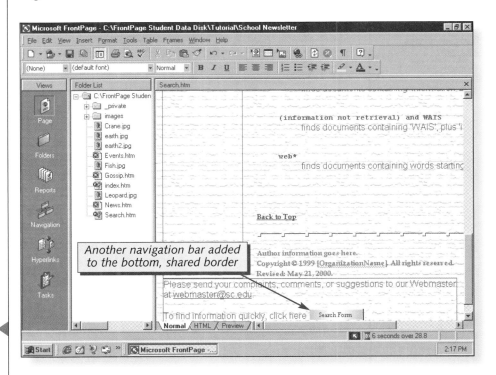

9. **Double-click *index.htm* in the Folder List, press** Ctrl**, then click the Search Form button to test the link.**

The link takes you to your search page. Note that adding your page to the navigation structure has also given you a page banner in the search page. At the bottom of the search page is the search button in the bottom, shared border. Since this hyperlink would only lead the visitor to the page they are already on, it is wise to eliminate the border from this page.

10. Right-click the *Search.htm* page, then click Shared Borders in the shortcut menu.

The Shared Borders dialog box appears.

11. Click the Current page option button, click to uncheck the Bottom box, and then click OK.

The shared border is removed from the search page.

12. Click the Save button 💾.

Creating a List of Keywords for a Search Engine

In this activity, you will use the FrontPage 2000 Help system to find out how to give certain search engines a list of keywords for your Web site.

1. Click Microsoft FrontPage Help on the Help menu.

2. Click the Answer Wizard tab, if necessary.

3. Select the text in the *What would you like to do?* text box and type How do I make a list of keywords for a search engine?.

Figure 4.20
Help page on creating a keywords index

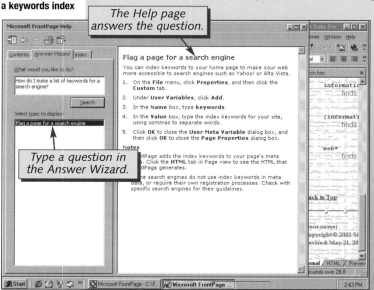

4. Click Search.

The topic *Flag a page for a search engine* appears in the *Select topic to display* list. The Help page appears as shown in Figure 4.20.

5. Read through this Help page.

The Help page explains the procedure for adding an index of keywords to your page's meta data to increase the likelihood that search engines will recognize your Web in search results.

6. Click the Close button ⊠ to close the Help window.

Changing Search Form Properties

With a few modifications the *Search Page* template is about ready to use. Once you add the page to the navigation structure, your new page takes on the look of the other pages according to the theme in effect.

You are not restricted to the text or appearance set by the template, however. You can make any additions, deletions, or changes to the text and/or format you want. You can also alter the way the search buttons and boxes look. The Search Form Properties tab of the Search Form Properties dialog box lets you enter new labels for the buttons and change the width of the keywords text box.

The Search Results tab lets you limit the pages visitors search by assigning a word list. The default is to search all pages in the Web. This tab also contains options that control the appearance of the date and time and the relevance, date, and size of pages meeting the search criteria. Figure 4.21 shows the features of the Search Form Properties dialog box.

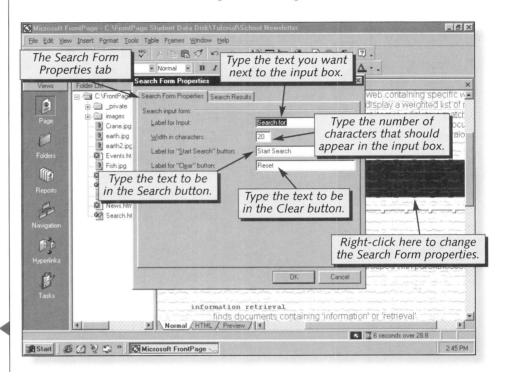

Figure 4.21
The Search Form Properties
dialog box

Changing the Appearance of the Search Form

In this activity, you will type new labels for the buttons on your search form. Then you will resize the text box and set how the search results will be displayed.

1. **Double-click *Search.htm* in the Folder List to display it in the workspace, if necessary.**

2. **Right-click the search form.**

The search form is the box containing the words Search for, a text box, and the search buttons in the middle of the search page.

To change the properties of most FrontPage objects, click the object and then press Alt + Enter←.

3. **Click Search Form Properties on the shortcut menu.**

The Search Form Properties dialog box is displayed in the Search Form Properties tab. The text *Search for* appears highlighted in the *Label for Input* text box.

Changing the Appearance of the Search Form

1. Right-click the search form.

2. Click Search Form Properties.

3. Type labels for the buttons.

4. Click the Search Results tab and change the results and display options.

5. Click OK.

Figure 4.22
The Search Results tab of the Search Form Properties dialog box

4. **Type the text** Type Keywords: **in the *Label for Input* text box.**

5. **Select the text in the *Width in characters* box and type** 40.

6. **Select the text in the *Label for "Clear" button* text box and type** New Search.

7. **Click the Search Results tab.**

The Search Results tab appears as shown in Figure 4.22.

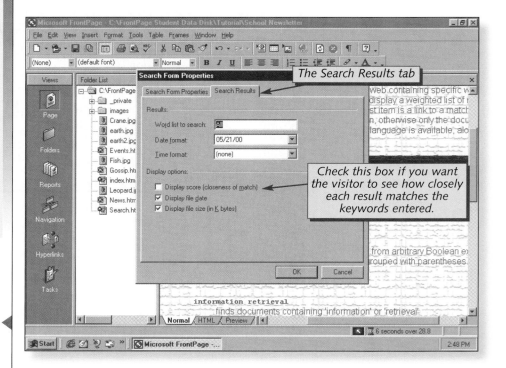

8. **Click to place a check mark in the Display score check box.**

This feature will allow visitors to see how closely a page matches the keywords they entered.

9. **Click OK.**

You return to *Search.htm*.

10. **Click to dehighlight the search form.**

Your search form has taken on the labels and text box width you just specified.

11. **Scroll to the bottom of the *Search.htm* page until you see the copyright notice.**

12. **Select the text *Author information goes here* and type your name.**

13. **Select *1999* (the copyright year) and type the current year.**

14. **Select *[OrganizationName]* and type** State College Gazette.

15. **Click the Save button** 💾.

16. **Close the Web and exit FrontPage.**

Test your knowledge by answering the following questions. See Appendix D to check your answers.

T F 1. A search page is a small box in a search form.

T F 2. The color wheel gives you a much wider choice of colors than the color scheme.

T F 3. Double-clicking the Format Painter icon lets you copy formatting to more than one location.

T F 4. The format of the Search Form is fixed.

T F 5. The spelling checker sometimes marks properly spelled words as misspellings.

ON*the*WEB

SEARCHING THE INTERNET

Search engines are Web sites that let you find pages of interest by entering keywords. You can register your site with popular search engines to help ensure your page will be found by users searching for related topics. In this activity, you will use your browser to learn more about search providers and how search engines find Web pages.

Note

This activity assumes you are using Internet Explorer as your Web browser. If you are using Netscape Navigator or a different browser, the steps will be slightly different.

1. **Click the Start button** **, point to Programs, and click Internet Explorer.**

The browser launches. You should be connected to the Internet; within a few moments, you should see your home page.

2. **Click the Search button** .

The left side of your screen displays the Search Explorer bar which provides a list of search category option buttons.

3. **Click Customize at the top of the Search Explorer bar.**

The Customize Search Settings dialog box appears as shown in Figure 4.23. In this window you can choose the search provider you would like to use for the various search categories.

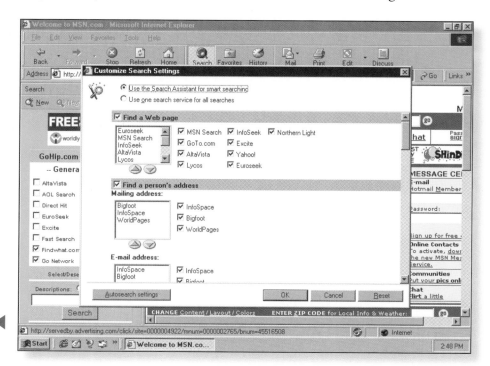

Figure 4.23 ◀
Customized Search
Settings dialog box

4. **Click the Use one search service for all searches option button** at the top of the dialog box.

The *Choose the search service* list box appears.

5. **Click Lycos, then click OK.**

The Customize Search Settings dialog box closes and the Lycos logotype, search form, and category links appear in the Search Explorer bar. Lycos will be used to conduct your Web page searches.

6. **Type keywords in the text box, then click Go Get It!.**

The Search Explorer bar displays a Categories and a Web Pages header, each followed by search results as hyperlinks.

7. **Click the first hyperlink under the Categories header: Computers > Internet > WWW > Website Promotion > Search Engine Submitting and Positioning > Help and Tutorials > Keywords.**

It is possible that this hyperlink may differ slightly in your search results since search engine content is updated regularly.

The right side of your screen shows the Lycos Network page containing the same topics as in the hyperlink you clicked. In the Lycos page each topic is a separate link leading to additional hyperlinks. All links are directly or generally related to using keywords in search engines and Web site development and promotion.

8. **Click the Help and Tutorials link.**

9. **Scroll down and explore the links that this topic provides, in particular: Search Engine Watch (*www.SearchEngineWatch.com*); 101 Searchengine (*www.101SearchEngine.com*); and A simple article on site submission basics (*www.stylusinc.com/website/promotion_article.htm*).**

10. **Use the Back button** to get back to the Lycos results page after exploring each of the links.

11. **Click the Lycos logo at the top of the Search Explorer bar (in the left pane).**

The Lycos home page appears on the right side of the screen.

12. **Scroll to the bottom of the Lycos home page.**

13. **Click the Add Your Site to Lycos link.**

14. **Press Ctrl + E to close the Search Explorer bar.**

The Lycos page expands to fill the entire screen.

15. **Read through the page.**

Lycos explains the procedure for getting users to find your site when they search Lycos.

16. **Explore the Web sites of search engines such as *www.Excite.com* (Add URL link at bottom of page); *www.GoTo.com* List Sites & Products link at the bottom of the page; or *www.AltaVista.com* (Add a URL link in left frame) to see how they provide the opportunity to include Web pages in their site.**

17. **Click Close on the File menu to close your Web browser.**

You may proceed directly to the exercises for this lesson. If, however, you are finished with your computer session, follow the "shut down" procedures for your lab or school environment.

Lesson Summary & Exercises

SUMMARY

The skills learned in this lesson will help you to distinguish your Web site from the millions of poorly designed amateurish sites on the Internet. To be considered as professional looking, a Web site has to have more than accurate content. It must have a consistent theme—that is, it must use an appropriate set of colors, fonts, and graphics. In this lesson, you chose and customized a theme. You used styles and the Format Painter to ensure your character and paragraph formatting was uniform throughout your Web.

Using Spelling, Find, and Replace, you gave the same attention to the content of your Web as you did to its appearance. And by adding a search form to your Web you provided visitors to your site with a convenient yet comprehensive method for locating the information they seek.

Now that you have completed this lesson, you should be able to do the following:

- Apply a theme to a Web using default settings. (page 116)
- Apply selected elements from a theme to a Web. (page 116)
- Select a color scheme for the entire Web. (page 120)
- Change colors in the theme using the color wheel. (page 120)
- Change the colors of individual items in a scheme using the Custom tab. (page 120)
- Save a custom theme. (page 120)
- Add a background graphic. (page 123)
- Change the font and text size of the page banner. (page 126)
- Modify font styles in a custom theme. (page 126)
- Apply styles to body and heading text. (page 127)
- Use the Format Painter to copy character and paragraph formatting from one place in your Web to another. (page 128)
- Spell check your body text as you type, one page at a time, or throughout the entire Web. (page 130)
- Use Find and Replace to locate and replace text. (page 138)
- Add a search form to your Web by creating a new page based on the *Search Page* template. (page 142)
- Use search engines to find Web sites and help them find your site. (page 146)
- Modify the search form by changing text in buttons and the display of search results. (page 147)

Lesson Summary & Exercises

CONCEPTS REVIEW

1 MATCHING

Match each of the terms on the left with the definitions on the right.

TERMS

1. Find
2. Replace
3. style
4. theme
5. search engine
6. color scheme
7. search form
8. Boolean
9. color wheel
10. Format Painter

DEFINITIONS

a. A built-in set of colors, fonts, and graphics that can be applied to an entire Web

b. Lets you copy text formatting from one location to another

c. A part of a page in a Web that contains a text box for visitors to enter a search expression

d. A way to make adjustments to a color scheme

e. A set of colors used in a theme

f. A command that locates and substitutes text

g. A Web site that lets you locate other Web sites based on keyword searches

h. Controls how multiple keywords are used in a search expression

i. A command that locates text

j. Lets you apply a set of saved formatting attributes from a drop-down list on a toolbar

2 COMPLETION

Fill in the missing word or phrase for each of the following statements.

1. In a Boolean search you should use the word _____ if you want both keywords to be present in order to find a match.

2. _____ elements change appearance when you point to them, click them, or double-click them.

3. You should check _____ in the Find dialog box if you want to search for *bat* but not find *bath*.

4. When modifying a theme, the _____ tab lets you choose a group of colors upon which to base your Web pages.

5. When the Check spelling as you type option is on, words not found in the dictionary appear _____.

6. Before you can display a navigation bar or page banner, the page must be added to the _____.

7. The _____ gives you an almost unlimited choice of colors from which you can modify a color scheme.

8. A(n) _____ is a graphics image that appears behind all of the text and other graphic elements.

9. A(n) _____ is a set of formatting attributes that you can apply to select text in your Web page.

10. A(n) _____ is a Web site that lets users enter keywords in order to locate other Web sites.

3 SHORT ANSWER

Write a brief answer to each of the following questions.

1. Briefly describe how to change the colors in a theme.

2. How would you use the Format Painter to copy a paragraph format of two consecutive paragraphs? What would you do differently if the paragraphs were not consecutive?

3. What options do you have when the speller selects a word that is not in its dictionary?

4. What entries would you make in the Replace dialog box if you wanted to change the name *Green* to *Wood* without changing the *green* chair or the name *Greenwood*?

5. Briefly describe the steps necessary to create a search form.

6. How can you ensure that a Web page will display properly if the page uses a font that is not on the user's computer?

7. What is a Boolean expression?

8. Describe how you apply a style to text.

9. What is the difference between running a spelling check from a Web page or from the Folders view?

10. How would you change the text that appears in the buttons of the search form?

4 IDENTIFICATION

Label each of the elements in Figure 4.24.

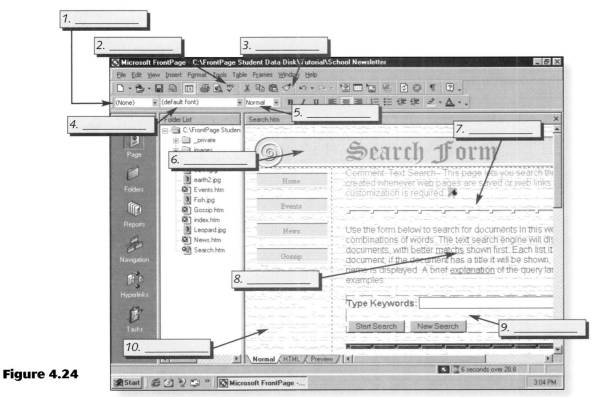

Figure 4.24

SKILLS REVIEW

Complete each of the Skills Review problems in sequential order to review your skills to apply a theme; customize a theme's colors, graphics, and text; apply a style; use the Format Painter; check spelling; find text in Web pages; replace text throughout the Web; add a search form; add navigation to a search page; and change the appearance of the search form.

1 Adding a Theme to a Web

1. Open the *Acme* Web in the *Skills Review* folder on your FrontPage Student Data Disk.

2. Display *index.htm* in Page view in the Normal tab.

3. Click **Theme** on the Format menu.

4. Click **Blends** in the themes list, then click **OK**.

5. Click **Yes,** if necessary, to confirm that you want to apply the theme.

6. Right-click the page banner, then click **Page Banner Properties**.

7. Click the **Picture option button**, then click **OK**.

8. Right-click the navigation bar, then click **Navigation Bar Properties**.

9. Click the **Buttons option button**, then click **OK**.

10. Click the **Save button** 🖫.

2 Modifying Theme Colors

1. Click **Theme** on the Format menu.

2. Click the **Modify button** [Modify ±], and then click the **Colors button** [Colors...].

3. Click **In Motion** in the Color Schemes tab.

4. Click the **Color Wheel tab**.

5. Click in the middle of the light blue area.

6. Click the **Custom tab**.

7. Click the **Item drop-down arrow** and click **Background**.

8. Click the **Color drop-down arrow** and click the **Gray color box**.

9. Click **OK**.

10. Click the **Background picture box** to uncheck it.

11. Click **No** when asked to save changes to the Blends theme.

12. Click **OK** to close the Themes dialog box.

Your Web page should now look like Figure 4.25.

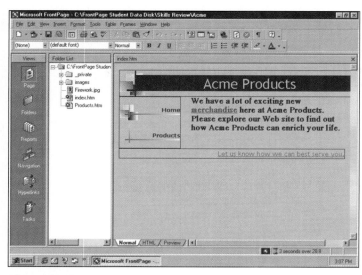

Figure 4.25

3 Modifying Theme Graphics

1. Click **Theme** on the Format menu.

2. Click the **Modify button** [Modify ±], then click the **Graphics button** [Graphics...].

3. Click the **Browse button** [Browse...], then click the **Select a file on your computer button** 🔍.

4. Double-click *acmeback* in the **Skills Review** folder.

5. Click the **Item drop-down arrow**, then click **Banner**.

6. Click the **Font tab**.

7. Click **Arial Rounded MT** or another font and click **OK**.

8. Click **OK** in the Themes dialog box.

9. Click **Yes** when asked to save the theme.

10. Type My Blends in the Save Theme box, and click **OK**.

11. Click **Theme** on the Format menu.

12. Click **My Blends** in the theme list.

13. Click to check the **Background Picture** check box.

14. Click **OK** to apply the *acmeback* background to *index.htm* and the *Acme* Web.

4 Modifying Theme Text

1. Click **Theme** on the Format menu.

2. Click the **Modify button** [Modify ±], then click the **Text button** [Text...].

3. Scroll the Sample of Theme window until you can see Heading 1 Style and Regular Text Sample.

4. Click the **Item drop-down arrow**, then click **Body**, if necessary.

5. Click **Book Antiqua** or a serif font of your choice.

6. Click the **Item drop-down arrow**, then click **Heading 1**.

7. Click **Bimini** or a headline font of your choice.

8. Click **OK** to close the Modify Theme dialog box.

9. Click **OK** in the Themes dialog box, and click **Yes** when asked to save changes.

5 Applying a Style

1. Select the body text in *index.htm*.

2. Click the **Font drop-down arrow**, then click **(default font)**.

3. Click the **Font Size drop-down arrow**, and then click **Normal**.

4. Click the **Bold button** [B].

5. Double-click *Products.htm* in the Folder List.

6. Select *Acme Leads the Way.*

7. Click the **Style drop-down arrow**, and then click **Heading 1**.

8. Click the **Font drop-down arrow**, and then click **(default font)**.

9. Click the **Save button** [💾].

6 Using the Format Painter

1. Double-click *index.htm* in the Folder List.

2. Select the body text again, if necessary.

3. Double-click the **Format Painter button** [🖌].

4. Double-click *Products.htm* to display it in Page view in the Normal tab.

5. Select the first paragraph of body text next to the fireworks picture.

6. Select the second paragraph of text material (the hyperlink).

7. Click the **Format Painter button** [🖌].

8. Click the **Save button** [💾].

Lesson Summary & Exercises

7 Checking Spelling

1. Delete the second letter *e* from the word *people* at the beginning of text in *Products.htm*.

2. Click the **Folders icon** 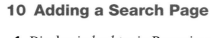.

3. Click the **Spelling button** .

4. Click the **Entire Web option button**, if necessary.

5. Click the **Start button**.

6. Double-click *Products.htm* in the Spelling dialog box and click **Change** to correct the spelling error.

7. Click **OK** to save and close the current document.

8. Click the **Close button** to close the Spelling dialog box.

8 Finding Text in Web Pages

1. Click the **Folders icon** , if necessary.

2. Click **Find** on the Edit menu.

3. Type Acme Products in the *Find what* text box.

4. Click **All pages under Search options**.

5. Click **Find in Web**.

6. Double-click the first page (*index.htm*) listed in the search results.

7. Click **Find Next** two times in the Find dialog box.

8. Click **Next Document** when asked to continue.

9. Click **Find Next** in the Find dialog box.

10. Click **OK** when asked if you are finished.

11. Click **Cancel** in the Find dialog box.

9 Replacing Text Throughout the Web

1. Click the **Folders icon** , if necessary.

2. Click **Replace** on the Edit menu.

3. Type Acme Products in the *Find what* text box, if necessary.

4. Type our company's products in the *Replace with* text box.

5. Click the **All pages option button**, if necessary.

6. Click the **Find in Web button**.

7. Double-click the page showing 1 occurrence (*Products.htm*).

8. Click **Replace**, click **OK**, and then click **Cancel**.

10 Adding a Search Page

1. Display *index.htm* in Page view in the Normal tab.

2. Right-click the Folder List and click **New Page**.

3. Double-click the *Search Page* template.

4. Click the **Save button** 🖫.

5. Type Search as the file name.

6. Click the **Change button**.

7. Type Search Form as the Page title, and then click **OK**.

8. Click **Save**.

11 Adding Navigation to a Search Page

1. Click the **Navigation view icon** 🖼.

2. Drag *Search.htm* from the Folder List to the right of the home page.

3. Click the **Page view icon** 🖺.

4. Double-click *index.htm*.

5. Click at the end of the hyperlink in the bottom, shared border.

6. Press [Enter⏎] and type Click here to search our Web followed by a space.

7. Click **Navigation Bar** on the Insert menu.

8. Click the **Top level option button** and uncheck the **Home page box**.

9. Click **OK**.

10. Click the **Save button** 🖫.

11. Press [Ctrl] then click the new button.

12. Right-click the *Search* page, and then click **Shared Borders**.

13. Click the **Current page button**, uncheck the **Bottom box**, and then click **OK**.

14. Click the **Save button** 🖫.

12 Changing the Appearance of the Search Form

1. Right-click the search form, then click **Search Form Properties**.

2. Type Enter keyword(s) here: in the *Label for Input* text box.

3. Type 30 in the *Width in characters* text box.

4. Type Begin search in the *Label for "Start Search" button* text box.

5. Click the **Search Results tab**.

6. Click the **Display score check box**.

7. Click **OK**.

8. Type your first and last name in place of *Author information goes here* at the bottom of the page.

9. Highlight 1999 *[Organization Name]* then type the current year and Acme Products.

10. Click the **Save button** 🖫.

11. Close the Web, click **Yes** when prompted to save changes, and exit FrontPage.

Lesson Summary & Exercises

LESSON APPLICATIONS

1 Apply and Modify a Theme, Apply Styles, and Use the Format Painter

Apply a theme, customize theme colors and fonts, and import a custom background to give the Web an attractive and consistent appearance.

1. Launch FrontPage and open the *Personal* Web in the *Lesson Applications* folder of your FrontPage Student Data Disk.

2. Display *index.htm* in Page view, Normal tab.

3. Add the Artsy theme to your Web.

4. Modify the theme's colors by choosing the Construction Zone color scheme and dark blue text from the color wheel. Use the Custom tab to change the color of the hyperlinks to purple.

5. Uncheck the background picture box, save your theme as *My Artsy,* and exit the Themes dialog box.

6. Click Theme on the Format menu to apply the *My Artsy* theme to the *Personal* Web.

7. Add *artsback.jpg* in the *Lesson Applications* folder as the background picture. Check the background picture box and save the background to the *My Artsy* theme. Modify the theme's graphics by changing the font for the page banner, and save changes to the *My Artsy* theme.

8. Modify the theme's body text to a serif font of your choice; modify Heading 1 text to a sans serif font of your choice. Save changes to the *My Artsy* theme and exit the Themes dialog box.

9. Apply the Heading 1 style to *Welcome to My Web Site!* within *index.htm*. Make sure the body text in *index.htm* is in the default font, normal size. Use the Format Painter to apply the *index.htm* body text format as necessary throughout the Web.

10. Save your changes.

2 Spell Check All Pages in a Web, Find Text, and Replace Text

Perform a spelling check of all pages of a Web and correct errors; search all pages of a Web and replace text.

1. Open *Family.htm* in the *Personal* Web in Page view in the Normal tab.

2. Select and delete the contents of the third paragraph (including the crane graphic, caption, and placeholder text).

3. Type the following as is, including misspellings which are underlined:

Cousin Anne has announced her <u>engagment</u> to her college beau, Steven Elliot. They don't have an exact date yet, but plan for a late summer <u>weding</u>. The couple expects to settle in Gary, Indiana, Steven's home town. Both Anne and Steven will be <u>gratuating</u> from State College this June. We wish them a long and <u>prosperus</u> life together.

4. Tab to the section to the right of the text, set the style to Heading 1, and type Anne and Steven Announce.

5. Select and delete the last three paragraphs on the page (including the fish graphic, caption, and placeholder text).

6. Spell check the page and correct the four spelling errors.

7. Switch to Folders view and spell check all pages, fixing any errors you find.

8. Use the Find command to locate the page containing the word *restaurant*.

9. Use the Replace command to change the word *web* to *Web*.

10. Save your changes.

3 Create a Search Page, Add a Navigation Button, and Modify Search Form Properties

Add a search page to a Web; add the search page to the navigation structure; add a navigation bar to the search page; remove a shared border from a search page; modify search form properties to customize the appearance of the search form.

1. Add a new page to the *Personal* Web based on the *Search Page* template. Name the page *Search Page* and the page title *Search*.

2. Add the new page to the navigation structure.

3. Add a new navigation bar to the bottom, shared border with the words Click here to search my Web.

4. Just above the bottom, shared border on the *Search.htm* page, edit the author name, organization, and current year information.

5. Remove the bottom, shared border from the *Search* page.

6. Modify the search form properties as follows: *Enter keywords to search for:* (Label for Input); *25* (Width in characters); *Begin* (Label for "Start Search" button); *Clear* (Label for "Clear" button). Add the Display score option to Search Results. When you're done, your search form should look similar to Figure 4.26.

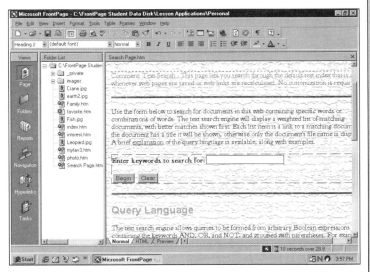

Figure 4.26

7. Close the Web, saving changes to all pages.

Lesson Summary & Exercises

PROJECTS

1 Scheming and "Theming"

The executive committee of the Benevolents is convinced that the Web site you designed and developed contains the right information. Now they would like you to dress it up a little by adding color and graphics to make the site appealing yet still business-like. You decide to add a theme and to make modifications to that theme, including a color scheme and graphics. Figure 4.27 gives you an example of an appropriate theme for the Web. (Note: there is a background picture in the *Projects* folder called *benevolents.jpg* that you can use.)

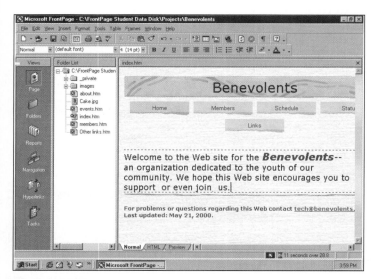

Figure 4.27

2 Do It with Styles

Now that you have given your *Benevolents* Web a theme, you need to apply a consistent format to your headings and body text. To simplify changes you may make later, you decide to modify your theme's text and to use styles for the body text and headings. Once you have your text styles set, apply the styles to each page of your Web using the Format Painter.

3 Good Looks Are Not Enough

Before submitting your improved Web to the committee, you want to put the same effort into improving the Web's content as you did to its appearance. Run the spelling program on all Web pages and correct any misspellings that are flagged by the spelling checker. Read over all pages to make sure they are grammatically accurate. The Victory Park cleaning event has been rescheduled. Rather than reading through the *Events* page, use the Find feature from Folders view to locate this event and make the necessary scheduling changes. You decide that the word *youth* should be replaced by the phrase *young persons* each time it occurs in your Web. To make sure you catch all occurrences in the Web, use the Replace feature from Folders view to make the change.

4 Seek and Ye Shall Find

One of the executive committee members suggests that you add a search page as a way for site visitors to find the information they need. You respond to the suggestion by creating a search page using the *Search Page* template. To make the search form as easy to use as possible, place a navigation bar in a shared border linking to the search page and make changes to the search form properties. Make sure to delete the navigation bar from the search page.

Project in Progress

5 Polish Your Collectibles

Dress up your collectibles store Web site with a custom theme. Use all of the techniques you learned in this lesson, including:

- Adding a theme
- Customizing the theme colors, graphics, and text
- Adding a background picture
- Applying styles to text
- Performing a spell check
- Adding and modifying a search form

(Note: there is a background picture in the *Projects* folder called *collectibles.jpg* that you can use.)

Building Webs with Pages

CONTENTS

OBJECTIVES

After you complete this lesson, you will be able to do the following:

- Create a Web using a Web wizard.
- Run tasks to customize Web wizard pages.
- Set table of contents properties.
- Add a blank page to a Web with the New button.
- Add a page to a Web while creating a hyperlink.
- Search for and repair broken hyperlinks.
- Change page titles and URLs.
- Add tables to a page and modify table properties.
- Type and format multilevel numbered and bulleted lists.

It is the ultimate goal of most Web sites to distribute information, whether for business, educational, or personal reasons. In this lesson, you will learn how to quickly set up a Web using a wizard, customize that Web, and add tables and lists with detailed information.

FrontPage
in the workplace

As more and more companies focus on the World Wide Web to attract customers, pressure is put on their competitors to do the same. Companies often hire Web designers to put their business on the Internet. The creation of an intricate, multimedia Web can take many months at a considerable expense. An alternative is the ready-made, formatted, and fully customizable Web that may be created using a wizard.

WORKING WITH WEB WIZARDS

In Lesson 2 you learned to create a Web using a template. Most of these Webs contain one or more pages with text and graphics placeholders and themes already applied. Once you've created one of these Webs with a template, it is up to you to revise the text and make any other alterations relevant to your needs.

Another way to create a Web is by using one of the three Web wizards installed with FrontPage 2000. Two of the Web wizards not only give you a set of related, hyperlinked pages with a theme, they also prompt you for information necessary to customize the contents of the Web. A third Web wizard lets you build a Web from existing files or Web pages. Creating a Web from a Web wizard gets your Web ready for publishing in a very short amount of time—as long as the Web wizard is close to what you need. Below is a description of the three wizards available in FrontPage 2000:

- Corporate Presence Wizard sets up a Web site containing pages of products and/or services offered, company information, company profile, a search form, and more. As the name says, this wizard is great if you want to get your business on the Web in a hurry.

- Discussion Web Wizard helps you set up a discussion forum on the topic of your choice. Pages let users search for articles of interest and contribute their own articles. Here is a wizard that is perfect for getting and encouraging an online exchange of ideas and opinions.

- Import Web Wizard creates a Web based on files stored on your computer or found on another Web site. Once you point to the folder for the Web or files, you can include all of the pages or files or select the ones you want to be in the new Web. If you have a Web you'd like to copy or if you have a lot of document files created by different programs, this wizard gets them ready to be published right away.

Creating a Web with a FrontPage Wizard

A wizard is really nothing more than a series of dialog boxes that prompt you to input information which is then used to complete the desired action. In Windows-based programs, there are wizards to install software and wizards to set up hardware, such as printers, microphone volume, or modems. There are wizards to connect you to the Internet and share that connection with other computers on the network; wizards to format letters and mailing labels; wizards to create graphs and charts; and wizards to customize your computer to increase accessibility to those with hearing, visual, or motor disabilities.

 *Note* *Microsoft Word 2000 also contains a Web page wizard designed to simplify the creation of a multi-page Web. To experiment with this wizard, click New on the File menu then click the Web Pages tab to locate the wizard.*

The Web wizards ask you questions about yourself, your company, which pages you want to include, and the theme you want to apply. Once you have completed answering all questions, FrontPage builds the Web and its navigation structure automatically. Adding more pages, changing themes, and editing the content is no different than if you created the Web and its pages from templates. If you answer the prompts correctly, however, you should have much less editing to do than if you created the pages from a template.

The Corporate Presence Web Wizard will ask you to supply the following information:

- The types of pages to be included in the Web (page selections include a home page, a products/services page, a What's New page, a table of contents page, and two forms— a feedback form and a search form).

- The topics to be listed on the home page and the What's New page. Each of the topics checked become another section on the page.

- The number of pages to be generated to support products and/or services offered and the topics to be on each page.

- The information to be included on the feedback form and how user responses should be collected.

- The options you want on the table of contents page.

- The elements you want placed in the shared borders.

- Whether or not to place an Under Construction icon on the pages. You would then delete the icon when the page is finished.

- The name and address of the company.

- Information about the name of the contact person.

- The theme to be applied to the Web.

- Whether or not to add tasks for each page that needs customization.

Note *You will work with the Corporate Presence Web Wizard in the following activities. As you work with the wizard, note that many of the dialog boxes that guide you through the creation of the Web contain selections that have been made for you by default. These can easily be changed, depending on your needs and preferences.*

Using the Wizard Dialog Box

Although each wizard asks a different set of questions and the number of dialog boxes varies from one wizard to another, there is a set of common dialog box elements you will see when working with any kind of wizard (not just a FrontPage 2000 wizard). Table 5.1 lists the names and functions of some of these elements.

TABLE 5.1	COMMON WIZARD DIALOG BOX ELEMENTS	
Button Name	**Button**	**Description**
Next button	Next >	Present in every dialog box (except the last). Click this button when you have read, typed, and selected the options you need.
Back button	< Back	Every dialog box (except the first) has one. This button lets you go back to the previous dialog box to either check or change your entries.
Finish button	Finish	Use this button to tell the wizard you are through making options.
Cancel button	Cancel	This button ends the entire wizard process. None of the options you selected are used and no new Web is built.
Progress indicator	▪▪▪▪▪▪	A horizontal bar that fills from left to right with blue squares, letting you know how far along you are in the wizard.

HANDS On

Creating a Web from a Wizard

In this activity, you will create a Web for a company using a Web wizard. Answering the prompts with the information you are given, you will see how quickly the Web can be built.

1. Start FrontPage 2000.
2. Click the New Page drop-down arrow 🗋, and click Web.

The New dialog box appears containing a group of Web templates and wizards. Although their icons look similar, note that the wizard icons contain a sparkling wand.

3. Click the Corporate Presence Wizard icon.

Do not double-click the icon or you will not have an opportunity to name the new Web—instead a default name will be assigned for you.

Creating a Web from a Wizard

1. Point to New on the File menu, then click Web.

2. Click the Web wizard, type the location for the new Web, and then click OK.

3. Choose the page options, theme, and identifying information for each dialog box; then click Next to advance the wizard.

4. Click Finish.

4. Type C:\FrontPage Student Data Disk\Tutorial\Sporting Greats **in the *Specify the location of the new web* text box.**

5. Click OK.

The first window of the Corporate Presence Web Wizard appears explaining the purpose of the wizard, as shown in Figure 5.1.

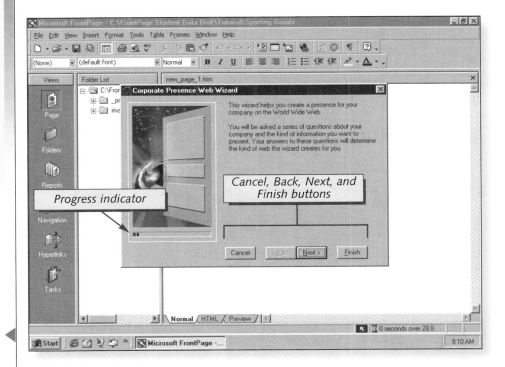

Figure 5.1
Corporate Presence Web Wizard

6. Click Next .

The second dialog box asks which pages to include in the Web. The progress indicator on the bottom left of the dialog box shows that you have a lot more information to enter before the Wizard is complete.

7. Make sure all of the boxes are checked, then click Next Next> .

This dialog box lets you choose the topics to be included on the home page.

8. Check all of the boxes, then click Next Next> .

Note

If you lose your place, click the Back or Next buttons to navigate within the series of dialog boxes.

A dialog box now asks you to decide what topics to put on the What's New page.

9. Make sure the Web Changes box is checked and the other boxes are not checked, then click Next Next> .

The next wizard dialog box asks you how many pages to create for products and services offered by the company. Of course, you can always add or delete pages later on, but your task is much easier if you choose an accurate number now.

10. Type 2 in the Products box, type 1 in the Services box, and then click **Next** ⌈ Next > ⌉.

This dialog box prompts you to select the topics to be included on each products and services page. By default, the *Pricing Information* and *Information request form* are checked in the Products section; and the *Information request form* is checked in the Services section.

11. Click **Next** ⌈ Next > ⌉.

A dialog box asks you to indicate the information to appear on the feedback form. The Full Name, Company Affiliation, Telephone Number, FAX Number, and E-mail Address are checked by default.

12. Click **Next** ⌈ Next > ⌉.

This wizard dialog box determines how data collected from the feedback form will be stored.

13. Click the **Yes, use tab-delimited format option button**, if necessary, then click **Next** ⌈ Next > ⌉.

This dialog box has options to be included in the table of contents page.

14. Check **Keep page list up-to-date automatically** and **Use bullets for top-level pages**; uncheck the second box and click **Next** ⌈ Next > ⌉.

This dialog box lets you choose the information to appear on the top and bottom shared borders.

15. Click to check the **Page title box** in the top section, then click to remove the other check marks from that section.

16. Click to check the **Links to your main web pages box** in the bottom section, then click to remove the other check marks from that section.

17. Click **Next** ⌈ Next > ⌉.

This dialog box determines whether an Under Construction icon should be placed on unfinished pages—Yes by default.

18. Click **Next** ⌈ Next > ⌉.

Finally, you get to enter information about the company.

19. Type Sporting Greats **as the full company name;** Greats **as the one-word version;** 1212 Appleton Road **as the address; then click Next** ⌈ Next > ⌉.

Now you are prompted for contact information. Accept the defaults since this is a fictitious company.

20. Click **Next** ⌈ Next > ⌉.

In this dialog box you have the opportunity to select a theme for the Web.

21. Click the **Choose Web Theme button** ⌈ Choose Web Theme ⌉.

The Choose Theme dialog box appears.

22. Click **Capsules** then check the **Vivid colors, Active graphics,** and **Background picture check boxes** and click **OK**.

23. Click **Next** [Next >].

The final wizard dialog box appears. The *Show Tasks View after web is uploaded* check box commands FrontPage to automatically add tasks for the jobs that should be done after the wizard is finished. The box is checked by default.

24. Click **Finish** [Finish].

The new Web appears in Tasks view with a set of tasks listed as shown in Figure 5.2.

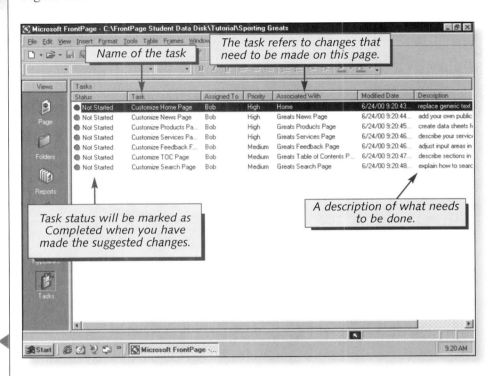

Figure 5.2
Tasks view after running Web Wizard

Customizing the Web

When a Web wizard has completed its work, there are still a number of jobs remaining to be done. The basic content of each Web page must be individualized with descriptions of the products, services, and company. The wizard has provided pages, hyperlinks, a structure, a navigation bar, a theme, and company details. All you have to do is start each task and type your information over the placeholder text.

Most of the placeholder text appears in colored type (often green or blue) and labeled as a "Comment." However, some placeholder text may be in black type or in the form of a hyperlink (such as "<u>Product 1</u>"). Whatever its appearance, this text suggests that it should be replaced by your meaningful content. Even if you don't replace it or delete it, the comment text will *not* appear when the Web is previewed or opened in a Web browser.

FrontPage
BASICS

Completing a Web Created by a Wizard

1. Start each task in Tasks view.

2. Replace the placeholder text with your company's information.

3. Save each page you change.

Figure 5.3 ◄
The Sporting Greats navigation structure

Completing a Web Created by a Wizard

In this activity, you will customize the pages created by the Corporate Presence Web wizard. Before doing this, you will take a look at the navigation structure created by the wizard.

1. Click the Navigation view icon ![icon].

The Corporate Presence wizard created the navigation structure shown in Figure 5.3. As you can see, there are four top level pages: Home, Feedback, Contents, and Search. The home page is parent to three child pages: News, Products, and Services. Products and Services each have as many child pages as you asked for when prompted by the wizard.

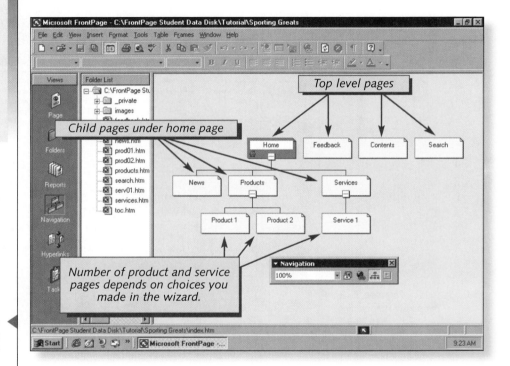

2. Click the Tasks view icon ![icon].

The task list appears.

3. Double-click Customize Home Page, the first task in the list.

The Task Details dialog box opens.

4. Click Start Task.

The home page opens in Page view in the Normal tab as seen in Figure 5.4.

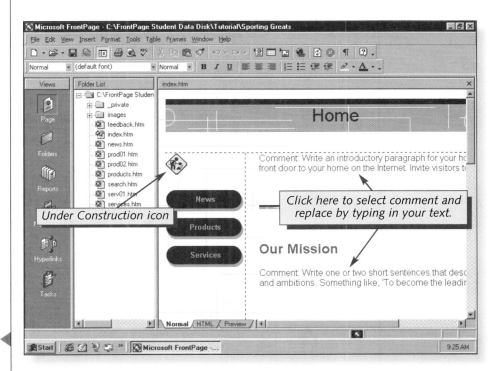

Figure 5.4
The Sporting Greats Home page

5. **Click the first comment section and type the following:** Welcome to the Sporting Greats Web site.

6. **Click the comment under the Our Mission section and type the following:** Our goal is to provide the highest quality products and services at the lowest prices possible.

7. **Replace the four comments in the Company Profile section with the following:**

Our sales staff knows all about the products and services we offer because they are experts in that field. Who better to help you with skiing equipment and lessons than a great skier?

We are members of several trade and professional organizations. Setting high standards for our company and our staff keeps us at the top of our field.

Ask the thousands of satisfied customers what they think about the quality of our products and services.

Our founder, Steve Almer, says, "Anybody can sell sporting goods. It takes a great organization to sell *Sporting Greats.*"

8. **Replace the comment in the Contact Information section with the following:** We want your experiences with us to be completely satisfying. Let us know how we can serve you better.

9. **Click the Construction icon near the top of the page and press** Delete.

10. **Click the Save button** 🖫 **, then click Yes to mark the task as completed.**

11. **Click the Tasks view icon** 📋**.**

12. **Double-click each of the tasks in the Tasks list and type the text provided in the following steps, replacing comments on each page.**

13. After you finish each task, click the **Save button**  then click **Yes** to mark the task as completed.

14. *Customize News Page*

May 22
Added a feedback form so you can easily give us your suggestions, advice, concerns, and so on.

January 10
Launch of the new Sporting Greats Web site.

15. *Customize Products Page*

Here are just two departments with some really special values this week.

Golf Clubs (Select and change the **Product 1** hyperlink.)
Check out the prices on these fine woods and irons.

Skates (Select and change the **Product 2** hyperlink.)
You won't find better deals than these anywhere . . . guaranteed!

16. *Customize Services Page*
We've lined up the best trainers in the area to teach anyone, in almost any sport.

Tennis, anyone? (Select and change the **Name of service 1** hyperlink.)

We have classes and private lessons to suit your needs, whether you're an absolute beginner or an advanced player trying to master tournament-clinching strategies.

17. *Customize Feedback Form*

Capitalize the *w* in *Web* in the first line of text.
(Leave the comment as is.)

18. *Customize Search Page*

Capitalize the *w* in *Web* in the first line of text.
(Leave the comment as is.)

USING SITE MAPS

Visitors to your Web site may not want to click through your navigation structure to find the page they want—especially if they know what they are looking for. Just as a book has a ***table of contents*** listing the location of the chapters and sections of the book, a Web site can have a table of contents listing all or some of the pages. Rather than listing the page numbers like a book, each page title is a hyperlink.

The table of contents is a type of ***site map.*** A site map is a Web page containing hyperlinks to pages within the Web site. A site map usually contains very little in the way of graphics or formatting—just the hyperlinks. FrontPage has two options for generating a site map—the table of contents created by the Web wizard and a site map by categories. The site map by ***categories*** asks you to create group names for pages such as Products, News Items, and so on. In each page's properties window, you choose the category to which the page belongs. When you point to Components and click Categories on the Insert menu, a site map by categories is created.

Creating a Table of Contents Page

You can insert a table of contents into a page by pointing to Components and clicking Table of Contents on the Insert menu. By default, FrontPage 2000 uses your navigation structure, beginning with the home page, to create the table of contents. Also by default each page will be shown only once, even if there are links from two or more pages to it; pages not linked to are not included; and the table of contents will be updated any time one of the pages is edited.

The Corporate Presence Wizard you worked with created a page to hold the table of contents called *toc.htm*. The actual entries cannot be seen until viewed in the Web browser. You can, however, set the format and other properties by right-clicking the table and clicking Table of Contents Properties in the shortcut menu. The Table of Contents Properties dialog box is illustrated in Figure 5.5.

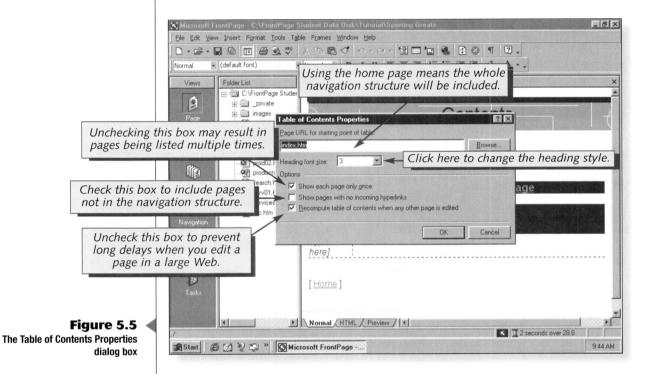

Figure 5.5
The Table of Contents Properties dialog box

If your table of contents starts at the home page, the entire navigation structure will be used. If you choose another page with which to start, only pages under that page become part of the table of contents. You can increase the font size for entries by selecting one of the font sizes in the drop-down list. There are check boxes to include pages under every page that links to them, to include pages that are not in the navigation structure, and to indicate whether the table of contents should be updated every time one of the pages is edited. In regard to the latter option, in a very large Web it may take the computer quite a while to rebuild the table of contents; in a small Web, only a minute or two.

Setting Up a Table of Contents

1. Point to Component and click Table of Contents on the Insert menu to create a new table of contents.

2. Right-click the table then click Table of Contents Properties to edit the features of an existing table of contents.

3. Enter the starting page, the heading font size, and the options you need, then click OK.

4. Save the page.

5. Click the Preview in Browser button to view the page titles within the table of contents.

Setting Up a Table of Contents

In this activity, you will change the table of contents properties for the *toc.htm* page created by the Web wizard.

1. Click the Tasks view icon  in the *Sporting Greats* Web.

The Customize TOC Page is the only task listed in the Tasks window.

2. Double-click the Customize TOC Page task and click Start Task in the Task Details dialog box.

3. Right-click a blank part of the table of contents area, then click Table of Contents Properties on the shortcut menu.

The Table of Contents Properties dialog box opens with *index.htm* listed as the starting point for the table.

4. Click the Heading font size drop-down arrow and click 2.

The heading font size relates to the heading styles. The lower the number, the higher the heading level. Thus, a small number is generally a large font size.

5. Check the Show each page only once box; check the Recompute table of contents when any other page is edited box.

The *Show pages with no incoming hyperlinks* box should remain unchecked.

6. Click OK.

The table of contents page seems unchanged.

7. Select and delete the comment above the Table of Contents heading.

8. Right-click the left shared border, then click Navigation Bar Properties.

The Navigation Bar Properties dialog box opens.

9. Click the Top level option button and make sure the Home page box is checked.

10. Click OK.

The navigation bar appears within the left shared border of *toc.htm*.

11. Click the Save button 🖫.

12. Click Yes when prompted by the dialog box to mark the task completed.

13. Click the Preview in Browser button 🔍.

14. Click Yes if a dialog box asks you to save your changes.

The table of contents page appears in your browser as shown in Figure 5.6. Now you can read the page titles and see the format of the table of contents as the Web visitor sees it.

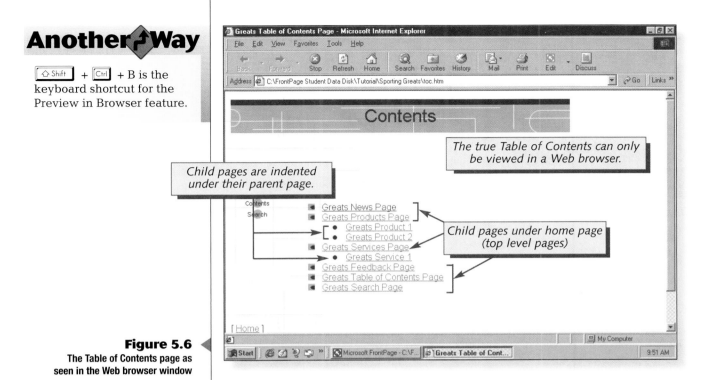

Child pages are indented under their parent page.

The true Table of Contents can only be viewed in a Web browser.

Child pages under home page (top level pages)

15. Click the **Close button** ☒ in the Browser window.

ADDING AND DELETING PAGES

The Web wizard usually creates a basic structure for a Web. It is not unusual, however, to have to add and remove pages to meet your particular needs. For example, assume that in the *Sporting Greats* Web the products pages are not really designed according to your needs. Rather than try to make a lot of modifications to these pages, it is sometimes easier to create new product pages and delete the ones created by the wizard.

Adding a New Page

In the following activity you will learn a new method for adding pages to a Web. While in the Page view, clicking the New Page button 🗋 sets you up with a page based on the Normal Page template, bypassing the New dialog box altogether. This new page has the same shared borders and default settings as other pages in the Web. If the Web design is based on a theme, the new page will use that theme as well. Once you add the page to the navigation structure, your page banner and hyperlinks will appear.

Creating a Page in Page View

1. Click the New Page button while in Page view.

2. Click the Save button, type a file name, and click Save.

3. Drag the page from the Folder List into the navigation structure in Navigation view.

4. Add a new page label in Navigation view.

Creating a Page in Page View

In this activity, you will delete the two products pages from the *Sporting Greats* Web and create a new page to replace one of them.

1. Click the **Page view icon** 🗐, if necessary.

2. Right-click *prod01.htm* in the Folder List, then click **Delete** on the shortcut menu.

3. Click **Yes** in the Confirm Delete dialog box.

4. Right-click *prod02.htm* in the Folder List, then click **Delete** on the shortcut menu.

5. Click **Yes** in the Confirm Delete dialog box.

The two products pages are removed from the Web.

6. Click the **New Page button** 🗋.

A new blank page appears based on the *Normal* template with a temporary file name (*new_page_1.htm*). As noted in comments in the new page, the top, bottom, and left shared borders appear blank until you add the page to the navigation structure.

7. Click the **Save button** 🖫.

The Save As dialog box appears.

8. Type Product 1 as the file name and click **Save**.

9. Click the **Navigation view icon** 🖫.

10. Drag *Product 1.htm* from the Folder List so it is a child page under the *Products* page.

The new page appears as *New Page 1*, a child page under *Products* in the navigation structure.

11. Click *New Page 1* within the page graphic, then type Golf Clubs as the page label.

12. Click the **Page view icon** 🗐.

 *When you change your Web's navigation structure in Navigation view by creating a new page or deleting a page, those changes are saved automatically when you switch to another view. However, you can easily save changes without changing views by right-clicking the view background then clicking Apply Change on the shortcut menu.*

Your new page now has a page banner and navigation bars as shown in Figure 5.7.

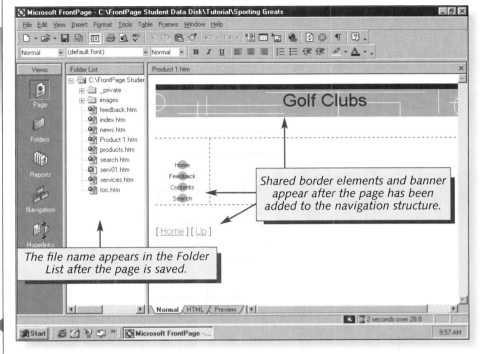

Figure 5.7
New page with new page title and
shared border elements

Creating a Page While Creating a Hyperlink

You can create a new blank page at the same time you create a hyperlink to
it. Suppose you are building a Web and you decide that rather than including
a lot of content on the current page, you will add a link to another page that
will hold the content. You can create the hyperlink and inform FrontPage
that the target page does not yet exist. At once the New dialog box will open
enabling you to choose the template upon which to base the new page.

Creating a Hyperlink to a New Page

In this activity, you will create a second products page in the *Sporting Greats*
Web while creating a hyperlink.

1. Display **Product 1.htm** in Page view in the Normal tab.

2. Click an insertion point in the text area to the right of the navigation bar and type
   More specials.

3. Select **More specials**, then click the **Hyperlink button** 🌐.

The Create Hyperlink dialog box appears.

4. Click the **Create a page and link to the new page button** 🗋.

The New dialog box opens providing the option to select a template upon
which to base the new page. The *Normal Page* template is selected by
default.

5. Click **OK**.

Creating a Hyperlink to a New Page

1. Type the text for the hyperlink within the current page.

2. Select the text and click the Hyperlink button.

3. Click the Create a page and link to the new page button.

4. Choose a template, then click OK.

5. Save the page, add it to the navigation structure, and type a new page label.

A new page based on the *Normal Page* template is created.

6. Click the **Save button** 🖫.

The Save As dialog box appears.

Type Product 2 as the file name, then click the **Save button**.

The new page *(Product 2.htm)* appears in Page view; it has been added to the Folder List.

7. Click the **Navigation view icon** 📶.

8. Drag *Product 2.htm* from the Folder List to a position to the right of the *Golf Clubs* page graphic to make it a child page of *Products*.

9. Click **New Page 1** in the page graphic and type Skates as the page label.

10. Click the **Page view icon** 📄.

The new product page appears (*product 2.htm*). It is formatted just like *product 1.htm*.

Understanding File Names and Hyperlinks

Hyperlinks are assigned to specific files, except for those that call up e-mail windows. Using relative URLs, hyperlinks can find files even when the Webs are moved from one location to another. You can even rename a file within FrontPage 2000, and if it is a target of a hyperlink you will be given the opportunity to update the link automatically.

If you change a file name outside of FrontPage 2000, such as in Microsoft Explorer, or if you delete a file and want to link to a different file, you will have to fix the hyperlink targets yourself. You can check for ***broken hyperlinks***— hyperlinks whose targets are no longer known—in the Reports view.

Good Web maintenance procedure should include a periodic check of the hyperlinks. The Recalculate Hyperlinks option on the Tools menu attempts to repair hyperlinks and update and synchronize all Web components. When you view the Site Summary report, you will see any errors that this check turned up. If you double-click on the Broken Hyperlink, you will display the Broken Hyperlinks report containing details for each of the errors. Double-clicking on an error line opens the Edit Hyperlink dialog box. In this window you may browse for and reassign the target to the hyperlink.

Updating Hyperlinks for Changed File Names

In this activity, you will search for and repair broken hyperlinks. Then you will change a file name and have FrontPage 2000 fix the hyperlink for you.

1. Click **Recalculate Hyperlinks** on the **Tools menu**.

The Recalculate Hyperlinks dialog box appears containing a list of actions that it will perform.

2. Click **Yes**.

3. Click the **Reports view icon** .

1. Click Recalculate
   Hyperlinks on the Tools
   menu, then click Yes.

2. Click the Reports view
   icon.

3. Double-click the
   Broken Hyperlinks row
   in the Site Summary
   report.

4. Double-click the broken
   hyperlink.

5. Click Browse, double-
   click the correct target,
   then click Replace.

Figure 5.8
The Site Summary report with
two broken hyperlinks

The Site Summary report appears, as shown in Figure 5.8. In the Broken hyperlinks row the count is 2, not surprising since you deleted two pages to which the *Products* page linked. You may also notice that there is a component error. This error references the Search page which, until the site is published, is unable to function.

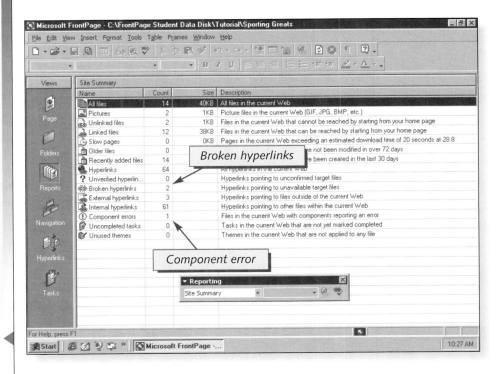

Note If you get a report other than the Site Summary, change the report type to Site Summary using the drop-down arrow in the Reporting toolbar.

4. Double-click the Broken hyperlinks row in the Site Summary.

The Broken Hyperlinks report appears with a row for each invalid link.

5. Double-click the *prod01.htm* row.

The Edit Hyperlink dialog box opens as shown in Figure 5.9. You have the option to change the target of the link or the page containing the link. An option button lets you change all pages linking to the deleted page with the new target page. In this case, however, only one page needs to be fixed.

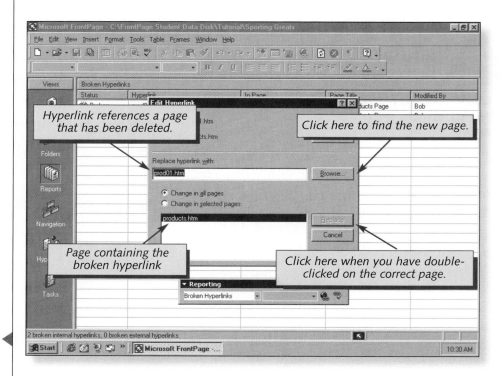

Figure 5.9
The Edit Hyperlink dialog box

6. Click Browse Browse.

The Select Hyperlink window appears.

7. Double-click *Product 1.htm*.

The Select Hyperlink window closes and you return to the Edit Hyperlink dialog box.

8. Click Replace.

9. Repeat steps 4 through 8, replacing *prod2.htm* with *Product 2.htm*.

No broken hyperlinks remain.

10. Click the Folders view icon 📁.

11. Click *serv01.htm* once in the Name column to select it then click it again to select the name.

Do not double-click, but click, wait, and click again. Double-clicking will take you to the Page view. If this happens, click the Folders view icon and try again.

12. Type Service 1.htm and press Enter⏎.

The Rename dialog box opens asking you if you want to update the page or pages that link to this file.

13. Click Yes.

After a moment the links are updated. As you can see, renaming files while in Folders view lets you update the links automatically.

If you change a file name in an application other than FrontPage 2000, use the Recalculate Hyperlinks tool and the Broken Hyperlinks report to reassign targets to the new file name.

Understanding Page Titles and URLs

It's easy to get page titles, page labels, and file names confused. As a quick review:

- Page titles appear as a page property in the Folders view (Title column) and in the title bar of the Web browser when the page is open. Depending on the Web browser, the page title is used for adding Favorites or Bookmarks.

- Page labels appear in the Navigation view, page banners, and navigation bars.

- File names appear in the Folder List, the heading of the Page view window, the Hyperlinks view, hyperlinks targets, and rows of the Tasks and Reports lists. File names and their paths are also the URL for the page; that is, the file name will appear in the Address or Location bar of the Web browser when it is open.

The file name is created when you first save the page—if you wish to change the URL you must change the file name. The page label is assigned when you add the page to the navigation structure. The page title is given the same name as the label; however, once you change the page title, the label is not changed. And, if you change the label at a later date, the title will not change. That is, once you have entered any of the three names, they remain independent of each other. If you want one of the three to be changed, you must change it yourself.

As you have learned, it is important for the page title to accurately represent the content of your Web since visitors will see it in the title bar of their browser. If visitors save your site as a Favorite or Bookmark in order to return to it, they will see the page title as they scan these lists in their browser.

Changing a Page Title

1. Right-click the page in Page view.

2. Click Page Properties on the shortcut menu.

3. Type the new page title.

4. Click Save.

5. Click Preview in Browser to see the page title in the browser's title bar.

Changing Page Titles and URLs

In this activity, you will change the page titles of the new pages you just created and see how this affects the title bar in the Web browser. Then you will change the file name of a page to change its URL.

1. Display **Product 1.htm** in Page view in the Normal tab.

2. Click the **Preview in Browser button** .

3. Click **Yes** if you are prompted to save your changes.

The default browser opens. Note that the page title, *New Page 1*, appears in the title bar; the file name, *Product 1.htm*, appears in the Address box at the end of the path in the URL. The page label, Golf Clubs, appears in the page banner.

4. Click **Close** to close the browser.

5. Right-click in the page and click **Page Properties** on the shortcut menu.

The Page Properties dialog box opens.

6. Type Sporting Greats Golf Clubs Specials **in the *Title* text box and click OK**.

7. Click **Save** .

8. Click the **Preview in Browser button** .

Changing a Page URL

1. Click the file name twice in Folders view.

2. Type a new file name.

3. Click Preview in Browser to see the new URL.

The page opens in the browser, as shown in Figure 5.10. Note that the new page title appears in the title bar. The URL and page banner remain unchanged.

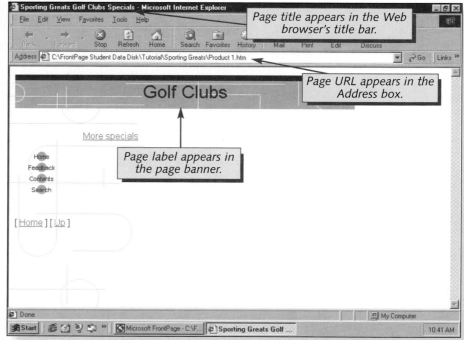

Figure 5.10

Web browser showing page title, page URL, and page label

9. Click **Close** ⊠ to close the browser.

10. Repeat steps 5 through 9 for the *Product 2.htm* page, typing the new page title as Sporting Greats Skates Specials.

11. Click *Product 1.htm* in the Folder List, then click it again.

A rectangle surrounds the file name.

12. Type GolfClubs.htm and press ⌷Enter◄┘ ⌷.

The Rename window opens, asking if you want to update the page with the hyperlink to this file.

13. Click **Yes**.

14. Click the **Preview in Browser button** 🔍.

15. Click **Yes** when prompted to save changes.

The page *GolfClubs.htm* appears in your browser. Note the change to the URL in the Address box—"GolfClubs.htm" appears at the end of the path.

16. Click **Close** ⊠ to close the Web browser.

17. Follow steps 11 through 16 to change the file name of the *Product2.htm* page to *Skates.htm*.

CREATING TABLES

As you've worked through these activities, you have encountered Web pages divided up into rectangular areas or sections. All of these areas have been on pages you created from a wizard or a template. However, you can manually divide up pages you create yourself by creating a table.

A *table* is a way to organize a page or a part of a page by dividing it into one or more rows and one or more columns. Each box created by the intersection of a column and row is called a *cell.* In FrontPage 2000, a cell can contain almost anything, including text or even a graphic image.

By default all rows have the same height and the columns have the same width; however, you have many options to fix the size of all or any cells. Each cell has a border, but you can customize the color and style of the lines that make up the border. Likewise, the vertical alignment of the table, the color, size, and attributes of text, the background of the cells, and many other factors give a wide variety of appearance and function to tables.

Some tables look like tables, especially when the rows and columns are evenly spaced and the borders are clearly drawn. At other times, a table may not look at all like a table, as when the cells are of uneven widths and heights and the borders have an unusual style.

Even the size of the table can be changed. You can add a row to the bottom of the table with the press of a key and it is also a simple matter to insert columns and rows into the middle of the table.

Setting Up Tables

There are three basic methods for creating a table. With the Insert Table toolbar button ▦, you can drag to select the number of rows and columns for the table. A second method is to point to Insert on the Table menu and click Table. With this technique you can choose to set many table properties in addition to determining the number of rows and columns. A third procedure allows you to "draw" the table by dragging the outline of the table and then dragging lines across to create rows and down to create columns. (Although this method can be used to create a table, more often it is used to divide a cell into two or more cells.)

HANDS On

Creating a Table with the Insert Table Tool

In this activity, you will add a table to a page using the Insert Table toolbar button ▦. Then you will add text to the table.

1. Display *GolfClubs.htm* in Page view in the Normal tab.

2. Click an insertion point at the end of the **More specials** hyperlink, then press `Enter⏎`.

The insertion point is now positioned where you want the top of the table to begin.

Creating a Table with the Insert Table Tool

1. Click an insertion point in the document where the table should begin.

2. Click the Insert Table button.

3. Drag down in the table grid for the number of rows and drag to the right for the number of columns you want.

3. Click the **Insert Table button** ▦.

A window opens containing an empty grid. Each box in the grid represents a cell in a table. As you move the pointer across the grid, a message at the bottom of the grid describes the size of the table. For example a "3 by 2 Table" will consist of 3 rows and 2 columns.

4. Point to the third row in the third column.

Three rows and three columns are highlighted. The message in the bottom of the window reads "3 by 3 Table."

5. Click the cell in the third row and in the third column.

The table appears in your document, as shown in Figure 5.11. Your insertion point is in the first cell.

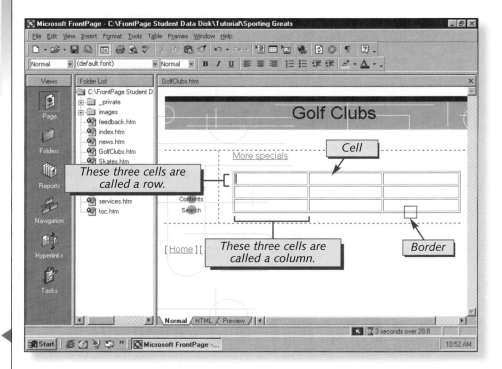

Figure 5.11
Empty table with 9 cells

6. Type Item **and press** Tab.

The Tab key moves the insertion point to the next cell to the right within a row. When you reach the end of a row, Tab moves the insertion point to the first cell in the first column to the left within the next row.

7. Type Description **and press** Tab.

8. Type Price **and press** Tab.

You now have a row containing headings for each column.

9. In the next two rows, type the following:

Williams Woods	1, 3, and 5	$149.99
MetalMax	Driver	$99.99

Note *Press* Tab *after each entry except the last ($99.99). If you press* Tab *after entering the price in the last cell, a new blank row will be created. Press* Ctrl *+ Z with the insertion point within the row to delete this blank row.*

10. Click Save 🖫.

HANDS On

Creating a Table with the Insert Table Dialog Box

In this activity, you will create a table using the Insert Table dialog box. Then you will add text to this table.

1. Display *Skates.htm* in Page view in the Normal tab.

2. Click an insertion point in the text box to the right of the navigation bar, if necessary.

3. Point to Insert on the Table menu and click Table.

The Insert Table dialog box appears, as in Figure 5.12. With this method of inserting a table you use counter buttons (arrows that count up or down) to choose the number of rows and columns for the new table.

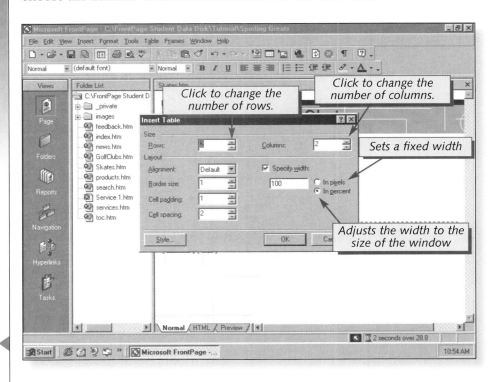

Figure 5.12
The Insert Table dialog box

4. Click the Rows up counter arrow two times.

The number of rows changes to 4.

5. Click the **Columns up counter arrow** one time.

The number of columns changes to 3.

6. Click **OK**.

A table containing 4 rows and 3 columns appears in the page.

7. Type the following as column headings using [Tab] to advance to the next cell after you type each entry:

Manufacturer	Description	Price

8. Type the following rows using [Tab] to advance to the next cell after you type each entry:

Ultimate	Men's two-piece molded boot	$79.99
BladeX	Adult's Roller Hockey	$129.99
BladeX	Youth's 3-buckle	$29.99

9. Click **Save** 💾.

Adjusting Table Properties

Tables created with either the Insert Table button ⊞ or the Insert table dialog box use the entire width of the page by default. If the page has a left and/or right shared border, the table will fill the rest of the available space. You can use several techniques to change the amount of space the table uses. The Table Properties dialog box (Figure 5.13) controls the layout, borders, and background for the entire table—each occupying its own portion of the window.

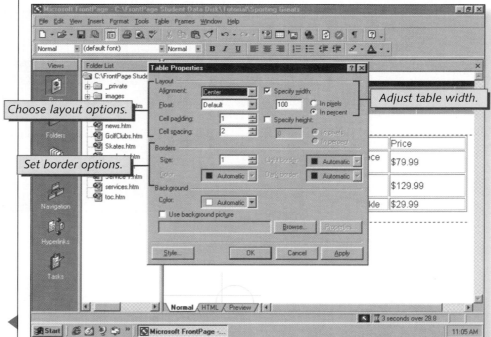

Choose layout options.

Adjust table width.

Set border options.

Figure 5.13
The Table Properties dialog box

- Layout options include alignment, table size, how text should wrap around the table, and the margins to be used within each cell.
- Border options set the width and colors of the lines that compose the border.
- Background options let you choose the color and/or picture that appears behind the text.

With the Specify width box checked, you are able to set the width to a specific size, as measured in pixels, or to a specific percentage of available space. Since the default is 100%, newly created tables fill the entire width of the page. It is important to remember that the choice you make affects the width of the table in the visitor's Web browser, not just in FrontPage. Just because your screen shows the entire table well, does not mean that another user with a smaller screen, lower resolution, or a windowed Web browser can see the entire table without scrolling. The percentage option ensures that the visitor's screen displays the table fully. Another method for setting the width of columns is called AutoFit. Applying this command forces the column to narrow or widen to the length of the longest item in that column.

If you uncheck the Specify width box, you have the ability to size the table as you see fit by dragging the table borders to increase or decrease the width of the table. The same options are available in determining the height of the table. The Specify height check box lets you choose the number of pixels or percentage of the page height for the table or lets you set the height manually.

The Alignment option is set to Default. It functions the same as in the Paragraph dialog box; that is, you can choose from left, right, center, or justify to position your table horizontally. As with font, font size, and other options, leaving the alignment set to Default allows you to change the default value and have all tables realign automatically.

The Float option tells FrontPage 2000 what to do with text near the table. The Left option forces text above the table to use any space on the left side of the table; conversely, the Right option pushes the text to the right of the table. If there is no room for the text on that side, the text will skip over the table and resume at the next blank line.

The Cell padding and Cell spacing set the distance from the borders to the text or from one cell to another, respectively.

The Cell Properties dialog box is very similar to the Table Properties dialog box, as shown in Figure 5.14. Essentially the options chosen here apply to the cell in which the insertion point is located or the cells that have been selected.

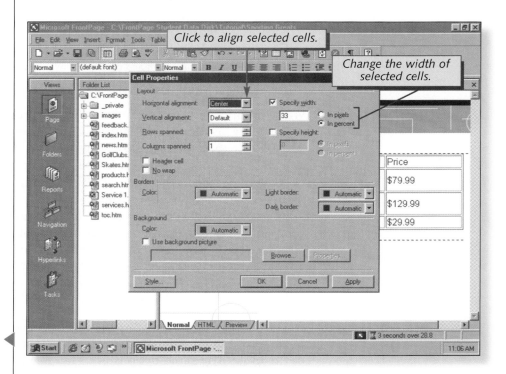

Figure 5.14
The Cell Properties dialog box

In this dialog box, you can set the horizontal and vertical alignment of cells, pick the width and height of cells, make cells take up several rows and/or columns, change the border, and choose a background. By using the percent button to size the cells in the Specify width section, you ensure that the cell size adjusts as the table size changes.

There are four options new to this dialog box. Rows spanned and Columns spanned increase the height and width of cells, respectively. The Header cell check box boldfaces text within the box so that it stands out from the rest of the detail text. Finally the No wrap check box prevents text from spanning two lines—the column will widen as much as possible to accommodate the text you enter. When you allow the text to wrap, words will jump to the next line when the text fills the width of the cell, thereby increasing the height of the entire row automatically.

Resizing Tables and Cells

In this activity, you will change the size of the tables and selected cells for the two tables you just created.

1. Display *GolfClubs.htm* in Page view in the Normal tab.

2. Right-click any cell in the table.

A shortcut menu appears.

3. Click **Table Properties**.

The Table Properties dialog box opens. By default, the *In percent* option button is active.

4. Select the number in the Specify width box and type 50.

5. Click OK.

The Table Properties dialog box closes. The table in *GolfClubs.htm* now occupies only 50% of the available width.

6. Right-click the table and click Table Properties on the shortcut menu.

7. Select the text in the Specify width box, type 100, and click OK.

The table is restored to full width.

8. Right-click the Description cell.

9. Click Cell Properties on the shortcut menu.

The Cell Properties dialog box appears.

10. Type 60 in the Specify width box, then click OK.

The column containing the cell expands to fill 60% of the table width.

11. Move the pointer to the border between the first and second columns.

The pointer changes shape to a double-headed arrow, pointing left and right.

12. Double-click.

The first column expands to the minimum width needed to contain the text. This is an example of how the AutoFit feature works.

13. Drag the border between the first and second columns to the right so the text *Williams Woods* in the second row fits on one line.

14. Position the pointer on the horizontal border between the first and second row.

The pointer becomes a double-headed arrow pointing up and down.

15. Drag the border down so that the height of the first row doubles.

16. Click Save 💾.

Selecting Cells

In the previous activity, you changed the width and height of rows or columns of cells using the Cell Properties dialog box. As long as your insertion point was in one of the cells in the column or row, the command worked. Many commands that act on less than an entire row or column require that you first select the cells to be changed.

As when selecting text, there are a number of techniques you can use to select more than one cell. Some use the keyboard, others the mouse, and still others use a combination of both. Table 5.2 describes these techniques.

| TABLE 5.2 | SELECTING CELLS |

Area	Menu Option	Keyboard/Mouse Shortcut
One cell	Click the table cell; point to Select and click Cell on the Table menu.	Press [Alt] and click cell.
Adjacent cells	None	Drag pointer over cells.
Nonadjacent cells	None	Press [Ctrl] + [Alt] and click individual cells.
Entire row	Click any cell in row; point to Select and click Row on the Table menu.	Move pointer to left border and click when it changes to a right arrow.
Adjacent rows	None	Move pointer to left border, click when it changes to a right arrow, then drag over the rows. *Or:* Select one row as just described, press [⇧ Shift], and select the last row you need.
Nonadjacent rows	None	Move pointer to left border then click when it changes to a right arrow. Press [Ctrl] and select other individual rows.
Entire column	Click any cell in column; point to Select and click Column on the Table menu.	Move pointer to top border and click when it changes to a down arrow.
Adjacent columns	None	Select first column by moving pointer to top border and clicking when it changes to a down arrow, then drag over additional columns. *Or:* Select one column as just described, press [⇧ Shift] and select the last column you need.
Nonadjacent columns	None	Select first column by moving pointer to top border and clicking when it changes to a down arrow. Press [Ctrl] and select other individual columns as just described.
Entire table	Click anywhere in table; point to Select and click Table on the Table menu.	Move the pointer to the left of the table border and double-click.

Changing Table and Cell Properties

Changing table properties:

1. Right-click any cell, then click Table Properties.

2. Adjust the Layout, Width, Borders, or Background.

3. Click OK.

Changing cell properties:

1. Select the cells.

2. Right-click the highlighted area, then click Cell Properties.

3. Adjust the Layout, Width, Borders, or Background.

4. Click OK.

Changing Table and Cell Properties

In this activity, you will change the properties of the tables and selected cells for the two tables you just created.

1. Display *GolfClubs.htm* in Page view in the Normal tab.

2. Point to the left border of the first row of the table.

The pointer takes the shape of a right arrow.

3. Click the border.

The entire row is selected.

4. Right-click any of the selected cells, then click Cell Properties on the shortcut menu.

The Cell Properties dialog box opens.

5. Click the Horizontal alignment drop-down arrow, click Center, and click OK.

The column headings are centered within their cells.

6. Click to the left of $149.99 then drag to select that cell and the cell below it containing $99.99.

7. Right-click the highlighted area, then click Cell Properties.

8. Click the Horizontal alignment drop-down arrow, click Right, and click OK.

9. Click Save 🖫.

10. Display *Skates.htm* in Page view in the Normal tab.

11. Click within the first row of the table, point to Select on the Table menu, and click Row.

12. Right-click the selected row and click Cell Properties on the shortcut menu.

13. Click the Horizontal alignment drop-down arrow, click Center, and click OK.

The headings in the table are centered.

14. Click outside the table to deselect the heading cells.

15. Press Ctrl + Alt then click each of the three Price cells containing numbers.

16. Right-click the selected cells, then click Cell Properties on the shortcut menu.

17. Click the Horizontal alignment drop-down arrow, click Right, and click OK.

The prices in the table appear right-aligned.

18. Click outside the table to deselect the cells then right-click in an empty area of one of the table cells.

19. Click Table Properties on the shortcut menu.

The Table Properties dialog box appears.

20. Click the Size up counter arrow until the border size is 5.

21. Click the Color drop-down arrow, click the light blue color box under Theme Colors, then click OK.

Hover the pointer over the background color boxes and the red/green/blue color values will display.

The table appears with a thicker border and a blue background.

The table should now look similar to Figure 5.15.

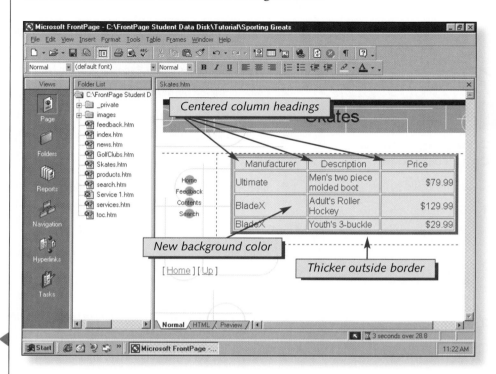

Figure 5.15
Table with Table and Cell
Properties changed

Adding and Deleting Table Rows and Columns

When you create a table, you must choose the number of rows and columns to be included. Once text is entered into the table, however, it is not uncommon to find it necessary to add or remove rows or columns. As with most table functions, there is more than one way to change the structure of a table.

The structure used in the two tables you have created is typical in that the columns represent categories of information and the rows describe individual items. Altering the number of columns represents a change in design and is done much less frequently than changing the number of rows. In the case of your tables, there is a far greater likelihood that you will have to add more individual items within new rows in a table. Expanding the number of rows needs to be done so often that most programs let you accomplish the task with one keystroke—by pressing the [Tab] key when within the last table cell.

Normally, the [Tab] key selects the next cell in the table. But when you are already in the last cell of the last row, pressing the [Tab] key adds a new row to the bottom of the table. This new row takes on the properties of the previous row; that is, the new row has the same number of cells that are in the same width as in the row above.

There are many ways to add rows or columns to a table. You can use the Table menu or right-click the table to use shortcut menus. You can also use keyboard shortcuts to accomplish many of the same tasks. Although there is a button on the standard toolbar (Insert Table) you may feel that there are not enough buttons to help you work with tables. Thankfully, Microsoft FrontPage 2000 has an entire toolbar devoted to tables.

Adding and Deleting Rows and Columns

In this activity, you will add a new row and a new column to a table. Then you will delete a row from a table. Before performing these tasks, you will display the Tables toolbar so you may accomplish many table functions with a single click.

1. Display *GolfClubs.htm* in Page view in the Normal tab.

2. Point to Toolbars and click Tables on the View menu.

The Tables toolbar appears. It has buttons for many common table modifications, as illustrated in Figure 5.16.

Hints & Tips

If you mistakenly delete a table element, click the Undo button on the Standard Buttons toolbar to reverse your action.

Figure 5.16
The Tables toolbar ◀

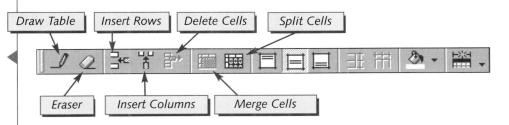

3. Drag the Tables toolbar by its title bar to a position just under and to the left side of the Formatting toolbar.

The Tables toolbar no longer floats independently in the window.

4. Click a cell in the Price column of the *Golf Clubs* table.

5. Click Insert Columns.

A new column appears to the left of the Price column.

6. Type Regular Price as the column header; type $250.00 in the second row; and type $120.00 in the third row of the new column.

7. Click the cell containing $99.99, then press [Tab].

A new row is added to the bottom of the table.

8. Type GolfPro, Putter, $62.50, and $44.99 from left to right in the cells of the new row, pressing [Tab] to advance to the next cell after each entry.

9. Select the first row containing the column headings.

10. Click Insert Rows.

A new row appears at the top of the table.

11. Click the first cell of the new row and type This Week's Specials.

12. Click Save.

13. Display *Skates.htm* in Page view in the Normal tab.

14. Select the third row.

15. Click Delete Cells.

The row is deleted and the last row moves up.

16. Click Save.

FrontPage BASICS

Adding and Deleting Rows and Columns

To add rows and columns:

1. Click an appropriate cell (a new column will be added to the left of the selected cell; a new row will be added above the selected cell).

2. Click Insert Columns or Insert Rows on the Tables toolbar.

To delete rows and columns:

1. Select the appropriate row(s) or column(s) to be deleted.

2. Click Delete Cells on the Tables toolbar.

Splitting and Merging Table Cells

Thus far your tables have had a uniform rectangular look with each cell in a row having the same height and the same width as other cells in its column. Tables built in FrontPage may vary from this structure. For example, sometimes you may want to have two cells within a single column. Or you might want to divide a cell horizontally.

You can *split* a cell vertically into several cells, all within the same column. You can also split a cell horizontally within a single row. Or you can select a group of two or more cells and combine them into a single cell, spanning more than one column and/or row.

There is a definite difference between inserting a new row or column into a table and splitting a cell. When you *insert* a new row into a table, for example, all rows are adjusted up or down to make room for the new row. However, when you *split* one or more cells in a table, the other cells in the row do not move.

Right-clicking a cell provides a shortcut menu. Clicking the Split Cells option displays the Split Cells dialog box. Here you choose the number of columns and/or rows into which the cell should be split. There is also a Split Cells button on the Tables toolbar and an option on the Tables menu.

Another way to split cells is to use the Draw Table feature. Clicking this toolbar button turns your pointer into a pencil. Dragging this pencil across a cell horizontally splits the cell into two rows. Dragging vertically splits the cell into two columns.

The opposite of splitting cells is *merging* or *spanning.* This feature combines individual cells into a single cell. Merging is especially useful when you are using tables to lay out text on a page.

In the Cell Properties dialog box, there are options for spanning rows and columns. The Rows spanned option lets you make a cell two rows high, for example. The Columns spanned option widens a cell.

You can select the cells to be combined and click the Merge Cells button ⊞ on the Tables toolbar; right-click and use the shortcut menu; or click Merge Cells on the Table menu. The Cell Properties dialog box, as described previously, lets you set the number of cells to combine without having to select the cells first. When you set the number of rows to span, cells that are in rows beneath the row the insertion pointer is in will be used to increase the height of the cell. Likewise, when you set the number of columns to span, cells to the right are used.

Note *If the cell already spans more than one column or row and you set the option to fewer columns and rows, the cell will decrease in size.*

Splitting Cells

1. Click the cell to be split.

2. Click the Split Cells button on the Tables toolbar.

3. Click the Split into columns or Split into rows option button.

4. Select the number of rows or columns into which the cell should be split.

Or:

1. Click the Draw Table button on the Tables toolbar.

2. Drag the pencil graphic vertically to split a cell into columns or horizontally to split into rows.

3. Click the Draw Table button again to end this action.

Figure 5.17
Cells split into two rows

Splitting and Merging Cells

In this activity, you will split and merge cells in your tables, using several different techniques.

1. Display *GolfClubs.htm* in Page view in the Normal tab.

2. Select the last three cells in the third row.

3. Click the Split Cells button ⊞ on the Tables toolbar.

The Split Cells dialog box appears. The Split into columns option button is selected by default; the default settings would split the cell into two columns.

4. Click the Split into rows option button.

5. Click OK.

The cells split in half horizontally, as shown in Figure 5.17.

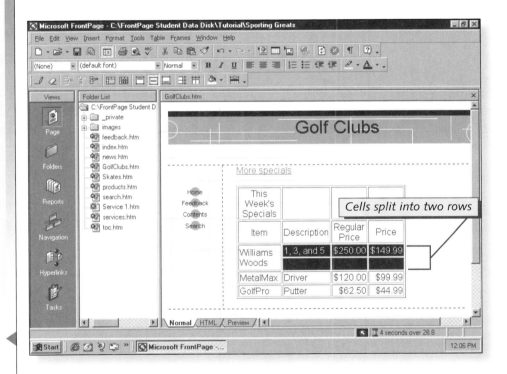

6. Type 1, 3, 4, 5; $335.00; and $240.99 into the new cells, from left to right.

7. Click Save 💾.

8. Display *Skates.htm* in Page view in the Normal tab.

9. Click Draw Table ✏️.

The pointer becomes a pencil graphic when positioned over the page.

Merging Cells

1. Select cells to be combined.

2. Click the Merge Cells button on the Tables toolbar.

Or:

1. Click the Eraser button on the Tables toolbar and drag across the cells to be merged.

2. Click the Eraser button again to end this action.

Did you know

In May 2000, the top five Web retailers included two bookstores, a ticket broker, a pet store, and a catalog shopping department store. Over two-thirds of those who shop the Internet several times a week are women.

---

10. Drag a line horizontally across the Price column heading cell.

A dotted line appears as you drag and the cell is split into two rows.

11. Drag a line vertically from the top of the new cell under the Price heading to the bottom of the table.

The three cells are split into two columns. The prices $79.99 and $29.99 move to the left of the new border.

12. Click **Draw Table** to make this function inactive.

13. In the two new cells under Price, type Was and Now Just, **from left to right.**

14. In the new cell under Now Just, type $72.49 **then type** $26.29 **below it in the bottom right cell.**

15. Click **Save**.

16. Display *GolfClubs.htm* in Page view in the Normal tab.

17. Click the **Eraser button**.

18. Click This Week's Specials and drag across the cells in the top row.

The borders turn red as you drag across them. When you release the mouse button, the cells are merged into one and the text is centered across the cell, as shown in Figure 5.18.

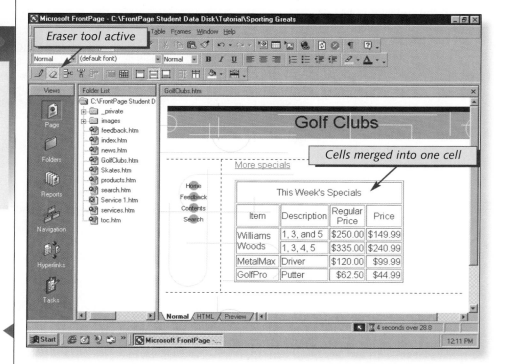

Figure 5.18
Merged cell

19. Click the **Eraser button** to deactivate it.

20. Click **Save**.

CREATING NUMBERED AND BULLETED LISTS

Tables are great for organizing and displaying information so that visitors to your Web site can easily locate the data they need. However, as the person responsible for the Web page content, you may wish to draw attention to certain items by formatting them in a numbered or bulleted list.

Using Numbered Lists

A ***numbered list*** takes paragraphs of text and assigns each one a sequential number, indention, and format according to the default style and theme in effect. The term *numbered* is not completely accurate since letters can also sequence the paragraphs, either in upper- or lowercase. You choose the style you want from the List Properties dialog box shown in Figure 5.19. You can access this dialog box by clicking Bullets and Numbering on the Format menu or by selecting the list, right-clicking, and clicking List Properties on the shortcut menu. The dialog box also has an option for starting the sequence with a number other than 1.

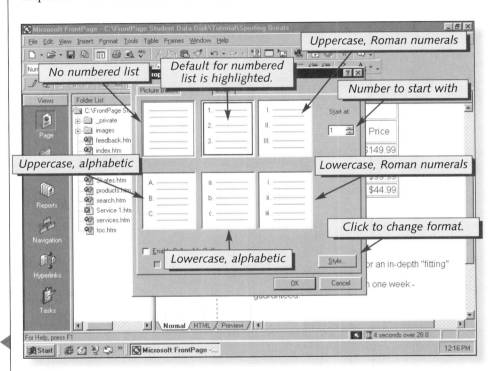

Figure 5.19
The List Properties dialog box

 You can quickly change the properties of the list by selecting the item, right-clicking, and clicking the List Item Properties option. Changing the style and/or number affects the current item and all following items in the list.

Entering the items for the list is simple—just click the Numbering button in the Formatting toolbar, and type. Whenever you complete an item, press ⏎. The next "number" appears, the text indents, and you can type the next item. When you have typed the last item, press ⏎ two times and you will be back to the regular text style.

Creating and Formatting a Numbered List

Creating a numbered list:

1. Click the Numbering button.

2. Type each item in the list, then press Enter.

3. Press Enter twice to deactivate the Numbering button or press the Numbering button to make it inactive.

Formatting a numbered list:

1. Select the list.

2. Right-click the list, then click List Properties.

3. Click a new number format, if desired, in the List Properties dialog box.

4. Click the Style button, then click the Format button.

5. Make desired formatting changes, then click OK to close each dialog box.

Figure 5.20
A numbered list

Creating and Formatting a Numbered List

In this activity, you will create a numbered list. Then you will change that list's properties.

1. Open *GolfClubs.htm* in Page view in the Normal tab.

2. Press Ctrl + End to put the insertion point below the table.

3. Press Enter to insert a blank line.

4. Type Ordering Custom Clubs is as Easy as 1-2-3, then press Enter.

5. Click the **Numbering button** on the Standard Buttons toolbar.

The number 1 followed by a period appears below the line you just typed. As long as the Numbering button looks active, pressing Enter will begin the next enumerated item in the list.

6. Type Purchase your clubs., then press Enter.

The number 2 appears.

7. Type Come to our practice range for an in-depth "fitting" from one of our pros., then press Enter.

8. Type Pick up your clubs in less than one week—guaranteed.

9. Press Enter two times.

Your list should look similar to Figure 5.20.

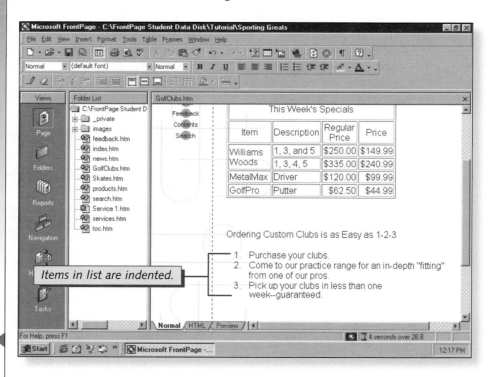

10. Right-click anywhere in the list, then click **List Properties**.

The List Properties dialog box appears.

11. Click the Style button [Style...].

The Modify Style dialog box appears.

12. Click the Format button, then click Font on the shortcut menu.

The Font dialog box appears.

13. Click Times New Roman in the Font list box; click 12pt in the Size list box.

14. Click the OK button to close the Font dialog box; click OK to close the Modify Style dialog box; then click OK to close the List Properties dialog box.

Your list now has new character formatting that you applied.

15. Click Save [save icon].

Using Multilevel Lists

Lists can be more complex than the single level list you just created. An outline is an example of a *multilevel* list. Each of the levels has its own sequencing format, and each subordinate level or *sublevel* is indented under its parent level. Creating a multilevel list in FrontPage is almost as easy as creating a simple, one-level list. There are only two basic differences:

1. You must make sure that each level begins at the proper indented location.

2. You can change the numbering style for each level.

The Enable Collapsible Outlines check box in the List Properties dialog box enables visitors to click on a level to display or hide sublevels. If you set the properties to have the list initially collapsed, visitors will have to click a level to make the sublevels appear.

You begin to create a multilevel list the same way that you created a single level list; that is, click the Numbering button and type each item in the list. As before, when you press [Enter] the next item begins with the next number. If you want this item to be a sublevel of the previous item, however, you first click the Increase Indent button [icon] two times. The first click indents the item without assigning a number; the second click assigns the number, starting with the first number of the style in effect.

To change the style, right-click the item, click List Item Properties, and choose a new style from the dialog box. When you press [Enter] you'll be ready to type the second item in the style and level of indention as the item immediately above it. If you need this item to be a sublevel of the sublevel, click the Increase Indent button [icon] two times and change the style, if necessary. If you want the new item to be at a higher level, click the Decrease Indent button [icon] two times and your style and level of indention will revert to the higher level already chosen.

Creating a Multilevel List

In this activity, you will create a multilevel list in the *Sporting Greats* Web.

1. Click the Navigation view icon [icon].

2. Right-click the *Service 1* page graphic, click Rename, and type Tennis Lessons as the page label.

3. Click the Page view icon [icon] then double-click *Service1.htm* in the Folder List.

Creating a Multilevel List

1. Click the Numbering button.

2. Type each item and press `Enter←`.

3. Click the Increase Indent button two times to enter a sublevel.

4. Click the Decrease Indent button two times to move up one level.

5. Press the Numbering button again to make it inactive.

Another Way

Within a single level list, you can deactivate the Numbering button by pressing `Enter←` twice after the last entry. In a multilevel list, press `Enter←` twice for each level to deactivate the Numbering button.

4. **Select the opening sentence then type** We can improve your game. Call for a free trial lesson.

5. **Select** Key Benefits, Benefit 1, Benefit 2, **and** Benefit 3, **then press** `Delete`.

6. **Click the** Numbering button .

The number 1 appears.

7. **Type** Group Lessons **and press** `Enter←`.

The number 2 appears in the list.

8. **Click** Increase Indent **two times.**

The next item is indented as a sublist under the first item and starts with the number 1.

9. **Type** Novice **and press** `Enter←`; **type** Intermediate **and press** `Enter←`.

Item 3 in the sublist appears.

10. **Click** Decrease Indent **two times.**

The next item is ready to be typed as item 2 at the top level.

11. **Type** Private Lessons **and press** `Enter←`.

12. **Click** Increase Indent **two times.**

The sublist appears again beginning with item 1.

13. **Type** Novice **and press** `Enter←`; **type** Intermediate **and press** `Enter←`; **then type** Advanced **and press** `Enter←`.

14. **Press the** Numbering button **to make it inactive.**

Your multilevel list should look like Figure 5.21.

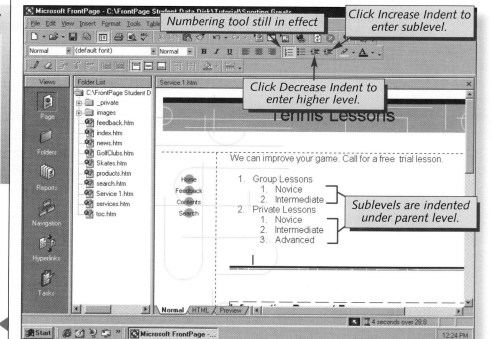

Figure 5.21
A multilevel list

15. Click Save.

Using Bulleted Paragraphs

FrontPage 2000 has a second way to create lists. This method does not use numbers or letters to highlight items; instead it uses graphical symbols called **bullets.** Usually round or square, bullets mark off a section of text, identifying each item as a key point, though not necessarily sequential as implied in a numbered list.

You use the Bullets button on the Formatting toolbar to create bulleted paragraphs. In creating a bulleted list, you can apply almost all of the techniques you learned regarding numbered lists. That is, every time you press Enter another bulleted item appears. You can press Increase Indent or Decrease Indent to set levels and sublevels. You can also set styles with the List or List Item Properties dialog box. With these dialog boxes you can choose the style of plain bullets to use such as a solid circle, an open circle, or a solid square.

If you use a theme, your bullets will have a more exciting appearance. Each theme has a bullet style that can be changed if you modify the theme. Even if you use a theme, you can choose plain bullets, if you wish.

Creating a Multilevel Bulleted List

1. Click the Bullets button.

2. Type each item and press Enter.

3. Click the Increase Indent button two times to enter a sublevel.

4. Click the Decrease Indent button two times to move up one level.

5. Press Enter twice for each level to make the Bullets feature inactive.

Creating a Multilevel Bulleted List

In this activity, you will add a multilevel bulleted list to a Web page in the *Sporting Greats* Web. First, you will enter the top level. Then you will insert sublevels into the list.

1. Display *Skates.htm* in Page view in the Normal tab.

2. Press Ctrl + End.

Your insertion point moves below the table.

3. Press Enter to add a new line.

4. Click the Bullets button.

The insertion point indents with a green and blue box. This bullet graphic is part of the theme for this Web.

5. Type Multi-purpose skates, press Enter; type Hockey skates, press Enter; and then type Speedskates.

6. Click at the end of the first bulleted item, press Enter, then click Increase Indent two times.

A bullet in the form of a blue circle marks the second bulleted level in this theme.

7. Type cross training/fitness, **press** ⏎; **then type** aggressive/street skates.

8. Click at the end of *Hockey Skates*, **press** ⏎, **then click Increase Indent** 📊 **two times.**

9. Type production models, **press** ⏎, **then type** component skates.

10. Click at the end of *Speedskates*, **press** ⏎, **then click Increase Indent** 📊 **two times.**

11. Type production 5-wheelers, **press** ⏎; **then type** component skates **and press** ⏎.

12. Click Increase Indent 📊 **two times.**

A bullet in the form of a green circle marks the third level.

13. Type racing frames, **press** ⏎; **type** boots, **press** ⏎; **type** bearings, **press** ⏎; **then type** wheels.

When you are done, your multilevel bulleted list will look like Figure 5.22.

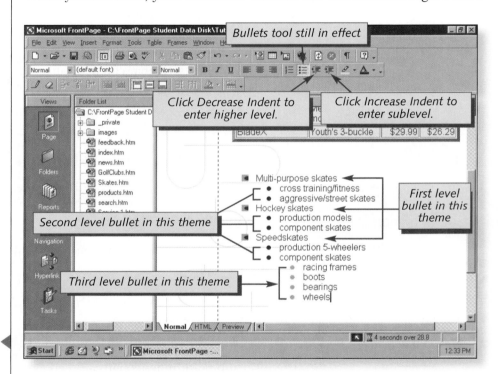

Figure 5.22
A multilevel bulleted list

14. Press ⏎ **six times (twice for each level) to make the Bullets feature inactive.**

15. Click Save 💾.

Web Pages with Frames

In this activity, you will learn how frames can be used to display multiple Web pages in the Web browser window.

1. Click Help ⍰.

The Help window opens.

2. Click the Contents tab.

3. Click the plus sign (+) to expand the Designing Web Pages book graphic.

4. Click the plus sign (+) to expand the Give Pages a Consistent Look book graphic.

5. Click the plus sign (+) to expand the Frames book graphic.

Two dozen Help pages are available on various topics relating to frames.

6. Click Understanding frames and frames pages.

7. Click the graphic in the right pane, then click the Maximize button ☐.

A window opens containing the Understanding frames and frames pages topic with an illustration of frames. On the left is a series of questions about frames. Clicking one of the questions displays the answer on the right side of the window. Figure 5.23 illustrates this format—typical of the way Help presents a complex feature.

Figure 5.23
Understanding frames and frames pages Help window

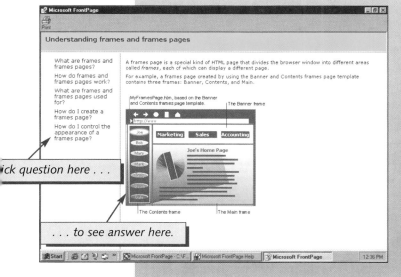

8. Click each of the questions on the left and read the answers on the right.

9. Click the Close button ☒ twice to close the Help window.

You return to the *Sporting Greats* **Web.**

10. Click Close Web on the File menu.

11. Click Yes when prompted to save the changes you made to each page.

12. Click Close ☒ to exit FrontPage.

Self CHECK

Test your knowledge by answering the following questions. See Appendix D to check your answers.

T F 1. Both Web templates and Web wizards use a series of dialog boxes to customize a new Web.

T F 2. Pressing ⌨Tab in the last cell of a table creates a new row.

T F 3. A table of contents page is a form of site map.

T F 4. Inserting a row is the same thing as splitting a cell horizontally.

T F 5. To change a page's URL, you must change the page's file name.

ON*the*WEB

FRAMES OR NO FRAMES

Frames are rectangular areas within a window that are each capable of displaying different information. Placed within separate frames, *frames pages* can display the content of two or more Web pages at the same time. These frames pages can operate independently, allowing the visitor to click on links changing the content in one frame only. Or one frame can control the display of content within another frame, much like a navigation bar in a shared border controls the page to be displayed by the browser.

FrontPage 2000 has several templates that include frames. Using frames gives the designer the convenience of banners and navigation tools but provides more flexibility than shared borders.

Framed Web pages present both advantages and disadvantages for both the Web designer and the Web site visitor. For the visitor, frames may give a Web a more consistent appearance since clicking a hyperlink changes one frame only and leaves the rest of the window alone. Visitors can also print or save one frame at a time rather than an entire page. On the downside, some Web browser versions have trouble saving a frames page as a favorite (called a *bookmark* in Netscape Navigator terminology). For the designer, each frames page must be created separately.

The use of frames is somewhat controversial—some designers love them, others hate them. To accommodate both groups, some Web sites offer two versions of their pages—one with frames and one without. Since some users are distracted by excessive graphics on a page and others have a problem with slow Internet connections, such options are welcome. For these users, many Web sites offer text-only or low-graphics versions of their pages. These accommodations help to increase the number of repeat "hits" to a Web site.

1. Click the Start button 📓Start **, point to Programs, and click your Web browser.**

Your start page launches in your Web browser and you should be connected to the Internet.

2. Type www.herald.com/ **in the Address box, then press** Enter↵ **.**

The home page of the Miami Herald Internet Edition opens. This Web site uses frames—the scroll bar on the right scrolls through the frames page, not the entire window.

3. Click the scroll arrow.

Only the frame scrolls.

4. Click Print on the File menu.

The Print dialog box opens, as in Figure 5.24. Near the bottom of the Print dialog box is a Print frames section. When you print pages that do not have frames, options in this section are dimmed.

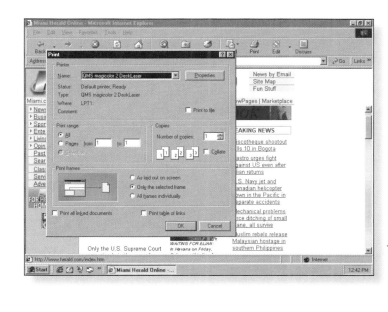

Figure 5.24
The Print dialog box with print frame options

5. Click **Cancel**.

6. Type www.boston.com/globe **in the Address box, then press** [Enter⏎].

The home page for Boston Globe Online appears. The site does not use frames.

7. Scroll down until you see the Alternative views section on the left.

8. Click the **Low-graphics version** link.

The screen changes to a less graphics-intensive version—a good alternative when using a slow modem.

9. Click **Print** on the File menu.

Note that the Print Frames section is dimmed.

10. Click **Cancel**.

11. Type www.sptimes.com/ **in the Address box, then press** [Enter⏎].

The home page for St. Petersburg Times Online appears. This site uses frames but has a text-only version for browsers that either do not support frames or may have slow connections.

12. Click the **Text-only version** hyperlink on the left side.

The browser now shows the text in the stories but does not display the graphic images.

13. Click the **Close button** ⊠ to close your Web browser.

Warning *You may proceed directly to the exercises for this lesson. If, however, you are finished with your computer session, follow the "shut down" procedures for your school or lab environment.*

SUMMARY

Companies that want to establish themselves on the Internet quickly can use one of the Web wizards in FrontPage 2000. In this lesson, you ran the Corporate Presence Web Wizard, chose options, and entered company data to create a multipage Web. You then ran tasks generated by the wizard to delete placeholder text, replace it with your content, and change the settings for the table of contents. After deleting some pages, you learned two additional methods for adding pages—the New button and the *Link to a new page when creating a hyperlink* button. When hyperlinks changed, you learned to find and fix broken hyperlinks.

Creating a Web quickly is only valuable if the information in the Web can be added quickly as well. You learned to change a page's file name to form a meaningful URL and to change the page title to display a meaningful name on the Web browser's title bar. You put data in an easy-to-read format by inserting tables. Changing the size, properties, and the number of rows and columns gave you flexibility to present the data in the best format. Finally, you typed and formatted multilevel numbered and bulleted lists.

Now that you have completed this lesson, you should be able to do the following:

■ Create a Web using a Web wizard. (page 168)

■ Run tasks to customize Web wizard pages. (page 172)

■ Delete placeholder text and replace it with meaningful information. (page 172)

■ Set table of contents properties. (page 176)

■ Add a blank page to a Web with the New button. (page 178)

■ Add a page to a Web while creating a hyperlink. (page 179)

■ Search for and repair broken hyperlinks. (page 180)

■ Change page titles and URLs. (page 183)

■ Add a table with the Insert Table tool. (page 185)

■ Add a table with the Insert Table dialog box. (page 187)

■ Resize tables and cells. (page 190)

■ Change table and cell properties. (page 193)

■ Insert and delete rows and columns. (page 195)

■ Split and merge cells. (page 197)

■ Type and format multilevel numbered and bulleted lists. (page 201)

■ Understand and view frames in a Web. (page 205)

Lesson Summary & Exercises

CONCEPTS REVIEW

1 MATCHING

Match each of the terms on the left with the definitions on the right.

TERMS

1. bullet
2. split
3. broken hyperlink
4. site map
5. table
6. frame
7. merge
8. multilevel
9. cell
10. page title

DEFINITIONS

a. A link in which the target has been deleted or moved

b. Combination of two or more cells

c. The intersection of a column and a row in a table

d. Sections of a browser window capable of displaying different information

e. A page layout feature consisting of columns and rows

f. Controls the name displayed on the browser's title bar

g. A page containing links to other pages in the Web

h. A graphical symbol that highlights items in a list

i. To break a cell into two or more rows and/or columns

j. A list containing both parent items and subordinate indented items

2 COMPLETION

Fill in the missing word or phrase for each of the following statements.

1. A(n) _____ is a subordinate part of a list that is indented beneath a parent level.

2. To change a page's URL you must change the _____.

3. A table of contents page is a type of _____.

4. When the Web wizard is finished, pages needing customization are set up as uncompleted _____.

5. The _____ button lets you split cells vertically or horizontally.

6. An outline is an example of a(n) _____ list.

7. To change the format of a list from the selected item down, right-click and then click _____.

8. To add a row to the bottom of the table, click in the last cell and press _____.

9. Clicking on the top border of a table selects an entire _____.

10. The _____ feature adjusts the width of a column to match the length of the longest item.

Lesson Summary & Exercises

3 SHORT ANSWER

Write a brief answer to each of the following questions.

1. Name two ways to add rows to a table.

2. Name two ways to add a table to a page.

3. List three methods for adding a blank page to a Web.

4. Describe the difference between the page title, the page label, and the file name.

5. What must you do to add a sublevel to a list?

6. What are the two types of site maps available in FrontPage?

7. Name three ways to merge two or more cells.

8. What should you do after clicking Finish in the last Web wizard dialog box?

9. What is the difference between inserting a row into a table and splitting a cell into two rows?

10. What must you do *before* filling out the first wizard dialog box to create a Web using a Web wizard?

4 IDENTIFICATION

Label each of the elements in Figure 5.25.

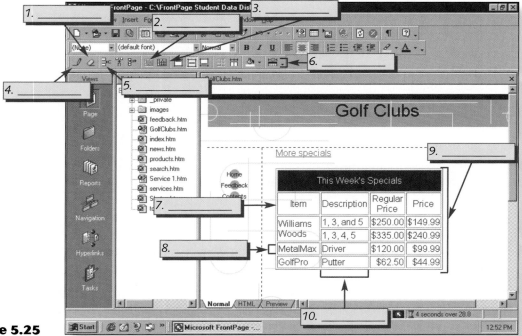

Figure 5.25

210 FrontPage 2000
LESSON 5

Lesson Summary & Exercises

SKILLS REVIEW

Complete each of the Skills Review problems in sequential order to review your skills to create a Web using a wizard; customize pages created by the wizard; set properties for a table of contents page; add and delete pages from the Web; change file names and update broken hyperlinks; change page titles and view URLs; create and modify tables; and type numbered and bulleted lists.

1 Creating a New Web Using a Wizard

1. Launch FrontPage 2000.
2. Click the **New Page drop-down arrow** 🗋, then click **Web**.
3. Click the **Corporate Presence Wizard**.
4. Type C:\FrontPage Student Data Disk\Skills Review\PetCare Clinic in the *Specify the location of the new web* text box, then click **OK**.
5. Click **Next** Next> in the Corporate Web Wizard opening dialog box.
6. Click to check **Products/Services** and **Table of Contents** in the main pages dialog box; click to uncheck all other boxes; then click **Next** Next>.
7. Click to check **Introduction** and **Contact Information** in the Home Page topics dialog box; uncheck the other boxes; then click **Next** Next>.
8. Click **Next** Next> through the next five dialog boxes until you reach the dialog box that asks *What is the full name of your company?*
9. Type PetCare Clinic as the full company name; PetCare as the one-word version; 87000 Easterday Ave. as the street address; then click **Next** Next>.
10. Click **Next** Next> in the telephone, fax, e-mail address dialog box.
11. Click the **Choose Web Theme button**, then click **Citrus Punch** as the theme.
12. Click to check the **Vivid colors**, **Active graphics**, and **Background picture check boxes**, if necessary.
13. Click **OK**, then click **Next** Next>.
14. Click **Finish** Finish in the last wizard dialog box.

2 Customizing Web Wizard Pages

1. Double-click the **Customize Home Page task**.
2. Click **Start Task**.
3. Select the comment, then type: We want you to trust us with the care of your pet. Our highly trained staff has a combined 87 years of experience. Call us and we'll set up a free introduction and tour of our facility.
4. Select the comment under Contact Information and press Delete.
5. Click the **Under Construction icon** and press Delete.
6. Click **Save** 🔲, then click **Yes** to mark the task as completed.
7. Click the **Tasks view icon** 📋, double-click **Customize Products Page**, then click **Start Task**.

Lesson Summary & Exercises

8. Select the comment then type We only stock the highest quality pet care products.

9. Select **Name of product 1** and type Cat Food to rename this hyperlink.

10. Select **Description of Product 1** and type Cans and bags for all sizes, ages, and needs.

11. Select **Name of product 2** and type Dog Food.

12. Select **Description of Product 2** and type Wet and dry for all types of dogs.

13. Click **Save** 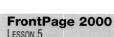, then click **Yes** to mark the task as completed.

14. Click the **Tasks view icon** 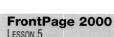, double-click the **Customize Services Page task**, then click **Start Task**.

15. Select the comment and type Leave your pet with us. We offer exercise areas, medical care, and TLC.

16. Select **Name of service 1** and type Boarding rates.

17. Select **Description of Service 1** and type We can board your pet for one day, a week, or longer at reasonable rates.

18. Click **Save** 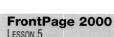, then click **Yes** to mark the task as completed.

3 Setting Properties for a Table of Contents Page

1. Click the **Tasks view icon** 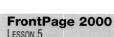, double-click **Customize TOC Page**, then click **Start Task**.

2. Right-click the Table of Contents area, then click **Table of Contents Properties**.

3. Click the **Heading font size drop-down arrow**, click **1**, then click **OK**.

4. Right-click the left, shared border and click **Navigation Bar Properties**.

5. Click the **Top level button**, then click **OK**.

6. Click **Save** 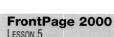, then click **Yes** to mark the task as completed.

7. Click the **Preview in Browser button** 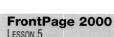, then click **Yes** when prompted to save changes.

8. Click **Close** 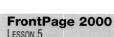 to close the browser window.

4 Adding Blank Pages and Removing Pages

1. Click *prod01.htm* in the Folder List, press 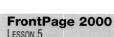, and click **Yes** in the Confirm Delete dialog box.

2. Click *prod02.htm* in the Folder List, press 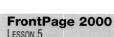, and click **Yes** in the Confirm Delete dialog box.

3. Click the **New Page button** 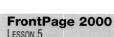, then click **Save** 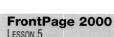.

4. Type *CatFood.htm* as the file name, then click **Save**.

5. Click the **Navigation view icon** 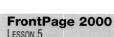.

6. Drag *CatFood.htm* from the Folder List to make it a child page under *Products*.

7. Click the page label to highlight it, then type Cat Food as the page label.

8. Click **Page view icon** 🗐.

9. Type next product in the text area to right of the navigation bar.

10. Select **Next product,** then click the **Hyperlink button** 🖼.

11. Click the **Create a page and link to the new page button** 🗋, then click **OK** in the New dialog box to choose the *Normal Page* template.

12. Click **Save** 🖫, type *DogFood.htm* as the file name, then click **Save** in the Save As dialog box.

13. Click the **Navigation view icon** 🗃, then drag *DogFood.htm* from the Folder List to the right of *Cat Food* to make it a child page of *Products*.

14. Click the **New Page 1 page label**, type Dog Food as the page label, then click the **Page view icon** 🗐.

5 Changing File Names and Updating Broken Hyperlinks

1. Click **Recalculate Hyperlinks** on the Tools menu, then click **Yes** in the Recalculate Hyperlinks dialog box.

2. Click the **Reports view icon** 🗐.

3. Double-click the Broken hyperlinks row.

4. Double-click the *prod01.htm* row, then click **Browse** [Browse...] in the Edit Hyperlink dialog box.

5. Double-click *CatFood.htm* in the Select Hyperlink dialog box, then click **Replace**.

6. Double-click the *prod02.htm* row then click **Browse** [Browse...] in the Edit Hyperlink dialog box.

7. Double-click *DogFood.htm* in the Select Hyperlink dialog box, then click **Replace**.

8. Click the **Folders view icon** 🗀, then click *serv01.htm* two times to highlight the file name.

9. Type Boarding.htm, press [Enter ←], and click **Yes** in the Rename dialog box.

6 Changing Page Titles and Viewing URLs

1. Display *CatFood.htm* in Page view in the Normal tab.

2. Right-click the page, then click **Page Properties**.

3. Change the page title to PetCare Cat Food, then click **OK**.

4. Click **Save** 🖫.

5. Display *DogFood.htm* in Page view in the Normal tab.

6. Right-click the page, then click **Page Properties**.

7. Change the page title to PetCare Dog Food, then click **OK**.

Lesson Summary & Exercises

8. Click **Save** 🖫.

9. Click the **Preview in Browser button** 📷; click **Yes** if prompted to save changes.

10. Read the new URL in the Address box, then click **Close** ☒ to close the browser window.

7 Creating Tables

1. Display *CatFood.htm* in Page view in the Normal tab.

2. Click at the end of the **Next product** hyperlink, then press `Enter←`.

3. Click the **Insert Table button** ▦, then drag down three rows and over four columns.

4. Type the following column headings and data:

Item	Description	Quantity	Price
Good Eats	For kittens	3 lb. bag	$3.99
Slim 'N Trim	For overweight cats	5 lb. bag	$7.95

5. Click **Save** 🖫.

6. Display *DogFood.htm* in Page view in the Normal tab.

7. Click an insertion point in the text area to the right of the navigation bar.

8. Point to **Insert** and click **Table** on the Table menu.

9. Click **4** for the number of rows and **4** for the number of columns, then click **OK**.

10. Type the following column headings and data:

Item	Description	Quantity	Price
Healthy Dog	For older dogs	10 lb. bag	$6.75
Pup-Ez	For puppies	8 lb. bag	$6.25
GoodDog	Treats	1 lb. box	$3.35

11. Click **Save** 🖫.

8 Resizing Tables and Cells

1. Right-click any cell in the *DogFood.htm* table, then click **Table Properties**.

2. Type **75** in the Specify width box, then click **OK**.

3. Right-click any cell in the Description column, then click **Cell Properties**.

4. Type **50** in the Specify width box, then click **OK**.

5. Double-click the border between the Item and Description columns.

6. Drag the border between the Quantity and Price columns until all quantities fit on a single line.

7. Drag the border below the column headings so that the row is doubled in height.

8. Click **Save** 🖫.

9 Changing Table and Cell Properties

1. Display *CatFood.htm* in Page view in the Normal tab.

2. Select the first row.

3. Right-click any selected cell, then click **Cell Properties**.

4. Click **Center** in the Horizontal alignment list box, then click **OK**.

5. Select the cells containing prices.

6. Right-click any selected cell, then click **Cell Properties**.

7. Click **Right** in the Horizontal alignment list box, then click **OK**.

8. Right-click any cell, then click **Table Properties**.

9. Change the Size of the borders to **3** and the Background Color to the **light green** in Theme Colors, then click **OK**.

10. Click **Save** 🖫.

10 Adding and Removing Rows and Columns

1. Display *DogFood.htm* in Page view in the Normal tab.

2. Click any cell in the Description column, then click **Insert Columns** ⬚.

3. In the new column, type Item # as the column heading and 120, 276, and 187 from top to bottom in the cells.

4. Select the second row, then click **Delete Cells** ⬚.

5. Click in the last cell, then press ⌊Tab⌋ to create a new row.

6. In the new row type Doggy Bits; 445; For overweight dogs; 10 lb. bag; $8.95.

7. Click **Save** 🖫.

8. Display *CatFood.htm* in Page view in the Normal tab.

9. Click any cell in the first row, then click **Insert Rows** ⬚.

10. Type Cat Food Specials in the first cell of the new row.

11. Click **Save** 🖫.

11 Splitting and Merging Cells

1. Display *DogFood.htm* in Page view in the Normal tab.

2. Select the last two cells in the third row.

3. Click **Split Cells** ⬚, click **Split into rows**, then click **OK**.

4. In the new cells type 5 lb. bag, $10.49.

5. Click **Save** 🖫.

6. Display *CatFood.htm* in Page view in the Normal tab.

7. Click **Draw Table** ⬚.

8. Split the lower three cells in the fourth column vertically, then click **Draw Table** ⬚ again.

Lesson Summary & Exercises

9. In the new cells, type Now as the heading, then type $3.09, $6.99 in the two cells below.

10. Click **Eraser** 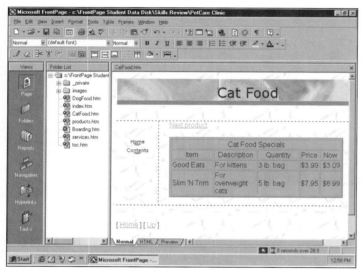, drag across the three borders between cells in the first row, then click **Eraser** again.

11. Click **Save** . Your table should look like Figure 5.26.

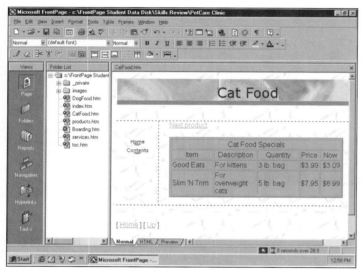

Figure 5.26

12 Creating a Numbered List

1. Display *Boarding.htm* in Page view in the Normal tab.

2. Select the comment and Key Benefits heading and bulleted items, then press Delete.

3. Type Boarding Rates and press Enter.

4. Select **Boarding Rates**, click the **Style drop-down arrow**, then click **Heading 1**.

5. Click to the right of *Boarding Rates* to deselect it, then click Enter to start a new line.

6. Click the **Numbering button** .

7. Type Cats; press Enter; type Small Dogs, press Enter; then type Large Dogs and press Enter two times.

8. Click an insertion point after Cats and press Enter.

9. Click **Increase Indent** two times, then type Daily - $15; press Enter; Weekly - $90; press Enter; and Monthly - $300.

10. Repeat steps 8 and 9 for Small Dogs, using the same sublevel data.

11. Repeat steps 8 and 9 for Large Dogs typing the amounts as Daily - $20; Weekly - $100; Monthly - $350.

12. Select the entire list, right-click the list, then click **Font** on the shortcut menu.

13. Click **Century Schoolbook** (or another serif font), click **14 pt** in the Size list box, and click **OK**.

14. Click to deselect the list, then click **Save** .

13 Creating a Multilevel Bulleted List

1. Click at the end of the last item in the *Boarding.htm* list and press Enter four times to start a new line.

2. Type We have:, select We have:, click the **Style drop-down arrow**, then click **Heading 1**.

3. Enter a new blank line after the heading, then click the **Bullets button** .

4. Type Great Facilities; press Enter; click **Increase Indent** two times; type Clean sleeping quarters; press Enter; type Multiple daily exercise periods; and press Enter.

5. Click **Decrease Indent** 🔳 two times; type Other services and press [Enter←].

6. Click **Increase Indent** 🔳 two times; type Grooming and press [Enter←]; type Obedience Training and press [Enter←].

7. Click **Increase Indent** 🔳 two times; type Beginning and press [Enter←]; type Intermediate and press [Enter←]; type Advanced and press [Enter←] two times.

8. Click **Save** 🔳.

9. Exit FrontPage, saving pages when prompted.

LESSON APPLICATIONS

1 Creating and Customizing a Web Using a Wizard

Create a new Web using a Web wizard and run the tasks necessary to customize the pages and give them meaningful content.

1. Start FrontPage and launch the Corporate Presence Web wizard typing the location for the Web as C:\FrontPage Student Data Disk\Lesson Applications\Office Supplies.

2. As you work through the wizard, include a products/services and a table of contents page; an Introduction and a Contact Information section on the home page; and 2 products and 0 services pages. Use defaults for the rest of the dialog boxes; however, type Office Supplies as the full company name, type Supplies as the one-word version of the name, and type 6010 Wilson St. as the address. Use the Blueprint theme for the Web.

3. Run the task to customize the *Home* page. Select the introductory comments on the *Home* page and type Welcome to the Office Supplies Web site. We hope you will find everything you need to stock your office. Delete the comment for the Contact Information section and the Under Construction logo. Save the page and mark the task as completed.

4. Run the task to customize the *Products* page. Select the comment and type Here are two of our departments featuring specials this week. Select the first hyperlink and type Binders; select the description and type We have binders in every color and size. Select the second hyperlink and type Paper. Select the description and type Whether you want reams or boxes, we can fill your copier or printer paper needs. Save the page and mark the task as completed.

2 Fixing the Table of Contents, Adding Pages, and Updating Hyperlinks

Change the properties of the table of contents and delete pages. Add a blank page using the New dialog box and add another while creating a hyperlink. Rename page titles and page labels and fix broken hyperlinks.

1. Start the task in the *Office Supplies* Web to customize the *TOC* page. Delete the comment. Right-click the table of contents and change the heading size to 2 in the Table of Contents Properties dialog box. Right-click the navigation bar and change the Navigation Bar Properties to Child pages under home. Save the page and mark the task as completed.

Lesson Summary & Exercises

2. Delete *prod01.htm* and *prod02.htm*. Add a new page based on the *Normal* template. Save it as *Binders.htm* and add it to the navigation structure as a child page under *Products*. Change the page label—type the new label as Binders. Change the page title—type the new title as Office Supplies Binders.

3. Insert a hyperlink named <u>Paper specials</u> and link it to a new page based on the *Normal* template. Save the new page as *Paper.htm* and add it to the navigation structure under *Products*. Type the page label as Paper and type the page title as Office Supplies Paper. Repair the broken hyperlinks so they point to your new pages.

3 Adding Tables and Lists

Create a table using the Insert Table button; create a second table using the Insert command on the Table menu. Type text, add and delete rows, split columns, merge cells, and format borders. Create a numbered and bulleted list and change its properties.

1. Create two tables in *Paper.htm* of your *Office Supplies* Web—one for copier paper and one for laser/inkjet paper. For the first table, use the Insert Table button to make a 3 x 3 table. Type the column headings as Manufacturer, Quantity, and Cost. Make up text to fill the second and third rows. Create a second table below the first table using the Insert command on the Table menu. This table should have three rows and four columns. Type column headings as Manufacturer, Quantity, Type, and Cost. Make up text for the second and third rows, using Inkjet, Laser, or Both in the Type column.

2. Make changes to the tables, adding a row and deleting a row from each. Change the border size and color. Split the last column of each table and type Quantity Discount as the new column heading. Type slightly lower costs in each new cell. Split one of the rows in each table to the right of the first column and fill the new cells with data regarding another product by the same manufacturer. Insert a row at the top of the first table, type Paper Specials in the first cell, and merge all cells in the row. Center the Paper Specials heading.

3. Create a numbered list in *Binders.htm*. Type five manufacturer names under the heading Most Popular Brands. Change the properties of the list to a font of your choosing. Under the numbered list, type a bulleted list with the heading Varieties of Binders. Type Colors and Widths at the first level in the list. As a sublevel to Colors, type several basic colors. As a third level in the Colors list, type a shade of each basic color. Under Widths include a sublevel of inches from 1/2" to 3". Save and close your Web.

PROJECTS

1 A Web for a Web Designer

You have decided to open a Web design consulting business. Although you don't intend to compete with large Web design businesses (at least for now), you plan to offer clients a fast Internet presence. Your Web service will be suitable for a business with immediate, basic needs or for a company looking to develop a more complex site at a later date. Your first step is to create a Web site describing the services you provide. Using the Corporate Presence Web wizard, create a Web on your FrontPage Student Data Disk in the *Projects* folder. Name the new Web *InstaWeb*. Include the pages, sections, and theme of your choice. You won't be offering any products—only services.

2 Make It Real

Customize *InstaWeb*, the site you created in Project 1. Run the tasks created by the wizard and set the properties for the Table of Contents page. Delete any services pages and create new ones, linking from one service to another. Add new pages to the navigation structure and assign meaningful page titles, page labels, and URLs. Repair broken hyperlinks.

3 Table It

Add tables to each of the services pages in *InstaWeb*, listing the types of services you intend to provide and the cost for each (you may wish to give an hourly rate). Add, delete, and resize rows and columns until you are satisfied with the results. Change the color, alignment, border width, and other properties of the table and cells. Split and merge cells as necessary.

4 Bite the Bullets

Add numbered and bulleted lists to the services pages in the *InstaWeb* site. Use a numbered list to describe the procedure you will use to create a Web—consultation, design, estimating, development, revisions, publishing. Use a multilevel bulleted list to promote your skills, to mention your concern for customer satisfaction, and point out the advantage of using your services over those of other companies.

Project in Progress

5 Keeping Up with the Joneses

Your competitor, Main Street Collectibles, has launched a Web site. You realize that you will lose a lot of business if you don't get online as well. While you consider what your ultimate Web site should contain, you decide to get online quickly using a Web wizard. You choose to build a site based on the Corporate Presence Web wizard. After fixing all the page content, add the elements you became familiar with and use the techniques you learned in this lesson. Your Web should include the following: meaningful content to replace all placeholder text; a table of contents; meaningful page titles and URLs; tables with split and merged cells; and multilevel numbered and bulleted lists.

Adding Multimedia Elements to a Web

CONTENTS

OBJECTIVES

After you complete this lesson, you will be able to do the following:

- Identify the sources of graphic images.
- Add a graphic image to a Web page from the Clip Art Gallery.
- Use the Clip Art Gallery Help to learn how to import images from Clips Online.
- Add graphic images from a file.
- Import graphic images from a file.
- Resize, rotate, flip, and bevel an image.
- Type text over an image in a text box.
- Add hotspots to an image creating an image map.
- Insert graphical elements such as a horizontal line, a hover button, a hit counter, and a scrolling marquee.
- Use the Office Clipboard to paste text and graphics from a FrontPage Web into a Microsoft Word document.
- Add and import images from a Web site into your Web.

All the content, formatting, themes, and pages in the world won't get many visitors to explore your Web site. Text-based pages are lucky to get a momentary glance from the Web surfers of today. Without multimedia—that is, graphic images, sound, video, and animation—a Web site is thought to be boring. In this lesson, you will learn how to incorporate multimedia elements into your Web.

USING IMAGES WITHIN A WEB

Most Web pages include elements that communicate to the visitor beyond what is possible with the written word. **Multimedia**—graphics, text, sound, video, and animation—combine to excite, entertain, and educate viewers in ways that plain text cannot. **Graphic images** are the pictures that you've seen in some FrontPage templates or in some Web pages you may have explored on the Web. In this lesson you will learn how to add graphic images to your Web pages. Before this, however, it is useful to understand where these images come from.

Understanding the Source of Images

All images are created by being either drawn or photographed. A program such as Microsoft Paint has the kinds of tools that let you draw digital pictures directly on the computer. Professional graphic artists use much more sophisticated software to produce various graphic images. The traditional tools of the graphic artist once included paper or canvas. Today a picture created on a traditional medium such as paper can be converted to digital format using a **scanner**—a device similar to a photocopier. Instead of making a paper duplicate like a photocopier, a scanner makes an electronic file that can be read by a computer and displayed on the screen.

Similarly, photographic images come to the computer using different methods. **Digital cameras** take pictures without film. The pictures are recorded in some form of memory or storage device from which they can be downloaded into the computer. Photographs developed onto film can either be scanned into the computer or stored on compact disk and transferred into computer storage from there.

Clip art consists of drawings and photographs you can buy and use in your own document. (The term "clip art" came from the books of pictures from which layout artists cut and pasted images.) Microsoft Office supplies a wide variety of different types of clip art. Additional clip art is available on compact disk or over the Internet.

Graphics must be digitized and stored on a medium the computer can use. These files must contain information regarding each of the millions of pixels a graphic can contain. To keep the size of graphic images from becoming unmanageable, **file compression** techniques are common. Compression reduces the file size so the image requires less disk space for storage. Different image sources, compression technologies, and other factors have resulted in many different file formats. The two most common formats are JPEG and GIF. While FrontPage 2000 can read other formats, it will convert them to one of these two formats when including them in a Web page.

Using Clip Art Images

The Clip Art Gallery is a collection of pictures, sound, and motion clips grouped into about fifty categories. In addition to the hundreds of clips in the Gallery, you can add your own images in categories of your own. The Clip Art Gallery is not for FrontPage exclusively—most of the other Microsoft Office programs can use it as well.

Adding a Clip Art Image

1. Point to Picture and click Clip Art on the Insert menu.

2. Click a Category.

3. Scroll and click the image you want.

4. Click Insert Clip.

Adding a Clip Art Image

In this activity, you will add clip art to your *School Newsletter* Web.

1. **Launch FrontPage 2000 and open the *School Newsletter* Web located in the *Tutorial* folder of your FrontPage Student Data Disk.**

2. **Display *index.htm* in Page view in the Normal tab.**

3. **Click an insertion point, if necessary, just to the left of the "*W*" in *Welcome* in the first line of text.**

4. **Point to Picture and click Clip Art on the Insert menu.**

The Clip Art Gallery window opens as shown in Figure 6.1. As you can see, there are tabs for pictures, sounds, and motion clips. You can search for images by typing keywords into the text box near the top of the window. More often, you will click and scroll through images using the categories links that dominate the window.

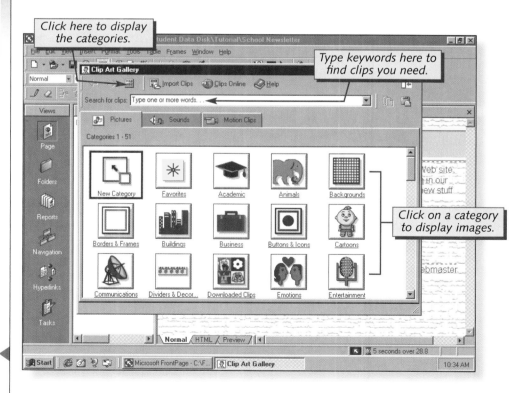

Figure 6.1
The Clip Art Gallery window

5. Click the **Academic** link.

Clips 1–60 in the Academic category load into the window.

6. **Scroll down to the bottom of the window.**

7. **Click the Keep Looking link.**

Another 60 images are displayed in the window.

8. **Scroll down until you see the portion of the window shown in Figure 6.2.**

9. **Click the school building.**

Usually not all clip art files are copied from the compact disks when FrontPage 2000 is installed. If you try to use one of the clip art files that wasn't loaded you will receive a message window with three options. If you have the CD, insert it and click Retry; if the file is stored on another drive or folder, click Look Elsewhere; if you don't have access to the file, click Cancel and find a different clip art image.

A list of options appears as shown in Figure 6.2. *Insert clip*, the first option, places the image in the document; *Preview clip*, the second option, enlarges the image so you can preview it; *Add clip to Favorites or other category*, the third option, lets you add the image to another category or to the Favorites list. *Find similar clips*, the last option, lets you search for other clips similar to the current clip.

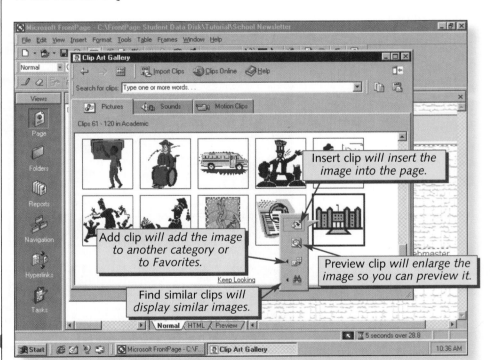

Figure 6.2
Clip art options

When you see an "X" inside a box (Internet Explorer) or a graphics icon with a dog-eared corner (Netscape Navigator) in your browser window, it means a graphic image file could not be found. This can happen when the file is not embedded in the page or has been deleted or moved from the *Web* folder.

Consider using the Preview clip option to enlarge an image before inserting it into your Web page. There may be details in the picture you don't notice while it is in its thumbnail view.

10. Click **Insert Clip** 🖼️.

The Clip Art Gallery closes and the image is placed in the page.

11. Press Enter←.

The text begins below the inserted image. Your Web page should now look like Figure 6.3.

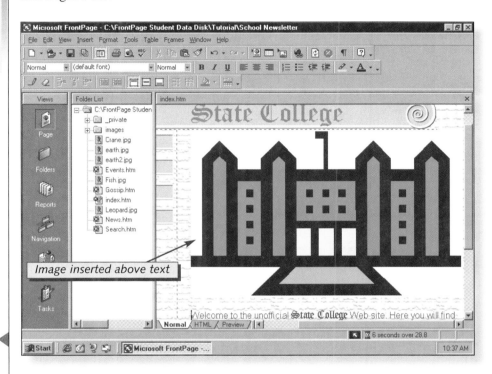

Figure 6.3
Clip art inserted into Web page

12. Click **Save** 💾.

The Save Embedded Files dialog box appears asking if you want to save the inserted (embedded) graphics image.

13. Click **OK**.

Importing Clip Art Using Clips Online

In this activity, you will use FrontPage 2000's Clip Art Gallery Help to learn how you can import additional graphic images from Clips Online—a special Web site for Clip Art Gallery users.

1. **Point to Picture and click Clip Art on the Insert menu.**

The Clip Art Gallery window opens.

2. **Click Help.**

The Microsoft Clip Gallery 5.0 Help window appears.

3. **Click the Maximize button** ☐.

4. **Click the plus sign (+) to expand the Importing clips book graphic.**

5. **Click Importing clips using Clips Online.**

Figure 6.4
The Importing clips using Clips Online Help page

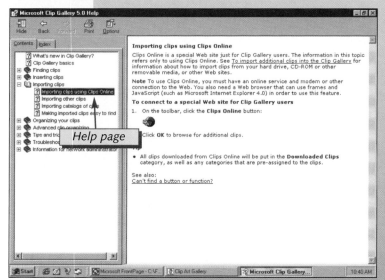

The Help page opens as shown in Figure 6.4.

6. **Read the Help window about using Clips Online.**

7. **Click Close ⊠ on the Help page window.**

8. **Click Close ⊠ on the Clip Art Gallery window.**

Adding Graphic Images from a File

Graphic images don't have to come in clip art packages. Images may have been drawn or photographed and scanned into a file. If you know the name of the file and its location, you can insert it into your Web page quite easily.

HANDS On

Adding an Image from a File

In this activity, you will replace an image on a Web page with an image stored on disk within your *School Newsletter* Web.

1. **Display *Events.htm* in Page view in the Normal tab.**

2. **Click the photograph of the earth and press ⌈Delete⌋.**

The image is removed from the page.

Adding an Image from a File

1. Point to Picture on the Insert menu, then click From File.

2. Click the Select a file on your computer button.

3. Navigate to the drive and folder containing the image to be imported.

4. Double-click the image file.

3. Select the words **Earth Photo Caption** and press Delete.

4. Point to **Picture** on the Insert menu, then click **From File**.

The Picture dialog box opens.

5. Click the **Select a file on your computer button** 📷.

The Select File dialog box appears.

6. Click the **Look in drop-down arrow** and click the drive in which your FrontPage Student Data Disk is located.

7. Double-click the *FrontPage Student Data Disk* folder then double-click the *Tutorial* folder.

8. Double-click *Cycling*.

The graphic image is inserted into the cell as in Figure 6.5.

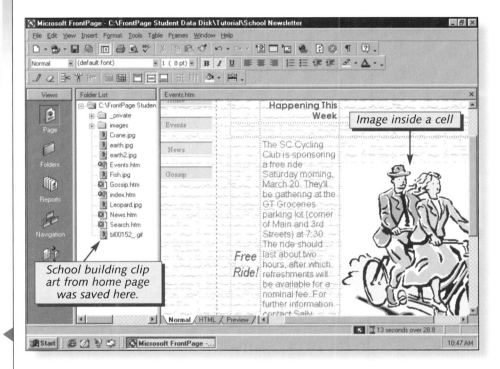

Figure 6.5
Graphic image added into page

9. Click Save 💾.

The Save Embedded Files dialog box appears. The dialog box asks if you want to save *Cycling.gif*.

10. Click **OK**.

Although FrontPage can use a wide variety of graphics file formats, it converts them to JPEG or GIF format, as necessary.

Importing Images from a File

1. Select the folder into which the imported files should be stored.

2. Click Import on the File menu.

3. Click Add File.

4. Locate and click a file to import.

5. Press Ctrl and click each additional file to import.

6. Click Open, then click OK.

Importing Graphic Images

Rather than searching for and adding individual pictures to your Web one at a time, you can move graphic files into your Web as a group. Then you can add them to your pages quickly and easily. The process of selecting and copying graphic files into your Web folder before they are inserted onto a page is called *importing graphics*.

There are a number of ways to import graphics into a folder in your Web. You can select and copy files using Windows Explorer and paste them into your Web folder. If the files are on your desktop, you can drag them into the Folder List or Contents pane of the Folders view. Or, you can use the Import option on the File menu, the method you will be using in the following activity.

Importing Images from a File

In this activity, you will import images from a file and then insert them into a page in your *School Newsletter* Web.

1. **Display *Gossip.htm* in Page view in the Normal tab.**

2. **Click the *images* folder in the Folder List.**

3. **Click Import on the File menu.**

The Import dialog box opens, as shown in Figure 6.6. From this dialog box you can select files, folders, or Web sites from which the files can be imported. The window displays the location and names of the files to be imported and the URL of files as they will be stored in the Web.

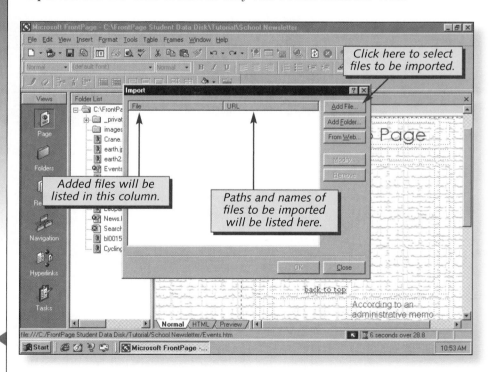

Figure 6.6 ◀
The Import dialog box

4. Click **Add File**.

The Add File to Import List appears.

5. Click the **Look in drop-down arrow,** then click the drive containing your FrontPage Student Data Disk.

6. Double-click the *FrontPage Student Data Disk* folder, then double-click the *Tutorial* folder.

7. Click *bs00975_.wmf*, press ⌷Ctrl⌷, then click *Pe00069_.wmf.*

The two files are selected.

8. Click **Open**.

The Import dialog box shows the two files with relative URLs indicating they will be stored in the *images* folder.

9. Click **OK**.

10. Click the **plus sign (+)** to expand the *images* folder.

The files have been copied into the *images* folder, as you can see in the Folder List.

11. Drag *pe00069_.wmf* from the Folder List to the cell to the right of the first article.

The graphic is immediately added to the page.

12. Scroll down until you see the empty cell to the left of the next article.

13. Drag *bs00975_.wmf* from the Folder List into the empty cell.

The second graphic appears in the page. Note how the cell enlarges to contain this image.

14. Scroll to the right and up until you can see the first graphic.

Figure 6.7
Web page with imported images added

Both imported graphics have been inserted into the page, as shown in Figure 6.7.

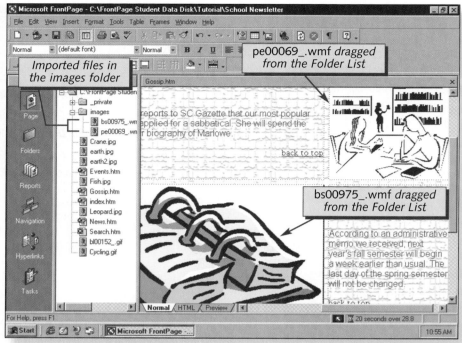

15. Click Save 📁.

UNDERSTANDING IMAGE PROPERTIES

The images in your Web are inserted in a particular size and orientation and have other characteristics. As with other objects in FrontPage 2000, you have many options as to how these images should appear. To make your choices easier to select, FrontPage has a toolbar for single click access to picture options—the Pictures toolbar. Table 6.1 describes the functions of the buttons on the Pictures toolbar.

Image Editing

Table 6.1 shows the variety of ways you can edit an image once it is inserted into your Web page. When you place an image on your page, its size is predetermined. You can change the dimensions of the image by either typing a specific length and width in the Picture Properties dialog box or by dragging its handles directly while in Page view. **Handles** are small black boxes that are located on the sides and corners of a resizable object. Handles appear when you click to select the object. Dragging a side handle (actually a *middle* black box on the top or bottom of an image) causes the image to be widened, narrowed, lengthened, or shortened. Such changes may result in the distortion of the image; for example, lengthening a picture of a face makes the face look long and narrow.

TABLE 6.1	THE PICTURES TOOLBAR	
BUTTON	NAME	FUNCTION
	Insert Picture From File	Enables you to locate and select a graphic image located on a storage device.
	Text	Creates a text box on top of a graphic image.
	Auto Thumbnail	Creates a smaller version of a graphic image to speed up downloading. Clicking on the thumbnail displays the full-size version.
	Position Absolutely	Lets you place the graphic anywhere in the page. Subsequent changes to the page will not affect the graphic's location.
	Bring Forward	Puts the selected graphic on top of any other object that covers any part of it.
	Send Backward	Puts the selected graphic behind any other object it is covering.
	Rotate Left	Turns the graphic 90° counterclockwise.
	Rotate Right	Turns the graphic 90° clockwise.
	Flip Horizontal	Makes a mirror image of the graphic.
	Flip Vertical	Turns the graphic upside down.
	More Contrast	Sharpens the graphic.
	Less Contrast	Makes the graphic softer.
	More Brightness	Makes the graphic lighter.
	Less Brightness	Darkens the graphic.
	Crop	Lets you remove parts of the graphic or change its proportions.
	Set Transparent Color	Lets you choose one color through which the background will appear.
	Black and White	Converts a color picture to black and white.
	Wash Out	Reduces the contrast and increases the brightness of a picture. Useful for turning an image into a background picture.
	Bevel	Adds a raised, three-dimensional border to a picture. Useful for using an image as a button.
	Resample	After an image has been reduced in size, this command reduces the file size as well.
	Select	Lets you click on an image to create handles around it. By default this tool is active when you select an image.
	Rectangular Hotspot	Lets you draw an invisible rectangle within an image that will serve as a hyperlink.
	Circular Hotspot	Lets you draw an invisible circle within an image that will serve as a hyperlink.
	Polygonal Hotspot	Lets you draw an invisible polygon within an image that will serve as a hyperlink.
	Highlight Hotspots	Makes it easier to view the hotspots in an image.
	Restore	Removes all editing changes you made since the image was last saved or added to the page.

When you drag corner handles instead of side handles, the ***aspect ratio*** is maintained since the length and width are changed proportionally. For example, if the width of the image is half of its length, cutting the size of the width by 40% results in an automatic 40% reduction in its length. Maintaining the aspect ratio allows you to resize an image without distorting it. The Picture Properties dialog box has a check box that keeps the aspect ratio intact.

 *You can remove uninteresting areas of a picture or change the proportions of a picture by using the Crop button in the Pictures toolbar (see Table 6.1). To do this, click the picture in Page view then click the Crop button on the Pictures toolbar. When the crop box appears on the picture, click and drag the handles on the box to define the area of the picture you want to keep.*

Resizing an Image

1. Select the image.

2. Drag the side handles to change one dimension of the image.

3. Drag the corner handles to maintain the aspect ratio.

Resizing an Image

In this activity you will find and place an image on a page in your *School Newsletter* Web. Then you will change the size of that image.

1. Display *News.htm* in Page view in the Normal tab.

2. Scroll down, click to the right of the side heading *Election Results*, and press Enter⏎.

3. Point to Picture and click Clip Art on the Insert menu.

The Clip Art Gallery window opens.

4. Type vote in the *Search for clips* text box, then press Enter⏎.

Several images appear.

5. Click the ballot image (the pencil writing an X), then click Insert clip .

The image is centered under the Election Results heading.

6. Point to Toolbars on the View menu, then click to check Pictures if the toolbar is not already active.

The dimmed Pictures toolbar appears at the bottom of the page.

7. Click the ballot image.

Handles appear around the picture and the Pictures toolbar becomes active. The selected image is ready for resizing or editing as shown in Figure 6.8.

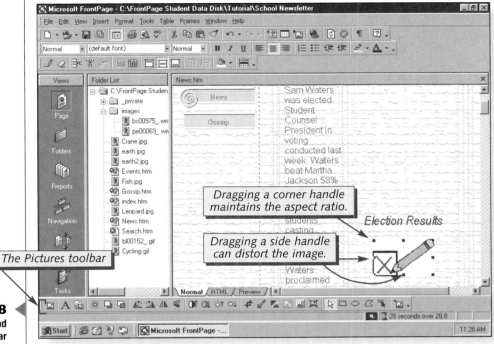

Figure 6.8
Selected picture and
Pictures toolbar

The Pictures toolbar

8. **Move the pointer to the middle handle on the right side of the image.**

The pointer changes to a double-headed arrow ⟷, indicating that dragging the border to the left or right is now possible.

9. **Drag the handle to the left, cutting the image width by half.**

The width of the image decreases while the height stays the same. Since the aspect ratio has been changed, the image is distorted.

10. **Move the pointer to the handle on the upper right corner of the image.**

The pointer changes to a double-headed arrow pointing diagonally ⟋, indicating that the aspect ratio will be maintained when you resize the image.

11. **Drag the handle diagonally to the right to double the size of the image.**

The height and width of the picture change simultaneously, keeping the aspect ratio the same.

12. **Click Save 🖫, then click OK in the Save Embedded Files dialog box.**

Rotating, Flipping, and Beveling an Image

Two pairs of toolbar buttons let you rotate or flip an image in order to position it differently on the page. When you **rotate** an image, you are turning it to the right or left 90° each time you click the button. Figure 6.9 shows the effect of rotating an image to the left or to the right.

Figure 6.9
(a) Original image;
(b) Image rotated to left;
(c) Image rotated to the right

a   b   c

If you want to turn the image upside down or create a mirror image of it, you can *flip* it using the Flip Vertical or Flip Horizontal buttons. When you flip an image vertically, the graphic is turned on the image's invisible vertical axis (upside down). When you flip an image horizontally, the graphic is turned on the image's invisible horizontal axis (mirror image). Figure 6.10 illustrates the effect of flipping an image.

a   b   c

Another effect you can easily add to a graphic is to draw a border that gives the image a raised, three-dimensional (3-D) look. The Bevel button applies this effect to any picture and is often used for an image that you want to appear as a button. Since the beveled border uses the existing picture, you should use an image that has color all around the edges. If you try to bevel a picture that is white on the edges, you may not notice the 3-D effect at all.

Rotating, Flipping, and Beveling

In this activity you will rotate and flip an image on a page of your *School Newsletter* Web. Then you will let the background picture show through the white areas of the image. Finally, you will bevel an existing image.

1. Display *News.htm* in Page view in the Normal tab.

2. Click the ballot graphic image.

Handles appear around the image indicating that it is selected.

3. Click the **Rotate Left button**.

The image turns 90° counterclockwise.

4. Click the **Rotate Right button** two times.

The image turns 180° to the right.

5. Click the **Flip Horizontal button**.

You get a mirror image of the picture.

6. Click the **Flip Vertical button**.

The image turns upside down. Other than the pencil and the check box, however, white makes up the majority of the space in the square graphic box, obscuring the background picture. You can choose one color in a GIF to be transparent.

7. Click the **Set Transparent Color button** and move the pointer over the image.

The pointer appears in the shape of a wand.

Rotating, Flipping, and Beveling

1. Select the image.

2. Click Rotate Left or Rotate Right to turn the image 90°.

3. Click Flip Horizontal or Flip Vertical to turn the image on an axis.

4. Click Bevel to give a raised, 3-D effect.

8. Click a white area in the image.

The area you clicked and the other white areas in the picture become transparent allowing the background picture to show through the image.

9. Scroll down and click the photograph of the leopard.

10. Click the Bevel button 🖼️.

The edges of the photograph now have a raised, 3-D effect. The image should look like Figure 6.11.

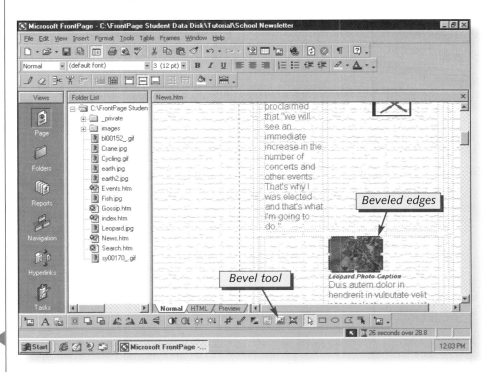

Figure 6.11
Beveled image

11. Select the caption and the placeholder text below the leopard picture and type Referendum result, "Keep the leopard as our mascot."

12. Delete the images and all the placeholder text in the cells below the text you just typed and above the bottom shared border.

13. Click Save 🖫, then click OK in the Save Embedded Files dialog box.

Typing Text Over an Image

A typical place for text to appear on the page is underneath a picture in the form of a caption or beside a picture as in the *News, Gossip,* and *Events* pages in your *School Newsletter* Web. Occasionally you may find it more effective to place text right on top of the image. The Text button 🅰 on the Pictures toolbar superimposes a text box on a selected graphic. Text you type then goes directly into the text box which can be resized by its handles. You can also use the regular text formatting commands to change the color, font, size, justification, and other attributes of the characters. Once you have finished typing the text, you can drag the box anywhere within the image.

Typing Text Over an Image

1. Select the image.

2. Click the Text button.

3. Adjust the text formatting as desired.

4. Type the text.

5. Drag the handles to resize the text box.

6. Drag the text box to position it within the image.

Typing Text Over an Image

In this activity you will resize an image on a page in your *School Newsletter* Web. Then you will type and format text within a text box on the image.

1. Display *Gossip.htm* in Page view in the Normal tab.

2. Click the calendar graphic and drag a corner handle to make the image small enough so the text in the column to the right fits within the workspace.

3. Click the **Text button** A.

A message window informs you that the image must be converted to GIF format to use this feature.

4. Click **OK**.

A text box (defined by drag handles) appears in the middle of the image.

5. Click the **Font drop-down arrow,** then click **Arial Black** or a similar sans serif headline font.

6. Click the **Font Size drop-down arrow,** then click **4 (14 pt)**.

7. Click the **Font Color drop-down arrow** A · on the Standard Buttons toolbar.

A list of color selections appears.

8. Click the **Red color box**.

9. Click in the text box, type School Starts, then press **Enter** .

10. Type Sept. 27th, **then click outside the text box.**

Depending upon the size of the box, the box expands to fit the text you entered.

11. Click on the text, then drag the box up to the middle of the image.

The text you typed floats on top of the image, as shown in Figure 6.12.

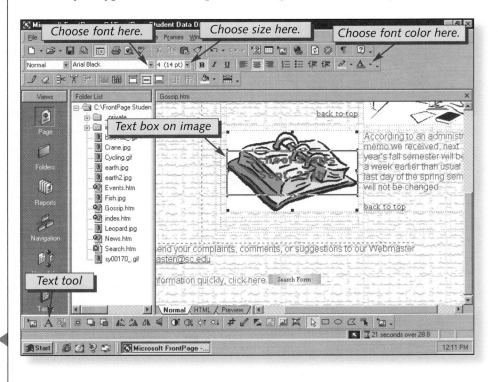

Figure 6.12 ◀
Text typed over a graphic image

12. Click Save 🖫 , then click OK in the Save Embedded Files dialog box.

Image Maps

An *image map* is a graphic with one or more invisible hyperlinks within it. Each of these hyperlinks is called a *hotspot*. The entire graphic may be one large hotspot, in which case clicking anywhere in the image takes you to the target of the hyperlink. Alternatively, the image can be divided into separate areas, each of which is covered by a different hotspot.

When you create an image map, you must give users some clue as to where to click. The clue can be part of the graphic, such as a door of a house to represent entering a section, page, or site. Sometimes the clue is implied, such as clicking a region in the map of a country or state. Of course, you can always type identifying text over an image to leave no doubt as to the target of the hyperlink.

FrontPage 2000 gives you three tools for creating hotspots—Rectangular, Circular, and Polygonal Hotspots. The Rectangular Hotspot 🔲 and Circular Hotspot ⬯ do as their names suggest—let you draw a square or circle to enclose the hyperlink. The Polygonal Hotspot 🔺 is somewhat more complex since it is used for areas with an irregular shape. Each click of this tool determines a point of the shape. Careful use of the Polygonal Hotspot tool lets you create a hotspot to conform to any part of the underlying image.

If you include many hotspots in an image, or if the image is complex or has vivid colors, you may have difficulty seeing the hotspots should you need to edit them. A fourth tool, Highlight Hotspots 🖾 , causes the image to disappear so all you see are the hotspots. Clicking Highlight Hotspots a second time restores the image.

HANDS ON

Adding Hotspots to an Image

In this activity, you will type some text on top of an image within your *School Newsletter* Web. You will then create hotspots to complete the image map.

1. Display *index.htm* in Page view in the Normal tab.

2. Click the school building graphic.

3. Click the Text button A .

A text box appears in the middle of the picture.

4. Click the Font Color drop-down arrow A ▾ , then click the white color box.

5. Click in the text box, type Events, click outside the box, and then drag the box to the left side of the picture.

6. Click the Text icon A , change the font color to white, click in the box, and type Gossip.

Adding Hotspots to an Image

1. Click the Rectangular, Circular, or Polygonal Hotspot button.

2. Draw the hotspot on the image.

3. For a Polygonal Hotspot, click each point of the shape then click the starting point or double-click when done.

4. Indicate the target of the hotspot in the Create Hyperlink dialog box then click OK.

7. **Click outside the box and then drag the box to the right side of the picture.**

8. **Click the Text button [A], change the font color to white, click in the box, and type News.**

A text box with the word *News* appears in the middle of the picture.

9. **Click the Rectangular Hotspot button □.**

The pointer becomes a pencil graphic.

10. **Click on the upper left corner of the building then drag to the bottom right corner of the left section of the building.**

The Create Hyperlink dialog box opens when you release the mouse button.

11. **Double-click *Events.htm*.**

12. **Repeat steps 9–11 to draw a rectangular hotspot on the right section of the building, using *Gossip.htm* as the target of the hyperlink.**

13. **Click the Polygonal Hotspot button [◁], then click points to enclose the middle section of the building, including the entrance at the bottom of the screen.**

The pointer becomes a pencil. When you click a starting point the pencil draws a straight line in any direction in which you point. You need to click a new point each time you turn in a new direction. Your three hotspots should be outlined as shown in Figure 6.13.

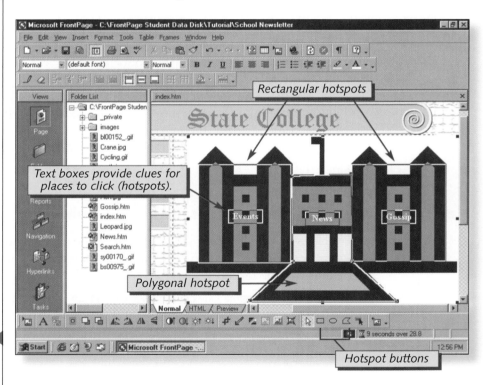

Figure 6.13
Hotspots with text boxes

14. **Click the last point of the polygonal hotspot which should be your starting point.**

The Create Hyperlink dialog box opens.

15. **Double-click *News.htm*.**

16. Click the **Highlight Hotspots button** 🔲.

The image of the school building disappears and all you see are the three hotspots.

17. Click the **Highlight Hotspots button** 🔲 **again to deactivate it.**

The image of the school building reappears.

18. Click **Save** 🔲.

19. Click **Preview in Browser** 🔲.

The page appears in your default browser.

20. Position the pointer over the Events hotspot and click.

The pointer changes to a hand when you move over the hotspot; the *Events* page appears in your browser when you click.

21. Click the **Back button** 🔲 on your browser's toolbar and click each of the other two hotspots.

22. Click **Close** 🔲 to close the browser window.

23. Click **Close Web** on the File menu, saving changes to pages, if necessary.

USING GRAPHICAL PAGE ELEMENTS

Pictures are not the only graphical elements you can put on a page. You have already created graphical page banners and navigation bars. When working with themes, you were able to add page backgrounds. Tables and lists are also types of page elements with graphical components. In this lesson, you will incorporate more graphical elements into your Web—including some special animation effects.

Horizontal Lines

Horizontal lines are page elements you can use to separate sections of a page. If your page has a theme, you can only set the alignment of the line—the theme sets the color, thickness, and width of the line.

Inserting a Horizontal Line

In this activity, you will add a horizontal line to your *Sporting Greats* Web. You will then change the alignment of the line.

1. Open the *Sporting Greats* Web in the *Tutorial* folder of your FrontPage Student Data Disk.

2. Display *index.htm* in Page view in the Normal tab.

Note the blue and green horizontal line running across the page. This line appears in the style determined by the theme in effect.

3. Display *news.htm* in Page view in the Normal tab.

4. Click at the end of the paragraph ending with the words . . . *take a look here first.*

5. Click **Horizontal Line** on the Insert menu.

A new blue and green line is inserted after the paragraph. The new line separates this paragraph from the next, as shown in Figure 6.14.

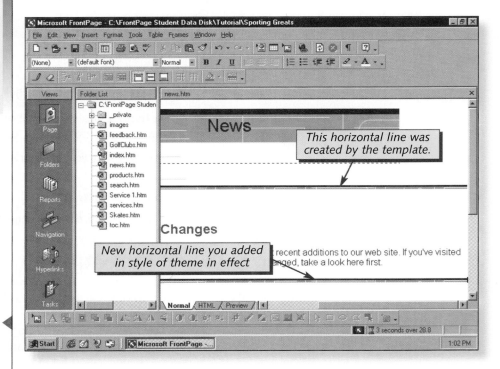

Figure 6.14
Horizontal line added to a Web page

6. Click **Theme** on the Format menu.

The Themes dialog box opens.

7. Scroll down in the Sample of Theme window until you can see a horizontal line.

For each highlighted theme, a unique horizontal line format appears in the Sample of Theme window.

8. Click on different themes to see how they display horizontal lines.

9. Click **Cancel**.

10. Click **Save** 🖫.

Creating a Hover Button

A *hover button* seems like any other button; that is, a graphical image which hyperlinks to another page or file when clicked. Unlike other buttons, however, a hover button also glows, displays a picture, or plays a sound when you click it or point to it.

When you first insert a hover button (or when you right-click to edit one), you must complete options within the Hover Button Properties dialog box. In the text box labeled *Button text*, you enter the word or phrase to be contained in the hover button. "Button Text" appears as the default text, but you will have to replace that with something more meaningful. To change the font of the button text, you have to click the Font button to the right of the text box.

In the *Link to* box, you must enter the target of the button's hyperlink. The Browse button presents a dialog box very similar to the Create Hyperlink dialog box in that you can link to a page, file, e-mail, blank page, or other Web site.

Drop-down lists let you set the color of the button and the background color. The latter is used when the button is a picture. There are two lists that control how the button will change when visitors point to it—Effect and Effect color. Table 6.2 describes each of the seven effects.

TABLE 6.2	HOVER BUTTON EFFECTS
Effect	**What Occurs When Pointed to**
Color Fill	The button changes from the button color to the effect color.
Color Average	The button changes from the button color to a mixture of the button color and the effect color.
Glow	The center of the button changes to the effect color and blends to the button color at the right and left edges of the button.
Reverse Glow	The center of the button remains the button color and blends to the effect color at the right and left edges of the button.
Light Glow	The center of the button changes to white and blends to the button color at the right and left edges of the button.
Bevel Out	The button appears to raise up from the page.
Bevel In	The button appears to sink back into the page.

Two text boxes let you control the width and height of the button. Such adjustments may be necessary if you enter a lot of text or need to match the size of a graphic image you want to use as the button. Finally, the Custom button lets you choose a sound clip to play or a picture to display when the button is pointed to or clicked.

Inserting a Hover Button

1. Click an insertion point in the page.

2. Point to Component and click Hover Button on the Insert menu.

3. Choose options in the Hover Button Properties dialog box.

4. Click OK.

Inserting a Hover Button

In this activity, you will add a hover button to a page in your *Sporting Greats* Web.

1. **Display *index.htm* in Page view in the Normal tab.**

2. **Click an insertion point at the end of *Welcome to the Sporting Greats Web site.* and press** [Enter←].

3. **Point to Component and click Hover Button on the Insert menu.**

The Hover Button Properties dialog box appears as shown in Figure 6.15.

4. **Type Specials in the *Button text* text box.**

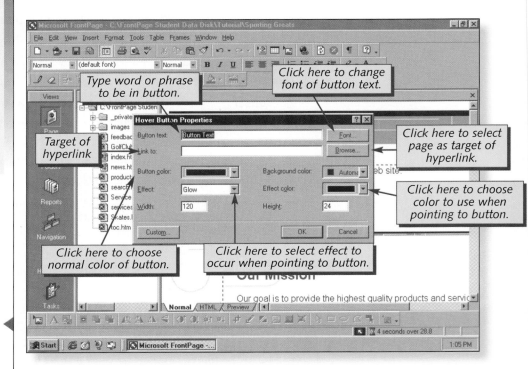

Figure 6.15
The Hover Button Properties dialog box

5. **Click the Browse button, then double-click *products.htm* as the target of the hyperlink.**

6. **Click the Button color drop-down arrow, then click the first box to the left under Theme Colors.**

The button will use a color already part of the theme in effect.

7. **Click the Effect drop-down arrow, then click Reverse glow.**

8. **Click the Effect color drop-down arrow, then click the second box from the left under Theme Colors.**

9. **Click OK.**

The button appears with the text you typed and color you selected.

10. Click **Save** .

Two files are added to the Folder List—one controls the button as it normally appears and the other controls the button when it is pointed to.

11. Click the **Preview tab**.

12. Point to the button.

The button takes on the reverse glow effect, as seen in Figure 6.16.

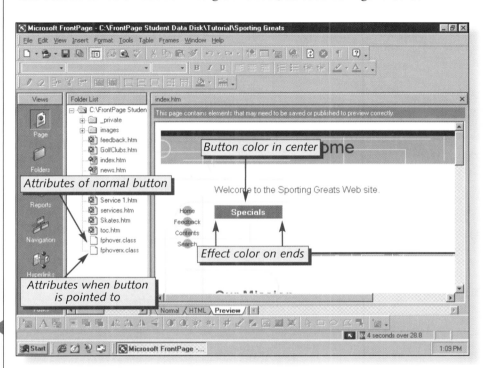

Figure 6.16
Hover button with Reverse glow effect

13. Click the button.

The hyperlink takes you to the *Products* page.

Creating a Hit Counter

A **hit counter** is a page element that displays a running total of the number of times visitors have viewed the page. Placing a hit counter on the home page lets both the Web designer and visitor see how popular the site is. The Hit Counter Properties dialog box contains five styles of hit counters from which you can choose.

The dialog box includes two other options. The *Reset counter to* text box lets you type a starting number for the hit counter. There are at least two reasons that Web designers start at a number other than zero. The hit counter may be replacing another hit counter and the designer may want to include the number of visitors counted in the previous list. Secondly, designers may want to make a site seem more popular than it is to visitors while still being able to get an accurate count.

The *fixed number of digits* option controls how many leading zeros will be displayed. For example, if there are 20 visitors and the option is set to 3 fixed digits, the hit counter will display 020; that is, a zero will be added to the leftmost position to force the display of 3 digits without changing the actual value. In the same scenario, 5 fixed digits will cause the hit counter to display 00020.

Inserting a Hit Counter

In this activity, you will add a hit counter to the *Sporting Greats* home page.

1. **Display *index.htm* in Page view in the Normal tab.**

2. **Scroll to the bottom of the page and click at the end of the Webmaster's e-mail address, then press** `Enter↵` **two times.**

3. **Type** You are visitor number **followed by a space.**

4. **Point to Component and click Hit Counter on the Insert menu.**

The Hit Counter Properties dialog box opens, as shown in Figure 6.17.

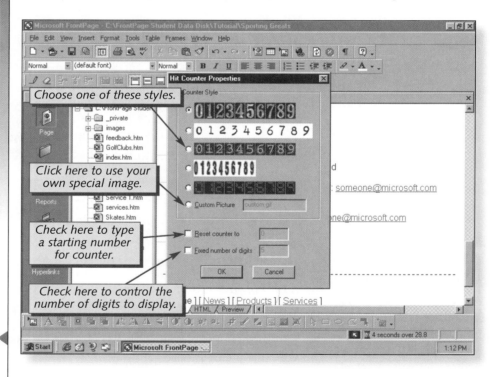

Figure 6.17
Hit Counter Properties dialog box

5. **Click the fifth option button in the Counter Style section.**

6. **Click the Reset counter to check box, and then type** 1000 **in the text box.**

7. **Click OK.**

A placeholder appears in the page with the words "[Hit Counter]." The actual graphic and number can only be viewed when the Web site is published on a Web server running the FrontPage Server Extensions.

8. **Click Save** 💾.

Creating a Scrolling Marquee

Animation enhances your Web by adding motion and other special effects. You can add animation and special effects to pictures, text, and almost any part of a page by applying ***dynamic HTML (DHTML) effects***. DHTML is an extension of the HTML language with specific codes for presentation effects. With DHTML you choose when the effect is to occur (such as mouse over or click) and what should occur (formatting change, adding a border or background, sound effect, and so on). More complex events can take place by *scripting*. Scripting requires an in-depth knowledge of a programming language but allows detailed control of page elements, transitions, timing, and transformations.

You've already used two types of animation that do not require scripting—page transitions and hover buttons. A third type of animation is a ***scrolling marquee***. A scrolling marquee is a box in which text moves thus drawing attention to an important message.

When you create or edit a scrolling marquee, you set options in the Marquee Properties dialog box. The *Text* text box is where you enter the message that will scroll. If you select text on the page before creating the scrolling marquee, the text will be entered automatically. The Direction option buttons determine whether the message will move toward the left or toward the right. In the Speed section of the dialog box, counter buttons set the Delay (how long before the message starts to appear) and Amount (the number of pixels per second the message moves).

Choosing an option button in the Behavior section of the dialog box causes the marquee to keep moving (Scroll); move to position and stop (Slide); or move back and forth (Alternate). The Align with text and Size sections are the same as other text and graphics dialog box options you have used.

By default, the message is set to scroll repeatedly, as long as the page is displayed. If you uncheck the *Continuously* box, you can enter the number of times you want the message to repeat—1 or more times. Finally, you can select a background color for the marquee, further highlighting the message.

Inserting and Editing a Scrolling Marquee

In this activity, you will add a scrolling marquee to a page in the *Sporting Greats* Web. Then you will make changes to the behavior of the marquee.

1. Display *Service 1.htm* in Page view in the Normal tab.

2. Select We can improve your game. Call for a free, trial lesson.

3. Point to Component and click Marquee on the Insert menu.

The Marquee Properties dialog box opens, as shown in Figure 6.18. The text you just selected before opening the dialog box appears in the *Text* box.

Figure 6.18
The Marquee Properties dialog box

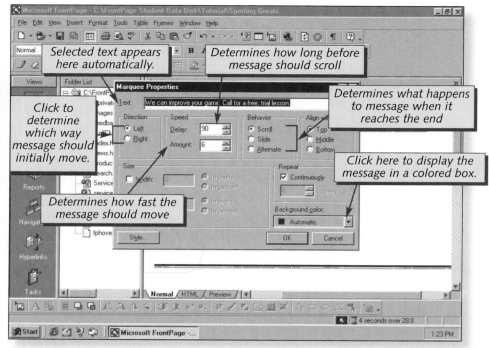

Selected text appears here automatically.

Determines how long before message should scroll

Click to determine which way message should initially move.

Determines what happens to message when it reaches the end

Click here to display the message in a colored box.

Determines how fast the message should move

Inserting and Editing a Scrolling Marquee

To insert a scrolling marquee:

1. Select text for the marquee.

2. Point to Component and click Marquee on the Insert menu.

3. Set direction, speed, behavior, alignment, size, repeat, and background color options.

4. Click OK.

To edit a scrolling marquee:

1. Right-click the marquee.

2. Click Marquee Properties.

3. Change any of the options.

4. Click OK.

Press [Alt] + [Enter ←] to display the properties for any selected item.

4. Click the **Right option button** in the Direction section.

5. Click the **Background color drop-down arrow**, click the first Theme Color on the left, then click **OK**.

The scrolling marquee appears in the page, but is static. To see this or any animation, you must view the element using the Preview tab in Page view or the Preview in Browser button.

6. Click the **Preview tab**.

The marquee appears and the message moves from left to right. Shortly after the message disappears off the right edge of the page, it reappears on the left.

7. Click the **Normal tab**.

8. Right-click the marquee and click **Marquee Properties** on the shortcut menu.

The Marquee Properties dialog box opens as before.

9. Click the **Left option button** in the Direction section, click the **Alternate option button** in the Behavior section, then click **OK**.

10. Click the **Preview tab**.

The message scrolls from right to left. Once it reaches the left edge of the page, it bounces in the other direction.

11. Click **Save** .

USING THE OFFICE CLIPBOARD

Importing files is a great way to bring large amounts of data from one program or document into another. For smaller amounts of data or parts of files, the **Windows Clipboard** is ideal. When you select and cut or copy all or part of a document, the data is automatically placed in the Clipboard. The Clipboard is a special area in memory set aside to temporarily hold data. Data in the Clipboard can be pasted into another part of the document, another document, or a document in another compatible program. Since the data remains in the Clipboard after it is pasted, you can paste the same data any number of times in as many different places as you want. However, when you cut or copy some new data, the new data replaces the old data—that is, the Windows Clipboard can only hold one thing at a time.

Office 2000 has its own Clipboard. The **Office Clipboard** works just like the Windows Clipboard, except it can hold up to 12 pieces of data. Each time you cut or copy data, the new data is added to the Office Clipboard. Although almost any Windows application can store data in the Office Clipboard, only Word, Excel, PowerPoint, Outlook, and Access can paste the data.

Copying and Pasting with the Office Clipboard

Within an Office 2000 application (such as Word) that can paste data from the Office Clipboard, the Clipboard toolbar lets you see the information you have copied. There are three commands on the toolbar—the first copies the selected text to the Clipboard; the second pastes all items from the Clipboard to the document; and the third deletes all data from the Clipboard (the Windows Clipboard, as well).

An icon indicates each separate piece of data you copied to the Clipboard. To paste any one piece of data, you just click the icon. To see what content is in an item, point to it. If it contains text, about the first 50 characters will appear; if the content is graphically based, a name will be assigned to it, such as Picture 1 or Picture 2.

HANDS On

Copying and Pasting

In this activity, you will launch Microsoft Word and display the Office Clipboard toolbar. Then you will switch to FrontPage 2000 and copy different page elements. Finally, you will switch back to Word and paste items from the Office Clipboard into the Word document.

1. Point to **Programs** on the Start menu, then click **Microsoft Word**.

The Word 2000 program launches and a blank document window appears.

You must have Microsoft Word 2000 installed on your computer in order to complete this activity.

Copying and Pasting

1. Launch an Office 2000 Office Clipboard-compatible program.

2. Display the Clipboard toolbar.

3. Switch to FrontPage.

4. Select data (text, page element, or graphic).

5. Click Copy or Cut.

6. Switch to the Office 2000 program.

7. Click items you wish to paste.

Another Way

Press Ctrl + C for copy; press Ctrl + X for cut; and press Ctrl + V for paste.

Another Way

Press Alt + Tab to switch from one open application to the next open application. If several applications are running on the taskbar, hold down Alt and keep pressing Tab until the name of the application you want appears on the screen. Then release Alt.

---

2. Point to **Toolbars** on the View menu and click to check **Clipboard**, if it is not already checked.

The Office Clipboard toolbar opens. If it is not floating over the workspace of the empty document, look to see if it is on another toolbar near the top of the screen.

You need only perform the next two steps if your Clipboard is attached to another toolbar.

3. Point to the **Drag Handle** at the left edge of the Clipboard toolbar.

The pointer becomes the Move Object pointer ⊕.

4. Drag the Clipboard toolbar down toward the center of the screen.

5. Click **Clear Clipboard** if the Clipboard is loaded with an icon.

The Clipboard becomes blank and the buttons appear dimmed.

6. Click the **Microsoft FrontPage taskbar button**.

The *Sporting Greats* Web appears.

7. Display *GolfClubs.htm* in Page view in the Normal tab.

8. Click the page banner, then click the **Copy button** on the Standard Buttons toolbar.

9. Select the table row for GolfPro, then click the **Copy button** .

10. Scroll down, select the numbered list with its heading, and then click the Copy button .

11. Click the **Microsoft Word taskbar button**.

The blank Word document reappears. This time, however, you should see icons representing three items in the Office Clipboard—the page banner, the table row, and the numbered list. The icons appear in the order in which you saved them, from left to right.

12. Click the third icon from the left.

The numbered list is pasted into the document.

13. Click the first icon.

The page banner graphic is pasted without its text.

14. Click the second icon.

The table row is pasted below the banner. Your document now resembles Figure 6.19.

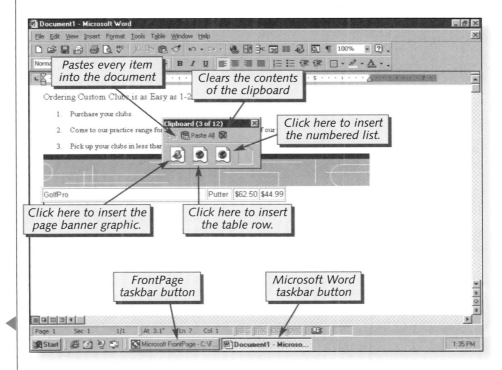

Figure 6.19
Word document with three
FrontPage elements

15. Click the Close button ⊠ to close Word; then click **No** when prompted to save changes.

The document is not saved. You return to FrontPage.

16. Close FrontPage 2000, saving changes to all Web pages, if prompted.

Test your knowledge by answering the following questions. See Appendix D to check your answers.

T F 1. Importing an image is the same as adding an image to a Web page.

T F 2. If you maintain the aspect ratio, an image will not be distorted when you resize it.

T F 3. Beveling an image creates a raised, 3-D effect.

T F 4. A hover button moves around the page when you click it.

T F 5. You can change the color of a horizontal line if the page has a theme.

ON*the*WEB

USING IMAGES FOUND ON WEB SITES

The World Wide Web is full of graphic images and elements that make Web surfing the popular and exciting activity it is today. Remember, most graphics you see belong to somebody. If you intend to use them, make sure you have the owner's permission or have a license permitting use. In this activity, you will be allowed to use graphics from a publisher's Web site for the purpose of completing this activity only.

Copying elements is simple using the Windows Clipboard—just right-click the image and click copy. Switch to your Web in FrontPage, position your insertion point, right-click and paste. Once the graphic is in your Web page, you can use any of the picture tools to edit it.

To import a file, locate the graphic you want, right-click it, and save it to your disk. Then use the Import option on the File menu to place it in your Web. You can also use Windows Explorer to drag files from one folder to another. In this activity, you will see how to drag a saved file from your desktop to your *Web* folder while in Folders view.

In this activity, you will locate a Web site with graphics you want to use. You will add a graphic to a Web page. Then you will import a page element for later use.

1. **Launch FrontPage 2000 and open your *School Newsletter* Web.**
2. **Display *News.htm* in Page view in the Normal tab.**
3. **Launch your Web browser.**

You are connected to the Internet. Your home page opens.

4. **Type** www.glencoe.com/norton/online/tutorials **in the *Address* text box and press** Enter.
5. **Right-click the photograph of Peter Norton then click** Copy **on the shortcut menu.**

The photograph is placed on the Clipboard.

6. **Click the** FrontPage taskbar button.
7. **Right-click in the left cell in the first empty row under the Leopard photo, then click** Paste.

The image is copied from the Clipboard into your Web page.

8. **Press** Tab, **then type the following:** Peter Norton to visit our campus next month. Details in next week's newsletter.
9. **Click** Save 💾, **then click** OK **in the Save Embedded Files dialog box.**
10. **Click the** Folders view icon 🗂.
11. **Click your browser taskbar button to return to your Web browser.**
12. **Right-click the Norton Tutorials Online image in the center of the page.**
13. **Click** Save Picture As.

The Save Picture dialog box opens.

14. Click the **Save in drop-down arrow**, then click **Desktop**.

15. Type Norton Online.gif **as the file name, and then click** **Save**.

The image will be saved on the Desktop.

16. Close your Web browser.

17. Click the **Restore button** 🖻 **on the top right of the screen.**

18. Resize and move the FrontPage window so you can see the Norton Online graphic file that you just saved on the Desktop.

19. Drag the file from the Desktop to the Contents pane of your Web.

The image file is copied into your Web and is ready to be added to a page whenever you are ready for it. Figure 6.20 shows the file added to the Contents page.

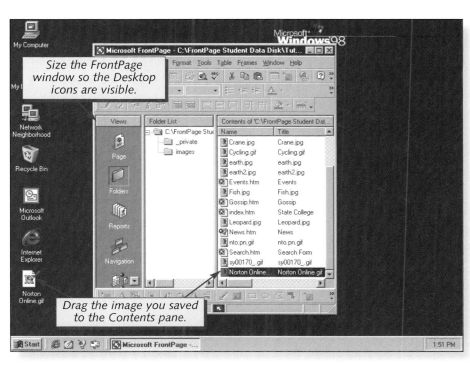

Figure 6.20
copied to a Web folder from the Desktop

20. Click **Close** ☒ **to exit FrontPage 2000.**

21. Click the image file you saved on the Desktop, press Delete, **then click** **Yes** **to confirm.**

The file is removed from your Desktop.

Warning

You may proceed directly to the exercises for this lesson. If, however, you are finished with your computer session, follow the "shut down" procedures for your school or lab environment.

Lesson Summary & Exercises

SUMMARY

Graphics can be used to enhance the content of a Web. In addition to providing visual information, Web sites are more attractive and entertaining when they contain pictures, animation, and other graphical page elements. Graphic images come from many sources—clip art, Web sites, scanned artwork, and digital photographs to name but a few. You learned how to insert pictures into your Web pages by adding them from the Clip Art Gallery and by importing them from a file. Once you put the images in place, you learned to resize, rotate, flip, and bevel them. You typed and located text on top of an image and added hotspots to create an image map. Adding a horizontal line, a hover button, a hit counter, and a scrolling marquee gave animation and interest to a page. You used the Office Clipboard to paste page elements from FrontPage into a Microsoft Word document. Finally, you used two techniques to add graphics from another Web site into your own Web page.

Now that you have completed this lesson, you should be able to do the following:

- Explain the importance of securing permission to use graphic images. (page 222)
- Identify the sources of graphic images. (page 222)
- Explain the significance of using multimedia in a Web. (page 222)
- Understand the importance of file compression and image formats. (page 222)
- Add a graphic image to a Web page from the Clip Art Gallery. (page 223)
- Use Clip Art Gallery Help to learn how to import images from Clips Online. (page 226)
- Add graphic images from a file. (page 226)
- Import graphic images from a file. (page 228)
- Explain how importing a graphic file differs from adding an image to a page. (page 228)
- Explain techniques for editing a graphic image. (page 232)
- Resize, rotate, flip, and bevel an image. (page 234)
- Type text over an image in a text box. (page 236)
- Define an image map and a hotspot. (page 237)
- Add hotspots to an image creating an image map. (page 237)
- Insert graphical elements such as a horizontal line, a hover button, a hit counter, and a scrolling marquee. (page 239)
- Use the Office Clipboard to paste text and graphics from a FrontPage Web into a Microsoft Word document. (page 247)
- Add and import images from a Web site into your Web. (page 250)

Lesson Summary & Exercises

CONCEPTS REVIEW

1 MATCHING

Match each of the terms on the left with the definitions on the right.

TERMS

1. aspect ratio
2. Clipboard
3. hot spot
4. image map
5. scripting
6. multimedia
7. hover button
8. handle
9. clip art
10. flip

DEFINITIONS

a. A special place in memory to hold cut or copied data

b. A graphic image that contains one or more hyperlinks

c. A small square box used to resize an image

d. To turn a graphic image horizontally or vertically

e. Page elements intended to excite and entertain viewers

f. A resizing option that prevents images from becoming distorted

g. A collection of drawings and photographs ready to add to a Web page

h. A programming language that is used to control complex events

i. A graphical image with a hyperlink that changes appearance when pointed to or clicked

j. A location on a graphic image that contains a hyperlink

2 COMPLETION

Fill in the missing word or phrase for each of the following statements.

1. A(n) _____ is a device that converts photographs or drawings from paper into electronic files.

2. An extension of the HTML language that adds codes for presentation effects is called _____.

3. A(n) _____ is a page element that displays the number of visitors to a Web page.

4. _____ is the means by which graphic files can be added to a Web before they are inserted onto a page.

5. Dragging a corner handle of a graphic image lets you keep the _____.

6. For a scrolling marquee's message to move back and forth to the left and right, you should choose the _____ option.

7. The _____ Clipboard can hold up to 12 pieces of copied or cut data.

Lesson Summary & Exercises

8. To type words or phrases on top of an image, click the _____ button on the Pictures toolbar.

9. The _____ is a collection of graphics, sound, and video clips that is a part of FrontPage 2000.

10. A(n) _____ is a graphic that contains one or more hotspots.

3 SHORT ANSWER

Write a brief answer to each of the following questions.

1. List three page elements that use animation.

2. Describe how you would turn an image upside down and a quarter turn counterclockwise.

3. List four sources of graphic images.

4. What is an image map and how would you create one?

5. Describe the steps you would take to display the Pictures toolbar. What would you do if the toolbar is attached to the end of another toolbar and you wanted it to float in the middle of the screen?

6. How does the use of a theme affect the options you can set on a horizontal line?

7. What is the difference between adding and importing a graphic?

8. Name two file types in which FrontPage saves embedded images.

9. Describe the steps you would use to find and insert an image from the Clip Art Gallery.

10. How could you import a graphic image from a Web site displayed in your browser window?

4 IDENTIFICATION

Label each of the elements in Figure 6.21.

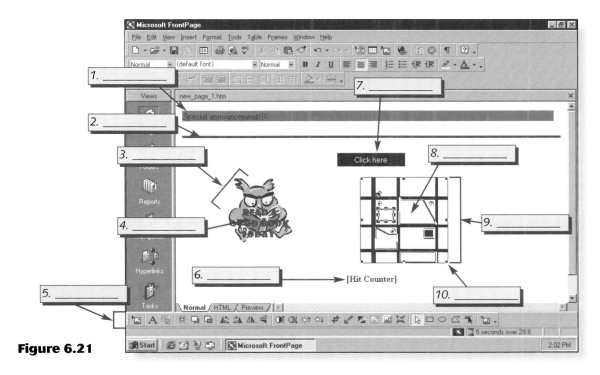

Figure 6.21

SKILLS REVIEW

Complete each of the Skills Review problems in sequential order to review your skills to add a clip art image; add an image from a file; import an image from a file; resize, rotate, flip, and bevel an image; type text over an image; add hotspots to an image; insert a horizontal line, hover button, hit counter, and scrolling marquee; and use the Office Clipboard to copy and paste page elements into a Microsoft Word document.

1 Adding a Clip Art Image

1. Launch FrontPage 2000.

2. Open the *Acme* Web in the *Skills Review* folder of your FrontPage Student Data Disk.

3. Display *index.htm* in Page view in the Normal tab.

4. Click at the end of the paragraph of text ending with . . . *enrich your life.,* and press Enter⏎.

5. Point to **Picture** and click **Clip Art** on the Insert menu.

Lesson Summary & Exercises

6. Click the **Animals** category link.

7. Click the first image in the second row (a man pulling a rabbit out of a hat), then click **Insert Clip** 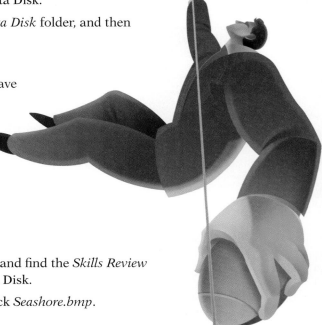.

8. Click **Save** , then click **OK** in the Save Embedded Files dialog box.

2 Adding an Image from a File

1. Display *Products.htm* in Page view in the Normal tab.

2. Click the image of the fireworks and press Delete.

3. Select **Fireworks Photo Caption** and press Delete.

4. Point to **Picture** and click **From File** on the Insert menu.

5. Click the **Select a file on your computer button** .

6. Click the **Look in drop-down arrow** and click the drive containing your FrontPage Student Data Disk.

7. Double-click the *FrontPage Student Data Disk* folder, and then double-click the *Skills Review* folder.

8. Double-click *AcmePeople.wmf*.

9. Click **Save** , then click **OK** in the Save Embedded Files dialog box.

3 Importing an Image from a File

1. Click the *images* folder in the Folder List.

2. Click **Import** on the File menu.

3. Click **Add File**.

4. Click the **Look in drop-down arrow** and find the *Skills Review* folder on your FrontPage Student Data Disk.

5. Click *CDs.bmp*, press Ctrl , and then click *Seashore.bmp*.

6. Click **Open**, then click **OK**.

7. Scroll to the bottom of the *products.htm* page.

8. Expand the *images* folder, if necessary.

9. Drag *cds.bmp* into the second column.

10. Drag *seashore.bmp* into the second column below *cds.bmp*.

11. Click **Save** .

4 Resizing an Image

1. Display *index.htm* in Page view in the Normal tab.

2. Click the image.

3. Drag a corner handle to reduce the size of the image by half.

4. Click **Save** .

5 Rotating, Flipping, and Beveling an Image

1. Display *Products.htm* in Page view in the Normal tab.

2. Click the image of the people holding hands around the world, then click **Flip Horizontal** ⚠.

3. Scroll down and click the image of the CDs.

4. Click **Rotate Right** 🔄.

5. Click the image of the seashore, then click **Bevel** 🖼.

6. Click **Save** 💾, then click **OK** in the Save Embedded Files dialog box.

7. Click **Close Web** on the File menu.

6 Typing Text Over an Image

1. Open the *PetCare Clinic* Web in the *Skills Review* folder on your FrontPage Student Data Disk.

2. Display *index.htm* in Page view in the Normal tab.

3. Click an insertion point on the line below the first paragraph.

4. Point to **Picture** and click **From File** on the Insert menu.

5. Click **Select a file on your computer** 🔍, then locate the *Skills Review* folder on your *FrontPage Student Data Disk*.

6. Double-click *Clinic.wmf*.

7. Click the image of the building just inserted into *index.htm*.

8. Click **Text** 🅰, then click **OK** if prompted to change the image format.

9. Type Dog Food, click the text box border, then drag the text box onto the left-most roof section.

10. Click **Text** 🅰, type Cat Food, and drag the text box onto the rightmost roof section.

11. Click **Text** 🅰, type Boarding, and drag the text box onto the center roof section.

12. Click **Save** 💾 and click **OK** in the Save Embedded Files dialog box.

7 Adding Hotspots to an Image

1. Click the image of the building within *index.htm*.

2. Click **Polygonal Hotspot** 📐 and click points to enclose the far right third of the building including the diagonal section of the roof.

3. Double-click *DogFood.htm* as the hyperlink.

4. Click **Polygonal Hotspot** 📐 and click points to enclose the far left third of the building including the diagonal section of the roof.

5. Double-click *CatFood.htm* as the hyperlink.

6. Click **Rectangular Hotspot**  and enclose the center of the building.

7. Double-click *Boarding.htm* as the hyperlink.

8. Click **Save**.

8 Inserting a Horizontal Line and a Hover Button

1. Display *products.htm* in Page view in the Normal tab.

2. Click the blank line between the Cat Food and Dog Food sections.

3. Click **Horizontal Line** on the Insert menu, then press `Enter←`.

4. Point to **Component** and click **Hover Button** on the Insert menu.

5. Type Boarding Services as the Button text and change the Button color to the first of the Theme colors.

6. Change the Effect color to the last of the Theme colors, and change the Effect to Color Average.

7. Click **Font**, change the font size to **12 pt**, then click **OK**.

8. Click **OK** then click **Save**.

9. Click the **Preview tab**.

10. Point to the hover button to see the effect.

9 Inserting a Hit Counter and a Scrolling Marquee

1. Display *index.htm* in Page view in the Normal tab.

2. Click an insertion point below the image and the horizontal line.

3. Point to **Component** and click **Hit Counter** on the Insert menu.

4. Click the option button for the third Counter Style.

5. Click to check the Reset counter and type **2000** as the starting number.

6. Click **OK**.

7. Select the words **Contact Information**.

8. Point to **Component** and click **Marquee** on the Insert menu.

9. Change the Direction to Right, the Behavior to Slide, and the Background color to the last Theme Color on the top row.

10. Click **OK**, then click **Save**.

11. Click the **Preview tab**, scroll down, and view the scrolling marquee.

10 Using the Office Clipboard

1. Launch Microsoft Word.

2. Point to **Toolbars** and click **Clipboard** on the View menu.

3. Drag the toolbar to the center of the screen, if necessary.

4. Click **Clear Clipboard** if your Clipboard is loaded.

5. Click the **Microsoft FrontPage taskbar button**.

6. Display *index.htm* in the Normal tab.

7. Click the horizontal line within *index.htm*, then click **Copy** 📋.

8. Click the scrolling marquee, then click **Copy** 📋.

9. Select the text from the heading *Telephone* to *Webmaster:*
   someone@microsoft.com and click **Copy** 📋.

10. Click the **Microsoft Word taskbar button**.

11. Click Item 2 in the Office Clipboard (the scrolling marquee); click Item 3 (the
    text), then click Item 1 (the horizontal rule). Your document should look like
    Figure 6.22.

12. Click **Close** ✕ to close Word; click **No** when prompted to save changes.

13. Click **Close Web** on the File menu, saving changes if prompted.

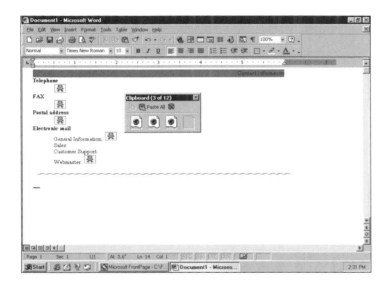

Figure 6.22

LESSON APPLICATIONS

1 Adding and Importing an Image

Add images from the Clip Art Gallery to a Web page. Import an image file into the Folder List and drag
it from the Folder List into a Web page.

1. Start Microsoft FrontPage 2000, if necessary, and open the *Personal* Web in
   the *Lesson Applications* folder on your FrontPage Student Data Disk.

2. Display *Family.htm*. Delete the graphic of the earth and its caption. Add an
   appropriate graphic from the Clip Art Gallery to the first story. (Hint: There is
   a graphic of river rafting you can use. Type rafting in the *Search for clips* box to
   find it.)

3. Click an insertion point above the text in the right column of the second story.
   Add the image file *Anniversary.wmf* from the *Lesson Applications* folder.
   (Point to Picture and click From File on the Insert menu to locate the image.)

4. Import *Engaged.wmf* from the *Lesson Applications* folder to the *images* folder in the Folder List. Then drag *Engaged.wfm* to the left cell above the text in the third story in *Family.htm*.

5. Save the page with its embedded graphics.

2 Editing Images and Creating an Image Map

Change image properties and type text onto a graphic. Add hotspots to make an image map.

1. Reduce the size of the *Engaged* graphic while maintaining the aspect ratio.

2. Flip the *Anniversary* graphic to display its mirror image.

3. Close the *Personal* Web saving all changes.

4. Open the *Office Supplies* Web in the *Lesson Applications* folder on your FrontPage Student Data Disk.

5. Display the home page and add the graphic *Supplies.wmf* from the *Lesson Applications* folder to an appropriate location in the page. Bevel the image. Add a text box, type Paper, and drag the box over the sheet of paper in the lower left corner of the image. Add another text box, type Binders, and drag it over the book in the image. Create hotspots to *Paper.htm* and *Binders.htm*. Save the page with the graphic.

3 Adding Page Elements and Animation Effects

Add graphical page elements to a Web including a horizontal line, a hover button, a hit counter, and a scrolling marquee.

1. Insert a horizontal line between the listings for binders and paper on the *Products* page of the *Office Supplies* Web.

2. Add a hover button on *Paper.htm* that hyperlinks to the *Binders.htm* page. Choose contrasting Button and Effect colors and use the Reverse glow effect.

3. Add a hit counter to the home page and start the counter at 500.

4. Change the first line of the *Products* page to a scrolling marquee. Set the direction to Right, set Behavior as Alternate, and choose a theme color for the background. Click the Preview tab to view the marquee.

5. Close the Web saving all changes.

PROJECTS

1 A Picture Is Worth 1K Words

Now that your *Benevolents* Web site is fully functioning, you and your Web design committee decide that the site needs some graphic images to make it more attractive to visitors. Using the Microsoft Clip Art Gallery or other sources of drawings and photographs, add images to each page. *Suggestions:* Add designs and/or pictures of youth activities to the home page; pictures or drawings showing growth and volunteerism on the *about* page; graphics representing each of the activities (basketball, meetings, cleaning up, dancing, and so on) on the *events* page; photographs or drawings for each of the individuals listed on the *members* page; and designs or images you think appropriate for the other links and search form pages.

2 Page Elements, My Dear Watson

Before publishing the *Benevolents* Web site, you decide to add some graphical page elements and animation effects to some of the pages. Add horizontal lines as appropriate; insert one or more hover buttons to create shortcut links from one page to another; place a hit counter on the home page; add an image map; and add scrolling marquees to pages needing some excitement.

3 Let Me Show You What I Mean

To gain business for your Web design consulting service *InstaWeb* (created in Projects 1–4 of Lesson 5), you realize your Web site must not only inform but must also attract clients by displaying the kinds of dynamic pages you can create for them. Using the skills you learned in this lesson, add, import, and edit graphical images that will enhance each of the pages in your Web.

4 Polishing Off the Web

To complete the design of *InstaWeb*, your Web design consulting services site, you need to add additional graphical elements and animations to your Web pages. Include page transitions, hit counters, an image map, hover buttons, horizontal lines, and scrolling marquees, as appropriate.

5 Staying Ahead of the Competition

Now that your competitor has a Web presence as well, you realize the need to improve the appearance and usefulness of your *Main Street Collectibles* Web site. Search for, add, and/or import graphic images that will enhance your Web pages, illustrate your products, show your store, and provide a map to your location. Include page elements and animations that you feel are necessary.

Overview: Congratulations! You have completed all the lessons in the FrontPage tutorial and now have the opportunity in this capstone project to apply the FrontPage skills you have learned. You will create a Web site for a company selling chocolates online. The site should include pages that introduce the company, its history, and contact information; pages that describe and illustrate the types of chocolates offered, including ingredients, prices, and sets for special occasions; and information on how to order chocolates as well as shipping charges and gift wrapping options. As you create the case study Web, try to incorporate these skills:

- Create a Web using a Web wizard, Web page templates, and/or build pages from scratch.

- Use online Help and Office on the Web as needed.

- Search the Internet.

- Add tasks to be completed later. Complete the tasks when appropriate.

- Add, proofread, import, and edit text content to your Web pages. Use the spell check, Find, and Replace commands.

- Apply page layout and formatting features, such as fonts, sizes, type styles, colors, alignment, and spacing.

- Build and print the navigation structure based on your Web design.

- Establish shared borders adding a page banner, navigation bar, and footer to Web pages.

- Create hyperlinks to bookmarks, other pages in the Web, other Web sites, e-mail message windows, and Office documents.

- Follow links and check the Web in Page view, the Preview tab, and by using the Preview in Browser command.

- Apply a custom theme to all pages with text, graphics, and colors of your choosing.

- Format text using styles and the Format Painter.

- Add and customize a search form.

- Include and modify the properties of a table of contents.

- Create, resize, and format tables.

- Add multilevel numbered and bulleted lists.

- Add, import, and edit graphic images.

- Insert image maps, horizontal lines, hover buttons, a hit counter, scrolling marquees, and page transitions.

- Print pages with a custom footer.

- Use the Reports view to locate slow pages or broken hyperlinks. Try to fix all problems.

- Change page tiles, page names, and URLs so they are meaningful when viewed by visitors.

Instructions: Read all directions and plan your work before you begin. You will be evaluated on these factors: (1) the number of skills involved in completing the case; (2) creativity; (3) practical applications for the task; (4) appropriate use of Web page features; (5) quality of the Web site produced, including mechanical accuracy, format, and written content; and (6) oral presentation of the case.

1. *Getting Started.* Research the subject of chocolate making and sales. Search the Web for chocolate manufacturers, whether they actually sell their products online or not. Research other sites selling gift items, such as flowers, fruits, candy, and so on. Add informative sites to your list of favorites/bookmarks in case you need to go back to complete the research.

2. *Design the Web.* Sketch the navigation structure before you begin to create the Web. If you plan to use the Corporate Presence Web wizard, base your design on the pages it will build, making modifications wherever you deem necessary. Your design should place each page on its appropriate level and include the page label. On separate pieces of paper, determine a page title, file name, and basic description of the page's intended contents. Indicate where graphics or other page elements should appear.

3. *Create the Web.* Choose whether to build a Web from a wizard or to add pages to a blank Web. If adding pages, base your pages on templates that are consistent with each other. Save the Web as *Chocolates Online* in the *Projects* folder on your FrontPage Student Data Disk. Modify the navigation structure to match the design you sketched.

4. *Create a Custom Theme.* Apply and make changes to a theme appropriate to the Web. Choose a background picture, text, graphics, and color options. Save the theme modifications and apply it to all pages in the Web.

5. *Modify Shared Borders.* Set or change page borders, leaving room for a page banner, navigation bar, and footer. Edit the properties of the page banner and navigation bar and include the e-mail address of the Webmaster in the bottom, shared border.

6. *Add Content.* Add and/or modify the text content, using the information you researched as well as your imagination. Import text you have created in another program, from a Web site, or other sources.

7. *Insert Hyperlinks.* Add hyperlinks to other pages, bookmarks, Office documents, and other Web sites.

8. *Add Tables and Lists.* Create and edit tables listing product details, prices, shipping costs, and so on. Include multilevel numbered and bulleted lists that highlight information that will attract customers.

9. *Add Graphics*. Insert and import graphic images from the Clip Art Gallery, Clips Online, other Web sites, or other sources. Resize, flip, rotate, bevel, and apply other editing techniques as appropriate.

10. *Add Animations and Graphical Page Elements*. Insert page transitions, horizontal lines, image maps, hover buttons, a hit counter, and scrolling marquees to highlight information or otherwise enhance the site.

11. *Request Reviewer Comments*. Ask one to five other students to review the presentation within a Web browser and to write reviewer comments. Read the comments and take appropriate action.

12. *Display the Web Site.* Print Web pages and open the Web in a Web browser. Demonstrate the overall appearance, hyperlinks, content, and practicality of the Web.

APPENDICES

CONTENTS

Portfolio Builder

WHAT IS A PORTFOLIO?

A *portfolio* is an organized collection of your work that demonstrates skills and knowledge acquired from one or more courses. The materials included in a portfolio should pertain to a specific educational or career goal. In addition to actual assignments, a portfolio should contain your self-reflection or comments on each piece of work as well as an overall statement introducing the portfolio.

Two types of portfolios exist. The first, which shows progress toward a goal over a period of time, is called a *developmental portfolio*. Developmental portfolios help you become more aware of your strengths and weaknesses and assist you in improving your abilities. The second type, called a *representational portfolio*, displays a variety of your best work. You can show a representational portfolio as evidence of your skills and knowledge. While you may use either type of portfolio when you are seeking employment, a representational portfolio is more effective.

WHY USE PORTFOLIOS?

Portfolios offer great advantages to you, your instructor, and potential employers. They allow you to reevaluate the work you have created, by determining which assignments should be included in the portfolio and analyzing how you can improve future assignments. If the goal of the portfolio is career related, portfolios also help you connect classroom activities with practical applications. A wide variety of genuine work is captured in a portfolio, rather than a snapshot of knowledge at a specific time under particular circumstances. Presenting a portfolio of your work to your instructor and potential employers gives them the opportunity to evaluate your overall skills and performance more accurately.

CREATING A PORTFOLIO

Creating a portfolio involves three steps—planning, selecting work to include, and providing comments about your work. First, you should plan the overall purpose and organization of the portfolio. After you plan your portfolio, you can begin selecting pieces of work to include in it. Ideally, you should select the work as you complete each Web page; however, you can review prior work to include as well.

Table A.1 recommends Web pages from the Projects assignments that you may want to consider for inclusion in your portfolio; however you may include additional pages, especially from the Projects section. If two pages demonstrate identical FrontPage 2000 skills, choose only one for your portfolio. If you apply your FrontPage 2000 skills in another course or elsewhere, include a sample in your portfolio.

TABLE A.1	POSSIBLE WEB PAGES TO INCLUDE IN YOUR PORTFOLIO
PAGE	**ACTIVITY**
Welcome page	Project 2 in Lesson 2
Events page	Project 4 in Lesson 2
Links page	Project 3 in Lesson 3
Home page	Project 5 in Lesson 3
Home page	Project 5 in Lesson 4
Search page	Project 4 in Lesson 4
Services pages	Project 4 in Lesson 5
Members page	Project 1 in Lesson 6
Home page	Project 5 in Lesson 6

Create a list or log that provides a summary of the contents of your portfolio. (Your instructor may provide a preformatted log that you can complete.) The log can include columns in which you can list the file name, page title, page label, description of the page, Web name, when and by whom the page was reviewed, whether the page was revised, and the grade you received on the assignment.

Lastly, you should prepare comments for each piece of work included in the portfolio. As you add work to your portfolio, generate comments about each piece. You may want to reflect on the skills used to create the page, or you can explain how the page is applicable to a specific job for which you are interviewing. Your instructor may provide you with a preformatted comments form or you may type your comments.

HANDS On

Building Your Portfolio

In this activity, you will plan your portfolio, select the pages to include in the portfolio, and prepare written comments about each piece of work included in the portfolio.

1. **Using Microsoft Word, or another word processor, answer the following questions to help you plan your portfolio:**

   ■ What is the purpose of your portfolio?

   ■ What criteria will you use in selecting work to include in the portfolio?

   ■ What is the overall goal that your portfolio will meet?

   ■ How will you organize your portfolio?

2. **Using Microsoft Word or another word processor, create a log that provides a summary of the contents of your portfolio. Follow the guidelines given by your instructor or provided in this appendix.**

3. **Remember the purpose and goal of your portfolio and select and print one Web page that you have completed to include in your portfolio. Enter information about the document in your log.**

4. **Prepare comments about the selected page and attach them to the printout.**

5. **Repeat steps 3 and 4 to select and prepare comments for other pages to include in your portfolio.**

6. **Using Microsoft Word, or another word processor, write a paragraph or two introducing your portfolio. Include some of the information considered in step 1.**

7. **Gather the pages to include in your portfolio and place them in a binder, folder, or other container in an organized manner.**

COMMAND SUMMARY

FEATURE	BUTTON	MOUSE ACTION	KEYBOARD ACTION
Basic Skills			
Maximize a window	▭	Double-click title bar	[Alt] + [Spacebar], X
Restore a window	▣	Double-click title bar	[Alt] + [Spacebar], R
Close a window	✕		[Ctrl] + [F4]
Open a Web	📂▾	Click Open or Open Web on the File menu	[Alt] + F, F or [Alt] + F, W
Close a File or a Web		Click Close Web on the File menu	[Alt] + F, L
Display Page view		Click Page on the View menu	[Alt] + V, P
Display Folders view		Click Folders on the View menu	[Alt] + V, F
Display Reports view		Point to Reports on the View menu and click the report	[Alt] + V, R and click the report
Display Navigation view		Click Navigation on the View menu	[Alt] + V, N
Display Hyperlinks view		Click Hyperlinks on the View menu	[Alt] + V, H
Display Tasks view		Click Tasks on the View menu	[Alt] + V, K
Save a page	🖫	Click Save on the File menu	[Ctrl] + S
Print a page	🖨	Click Print on the File menu then click OK	[Ctrl] + P, [Enter]
Undo	↩▾	Click Undo on the Edit menu	[Ctrl] + Z
Preview in Browser		Click Preview in Browser on the File menu	[Ctrl] + [⇧ Shift] + B
Display Tables toolbar		Point to Toolbars and click Tables on the View menu	[Alt] + V, T, [↓] to Tables, [Enter]
Display Pictures toolbar		Point to Toolbars and click Pictures on the View menu	[Alt] + V, T, [↓] to Pictures, [Enter]
Switch between open applications			[Alt] + [Tab]

APPENDIX B

COMMAND SUMMARY

FEATURE	BUTTON	MOUSE ACTION	KEYBOARD ACTION
Create a new Web		Point to New and click Web on the File menu	`Alt` + F, N, W
Create a new page	🗋▾	Point to New and click Page on the File menu	`Ctrl` + N

Entering and Formatting Text

FEATURE	BUTTON	MOUSE ACTION	KEYBOARD ACTION
Change font	Times New Roman	Click Font on the Format menu	`Ctrl` + `⇧ Shift` + F, `↑` or `↓`
Change font size	4 (14 pt)	Click Font on the Format menu	`Ctrl` + `⇧ Shift` + P, `↑` or `↓`
Bold Text	**B**	Click Font on the Format menu	`Ctrl` + B
Align Right		Click Paragraph on the Format menu	`Ctrl` + R
Align Left		Click Paragraph on the Format menu	`Ctrl` + L
Center		Click Paragraph on the Format menu	`Ctrl` + E
Import Text		Click File on the Insert menu	`Alt` + I, F
Insert a hyperlink		Click Hyperlink on the Insert menu	`Ctrl` + K
Follow a hyperlink within Page view		`Ctrl` + click	
Update hyperlinks		Click Recalculate Hyperlinks on the Tools menu	`Alt` + T, R
Insert a bookmark		Click Bookmark on the Insert menu	`Alt` + I, K
Apply a theme		Click Theme on the Format menu	`Alt` + O, T
Apply a style	Normal	Click Style on the Format menu	`Ctrl` + `⇧ Shift` +S, `↑` or `↓`
Apply Normal style	Normal	Click Style on the Format menu	`Ctrl` + `⇧ Shift` + N

FEATURE	BUTTON	MOUSE ACTION	KEYBOARD ACTION
Apply Heading (number) style	Normal	Click Style on the Format menu	Ctrl + Alt + (Number)
Use Format Painter			Ctrl + Shift + V to copy, then Ctrl + Shift + V to apply format
Spell check	ABC✓	Click Spelling on the Tools menu	F7
Find text		Click Find on the Edit menu	Ctrl + F
Replace text		Click Replace on the Edit menu	Ctrl + H
Cut text	✂	Click Cut on the Edit menu	Ctrl + X
Copy text		Click Copy on the Edit menu	Ctrl + C
Paste text		Click Paste on the Edit menu	Ctrl + V

Tables

FEATURE	BUTTON	MOUSE ACTION	KEYBOARD ACTION
Insert a Table		Point to Insert and click Table on the Table menu	Shift + Ctrl + Alt + T
Select Table		Point to Select and click Table on the Table menu	Alt + A, C, T
Select Column		Click top border of column	Alt + A, C, C
Select Row		Click left border of row	Alt + A, C, R
Select Cell		Alt + click cell	Alt + A, C, E
Select Next Cell		Alt + click next cell	Tab
Select Previous Cell		Alt + click previous	Shift + Tab
Resize Table		Drag border	Alt + A, R, T

COMMAND SUMMARY

FEATURE	BUTTON	MOUSE ACTION	KEYBOARD ACTION
Resize Cell		Drag border	[Alt] + A, R, C
AutoFit column		Click AutoFit on the Table menu	[Alt] + A, [↓], [Enter⏎]
Insert Columns		Point to Insert and click Rows or Columns on the Table menu	[Alt] + A, I, N
Insert Rows		Point to Insert and click Rows or Columns on the Table menu	[Alt] + A, I, N
Delete Cells		Click Delete Cells on the Table menu	[Alt] + A, D
Split Cells		Click Split Cells on the Table menu	[Alt] + A, P
Merge Cells		Click Merge Cells on the Table menu	[Alt] + A, M

Numbered and Bulleted Lists

FEATURE	BUTTON	MOUSE ACTION	KEYBOARD ACTION
Create a numbered list		Click Bullets and Numbering on the Format menu	[Alt] + O, N, [Ctrl] + [Tab]
Create a bulleted list		Click Bullets and Numbering on the Format menu	[Alt] + O, N
Create a sublevel	(2 times)		[Ctrl] + M, [Ctrl] + M
Create a higher level	(2 times)		[Ctrl] + [⇧ Shift] + M, [Ctrl] + [⇧ Shift] + M

Page Elements

FEATURE	BUTTON	MOUSE ACTION	KEYBOARD ACTION
Page Banner		Click Page Banner on the Insert menu	[Alt] + I, N
Shared Borders		Right-click page and click Shared Borders	[Alt] + O, D
Navigation Bar		Click Navigation Bar on the Insert menu	[Alt] + I, V
Page Transition		Click Page Transition on the Format menu	[Alt] + O, A

FEATURE	BUTTON	MOUSE ACTION	KEYBOARD ACTION
Change object properties		Right-click, and click (object name) Properties	
Insert a horizontal line		Click Horizontal Line on the Insert menu	[Alt] + I, L
Insert a hover button		Point to Component and click Hover Button on the Insert menu	[Alt] + I, O, H
Insert a hit counter		Point to Component and click Hit Counter on the Insert menu	[Alt] + I, O, C
Insert a scrolling marquee		Point to Component and click Marquee on the Insert menu	[Alt] + I, O, M

Graphics

FEATURE	BUTTON	MOUSE ACTION	KEYBOARD ACTION
Insert clip art		Point to Picture on the Insert menu and click Clip Art	[Alt] + I, P, C
Insert picture from file		Point to Picture on the Insert menu and click From File	[Alt] + I, P, F
Import a graphics file		Click Import on the File menu and click Add File in the Import dialog box	[Alt] + F, M, A
Vertical resize			
Horizontal resize			
Diagonal resize			
Move object			
Rotate a graphic clockwise			
Rotate a graphic counterclockwise			
Flip a graphic horizontally			

COMMAND SUMMARY

FEATURE	BUTTON	MOUSE ACTION	KEYBOARD ACTION
Flip a graphic vertically	◁		
Bevel a graphic	🖼		
Make a color transparent	✎		
Type text over an image	A		
Create rectangular hotspot	▭		
Create circular hotspot	⬭		
Create polygonal hotspot	◺		
Show hotspots	↖		

Help

Microsoft FrontPage Help	?	Click Microsoft FrontPage Help on the Help menu	F1

TOOLBAR SUMMARY

Standard Buttons Toolbar

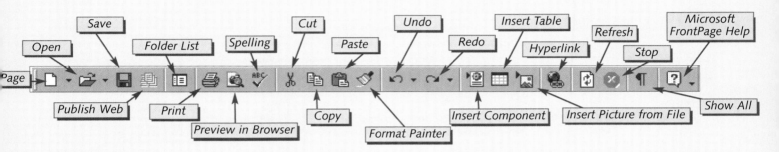

Formatting Toolbar

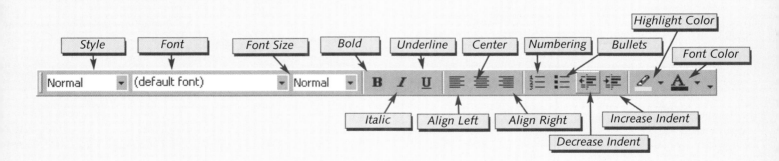

APPENDIX C

TOOLBAR SUMMARY

Tables Toolbar

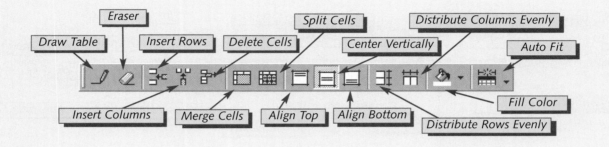

Eraser

Draw Table | Insert Rows | Delete Cells | Split Cells | Center Vertically | Distribute Columns Evenly | Auto Fit

Insert Columns | Merge Cells | Align Top | Align Bottom | Distribute Rows Evenly | Fill Color

Pictures Toolbar

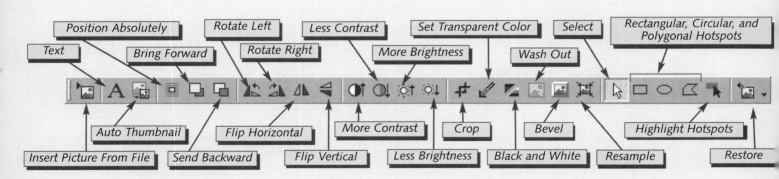

Position Absolutely | Rotate Left | Less Contrast | Set Transparent Color | Select | Rectangular, Circular, and Polygonal Hotspots

Text | Bring Forward | Rotate Right | More Brightness | Wash Out

Auto Thumbnail | Flip Horizontal | More Contrast | Crop | Bevel | Highlight Hotspots

Insert Picture From File | Send Backward | Flip Vertical | Less Brightness | Black and White | Resample | Restore

ANSWERS TO *Self* CHECK

Lesson 1

1. false
2. true
3. true
4. true
5. true

Lesson 2

1. false
2. false
3. true
4. true
5. false

Lesson 3

1. false
2. false
3. true
4. true
5. false

Lesson 4

1. false
2. true
3. true
4. false
5. true

Lesson 5

1. false
2. true
3. true
4. false
5. true

Lesson 6

1. false
2. true
3. true
4. false
5. false

Glossary

A

absolute URL   The address of a file, such as a Web page, that includes the entire path. The location of the file is independent of the location of the hyperlink that is referencing it.

active graphic   A set of page elements that change appearance when pointed to, clicked, or double-clicked.

adaptive menu   A feature that allows each user to customize menus. When you select a less frequently used command from an expanded menu, you automatically add that command to the short menu. Compare with *short menu* and *expanded menu*.

alignment   The position of text, objects, or graphics in relation to the top, bottom, left, and right margins.

animation   Motion effects available with FrontPage, such as page transitions, hover buttons, and scrolling marquees.

applications   Specialized software program used to create or process data, such as creating text in a word processing document, manipulating financial information in a worksheet, tracking records in a database management file, creating a presentation with a presentation or graphics program, or creating a Web page with FrontPage.

aspect ratio   The width-to-height ratio of an image. Altering the aspect ratio distorts the image.

attribute   See *effect*.

B

bevel   A graphics effect in which the edges of the image are altered so the image appears to have a raised, three-dimensional appearance.

bookmark   (1) A specified location within a document created for quick navigation to it from another place in the document. (2) A tool used within the Netscape Navigator browser to provide a shortcut to the location of a specific file, folder, or Web site so a user can return to it later without typing the address.

Boolean search   A method for locating information based on keywords linked by "AND," "OR," and "NOT."

broken hyperlink   A hyperlink whose target has been deleted or moved.

browsing   The process of clicking links of interest through a series of Web sites on the World Wide Web. Also called *surfing*.

bullet   A character, symbol, or graphic used as an effect to highlight paragraphs.

buttons   A box labeled with text or pictures that you can click to select a setting or put a command into effect.

C

category   A name under which Web pages can be grouped for a table of contents.

cell   A box formed by the intersection of a column and a row in a table. Each cell can hold a single value or text entry.

character formatting   Design features that are applied to the letters, numbers, and symbols in a Web page, such as fonts, sizes, and effects.

child-level page   A page on the same level as other child pages.

child page   A page directly connected to a parent page above it.

choose   See *select*.

click   The technique of quickly pressing and releasing the left button on a mouse or trackball.

clip art   A graphic file made of lines and curves that you can insert into a file and then resize, move, and modify as desired.

compression   See *file compression*.

D

default   A preset condition that remains in effect unless canceled or overwritten by a user.

desktop   The working area of the screen that displays many Windows tools and is the background for computer work.

digital camera   A video or still camera that converts light intensities into digital data. Digital cameras are used to record images that can be viewed and edited on a computer.

double-click   The technique of rapidly pressing and releasing the left button on a mouse or trackball twice when the mouse pointer on screen is pointing to an object.

downloading   The process of copying a file from a remote computer to a local computer (often accomplished through the Internet).

download time   The amount of time it takes for information to get to your computer from another computer, such as the time needed to display a Web page.

drag   The technique of moving an object on screen by pointing to the object, pressing and holding the mouse button, moving the mouse to a new location, and then releasing the mouse button. Also called *drag-and-drop*.

drag-and-drop   See *drag*.

dynamic HTML (DHTML) effects   DHTML is an extension of the HTML language that allows you to add presentation effects to objects such as buttons, graphic images, and Web pages.

E

edit   To make modifications to a document, such as a Web page.

effect   A characteristic of characters, such as small caps.

electronic mail (e-mail)   The exchange of messages and computer files through the Internet and other electronic data networks.

expanded menu   A list of all of the commands available on a menu that displays when a user clicks the double arrow at the bottom of a short menu. Compare with *short menu*.

external hyperlinks   A link from a Web page to another location outside the current Web.

F

file compression   The process of reducing file size by using a mathematical algorithm that analyzes groups of bits and encodes repeating sequences of data.

Find   A FrontPage command that locates the next occurrence of a given word or phrase.

fixed-width font   A font in which each character occupies exactly the same amount of horizontal space.

flip   The process of turning an image upside down by flipping it vertically or making it a mirror image by flipping it horizontally.

following   See *verifying*.

font   The design of a set of characters that includes a specific typeface, one or more effects, and a specific size.

footer   Text that appears at the bottom of every page of a printed document.

Format Painter   A tool that copies formats and applies (or "paints") the formats to other locations.

frame   One of several sections or panels in the window of a frames page. Frames can be scrolled and resized without affecting other frames in the window.

frames page   A Web page that divides the browser window into different areas or frames, each capable of displaying a different Web page.

Frequently Asked Questions (FAQ)   An online support feature in which answers are provided to common problems.

G

graphic image   A picture, drawing, or photograph that can be inserted into a Web page.

H

handles   Squares that surround an object and allow you to resize the object. Corner handles maintain the image's aspect ratio, while side handles allow the image to be distorted.

header   Text that appears at the top of every page of a printed document.

hit counter   A page element that displays the number of times visitors have viewed the page.

home page   The first page in a navigation structure, usually given the name *index.htm*, or *default.htm*.

horizontal line   See *horizontal rule*.

horizontal rule   A line that runs across a page or column within a page that separates sections.

hotspot   An area in an image map containing a hyperlink.

hover button   A page element that appears as a button containing a hyperlink. The button can change shape, color, or image when pointed to or clicked.

hovering   The act of pointing to a page element and waiting. The element may change appearance, position, or display Help text.

HTML   See *Hypertext Markup Language*.

hyperlinks   Connections usually within a Web page that move you to another location when you click on them. The location can be another Web page, another Web site, an e-mail address, or a file. Most commonly, a hyperlink is a graphic or text.

Hypertext Markup Language (HTML)   The language that serves as the basis for Web pages and the World Wide Web.

I

icons   A small image that represents a device, program, file, folder, or command.

image map   A graphic divided into regions or hotspots, each associated with a hyperlink. The image map generally contains visual clues so the visitor knows where to click.

importing   An operation in which a file created by one application is inserted into the current document of another application.

importing graphics   The process of copying a graphic image into a Web folder so it can be placed within a Web page.

internal hyperlinks   A link from a Web page to another location within the same Web.

Internet   A worldwide network of computers that connects each user's computer to all other computers in the network and allows the exchange of digital information in the form of text, graphics, and other media.

Glossary

Internet Service Provider (ISP)   A company that provides Internet access to users, usually for a monthly or an annual fee.

J

joystick   An input device used to control the on-screen pointer; a small joystick is often found in the middle of keyboards on laptop computers.

K

knowledge base   A collection of documents in a software company's Web site that can be queried to answer questions about a program's features and idiosyncrasies.

M

menu bar   An area below the title bar of all application windows containing menu names that, when clicked, display a list of commands.

merging   The combination of one or more adjacent table cells into one cell. Also called *spanning*.

mouse   A hand-held, button-activated input device that when rolled along a flat surface directs an indicator to move correspondingly about a computer screen. This allows the user to move the indicator freely to select operations or to manipulate data or graphics.

mouse pointer   See *pointer*.

multilevel list   A numbered or bulleted list containing main levels and indented sublevels. Each level may have a different numbering style or bullet type.

multimedia   The combined use of several media, such as movies, slides, music, and lighting, for educational or entertainment purposes.

N

navigation bar   Formatted text or graphic images of hyperlinks to other pages in the Web. Navigation bars are usually located in shared borders.

navigation structure   See *Web structure*.

network   A group of connected computers that permits the transfer of data and programs between users.

numbered list   A format in which numbers are sequentially assigned to paragraphs automatically.

O

Office clipboard   An area in memory used to store up to 12 cut or copied objects. Compatible Office 2000 software (Word, Excel, PowerPoint, Access, and Outlook) can paste any or all of the objects as needed.

operating system   A collection of programs that allows you to work with a computer by managing the flow of data between input devices, the computer's memory, storage devices, and output devices.

P

page banner   Formatted text or graphic image of the page label, usually located on the top shared border of Web pages.

page label   The name by which a Web page is known when in the Navigation view or in the page banner.

page title   A name for a Web page that appears on the title bar of a visitor's Web browser and in the Favorites or Bookmarks lists.

parent-level pages   The parent page plus pages on the same level as the parent page.

parent page   Page that has child pages below it.

path   The location of a file as defined by the drive letter and hierarchy of folders in which it is stored.

point   A unit of measure for font sizes, equivalent to 1/72 of an inch.

pointer   An arrow or other on-screen image that moves in relation to the movement of a mouse or trackball.

pointing   Moving the mouse pointer over an on-screen object.

proportional font   A font in which characters occupy variable amounts of horizontal space (for example, a *w* takes up more space than an *i*).

protocol   A set of rules and procedures that determine how a computer receives and transmits data. Common Internet protocols include *http* for the Web or *ftp* for transferring files.

R

relative URL   The address of a file, such as a Web page, *not* including the entire path. The location of the file is at least partially dependent on the location of the hyperlink that is referencing it.

Replace   A FrontPage command that substitutes a word or a phrase for another word or phrase. The command can be configured to prompt the user to make the substitution in each instance or to make all changes automatically.

right-click   The technique of quickly pressing and releasing the right button on a mouse or trackball.

rotate   The process of turning an image either clockwise (to the right) or counterclockwise (to the left).

S

same-level pages   Pages that are on the same level in the navigation structure and have the same parent page.

sans-serif typeface   A font with characters *not* adorned with serifs (for example, Arial).

scanner   An input device used to copy a printed page into the computer's memory and transform the image into digital data. Various scanners can read text, images, or bar codes.

ScreenTip   A text box showing a name and description of elements on the screen when you point to it.

script   A type of computer code that the computer can execute directly. Scripts can be written to control complex effects in FrontPage.

scrolling marquee   Animated text that moves horizontally across the Web page.

search engine   An Internet tool that allows a user to search for information on a particular topic.

search form   A Web page based on a template that allows visitors to enter keywords to find information located in the Web.

select   To designate or highlight (typically by clicking an item with the mouse) where the next action will take place, which command will be executed next, or which option will be put into effect.

serif   Finishing strokes on the characters of some fonts (for example, Times New Roman) that form a fine line.

serif typeface   A font with characters that are adorned with serifs.

shared borders   Areas on the edges of a Web page that can contain page elements or text that will appear on every page, such as a page banner, navigation bar, and so on.

short menu   A list of the most commonly used commands that appears when you click a menu name on the menu bar. Compare with *expanded menu*.

site map   See *table of contents*.

spanning   See *merging*.

split   The division of a table cell into one or more cells, either vertically or horizontally.

start page   See *home page*.

style   A named set of character and paragraph formats that can be applied to text—for example, headings or body text.

sublevel   An item in a numbered or bulleted list that is indented so as to be subordinate to a higher level item above it.

surfing   See *browsing*.

T

table   A format in which data is arranged into columns and rows of cells.

table of contents   A special Web page that includes hyperlinks to all or some of the pages within a Web. The table of contents can list the pages within categories defined by the Web designer. Also called a *site map*.

taskbar   An area on the Windows 98 Desktop that displays a button for the Start menu, icons for commonly used Windows 98 features, a button for each application running, and a button for the clock.

tasks   A to-do list within FrontPage for the design and maintenance of Web pages. Tasks can be viewed in Tasks view within FrontPage.

template   A preformatted page or Web that a user can base a new page or Web upon. The template may include various page elements and placeholder text.

theme   A set of unified design elements and color schemes for enhancing Web pages.

toolbar   A row of buttons representing frequently used commands. Toolbar buttons are used to execute commands quickly.

top-level page   Pages on the same level as the home page.

touch-sensitive pad   An input device used to control the on-screen pointer by pressing a flat surface with a finger—usually found on laptop computers.

trackballs   An input device that functions like an upside-down mouse, consisting of a stationary casing containing a movable ball that is rolled by the thumb or fingers to move the on-screen pointer. Used frequently with laptop computers and video games.

transition effect   A special effect associated with a Web page. The effect can occur when the page is entered or exited or when the Web is entered or exited.

typeface   A family of printed or displayed characters with particular design or style characteristics.

U

Uniform Resource Locator (URL)   The address of a Web site. A URL can be made up of letters, numbers, and special symbols that are understood by the Internet.

uploading   The process of copying a file from a local computer to a remote computer.

Glossary

V

verifying Testing that a hyperlink jumps to the intended target. Also called *following*.

Views bar A vertical bar at the left side of the FrontPage window that contains six icons through which you can navigate, edit, and organize a Web: Page, Folders, Reports, Navigation, Hyperlinks, and Tasks.

W

Web A group of connected Web pages usually with a common theme or purpose.

Web browser A program, such as Internet Explorer or Netscape Navigator, specially designed to read documents that are formatted in Hypertext Markup Language (HTML).

webmaster The individual responsible for the maintenance of a Web site. Questions, comments, or problems with the Web are usually e-mailed to the webmaster.

Web pages Documents in Hypertext Markup Language (HTML) most often viewed by a Web browser.

Web server Publishes Webs on the Internet so they can be viewed by others. The Web server accepts requests from browsers and returns appropriate HTML documents.

Web structure The way pages within a Web relate to one another. In FrontPage, this structure may be viewed within Navigation view.

Windows clipboard An area in memory used to temporarily store cut or copied objects. Objects include text, graphics, and files. The contents in the clipboard may be pasted into another location in the same document, another document in the same application, or into a document in another application that is compatible with the object.

wizard An interactive Help tool that guides a user through an operation step by step. In FrontPage 2000, there are wizards for creating a new Web or Web page.

World Wide Web An Internet service that allows users to view documents containing jumps to other documents anywhere on the Internet. The graphical documents are controlled by companies, organizations, and individuals with a special interest to share.

A

Absolute URL, *def.*, 92, 278
Active graphic, *def.*, 278
Active graphic elements, *def.*, 123
Adaptive menu, *def.*, 8, 278
Adding
    table rows and columns, 194–198
    Web pages, 177–184
Alignment, *def.*, 56, 278
Animation, *def.*, 245, 278
Answer Wizard, using, 46
Applications, *def.*, 4, 278
ARPANET, 38
Art. *See* Clip art.
Aspect ratio, *def.*, 232, 278
Attribute, *def.*, 54, 278

B

Banners, adding page, 79–81
Bevel, *def.*, 278
Beveling image, 233–235
Bookmark, 98, 206, *def.*, 278, *illus.*, 100
    creating hyperlink to, 100–101
    using, 98–101
Boolean search, *def.*, 142, 278
Border
    adding a banner to a, 80–81
    adding a shared, 77–79
    See also Shared border.
Broken hyperlink, *def.*, 180–182, 278
Browser
    opening an Office document in, 94–95
    previewing Web in, 87–90
    viewing Web with, 26–27
Browsing, *def.*, 278
Bullet, *def.*, 203, 278
Bulleted list
    creating, 199–205
    creating multilevel, 203–204
Bulleted paragraphs, using, 203–204
Button, *def.*, 4, 278
    creating a hover, 240–243

C

Category, *def.*, 174, 278
Cell(s), *def.*, 185, 278
    merging, 196–198
    resizing, 190–191
    selecting, 191–192
    splitting, 196–198
Cell properties, changing, 193–194
Character formatting, 50–51, *def.*, 50, 278
Child-level page, *def.*, 278
Child page, *def.*, 278
Choose, *def.*, 5, 278
Click, *def.*, 5, 278
Clip art, *def.*, 222, 278, *illus.*, 223, 224
    importing, 226
    using, 223–226

Clipboard, using Office, 247–249
Clips Online, using, 226
Code, finding, 138
Colors, changing theme, 119–122
Color scheme, creating a, 120–122
Color Schemes tab, 119
Color wheel, *illus.*, 121
Color Wheel tab, 120
Columns, changing table, 194–198
Command summary, 269–274
Compression, *def.*, 278
Contents, creating a, page, 175–177
Copying
    formats, 128–129
    with Office clipboard, 247–249
Corporate Presence Web Wizard, 166, 167,
    illus., 169
Counter, creating a hit, 243–244
Custom tab, 120
Custom theme, creating, 119–127

D

Default, *def.*, 278
Default font, *def.*, 50
Deleting
    table rows and columns, 194–198
    Web pages, 177–184
Desktop, *def.*, 4, 278
Developmental portfolio, *def.*, 266
Digital camera, *def.*, 222, 278
Discussion Web Wizard, 166
Double-click, *def.*, 5, 278
Downloading, *def.*, 91, 278
Download time, *def.*, 278
Drag, *def.*, 5, 278
Drag-and-drop *def.*, 5, 278
Dynamic HTML (DHTML) effects, *def.*, 245, 278

E

Edit, *def.*, 41, 279
    Web page, 41–43
Effect, *def.*, 54, 279
Electronic dictionaries, 129
Electronic mail (e-mail), *def.*, 95, 279
    using, 91
E-mail link
    creating, 96
    using, 95–96
Exiting FrontPage, 24–25
Expanded menu, *def.*, 8, 279
External hyperlinks, *def.*, 19, 279

F

Favorite, 206
File
    adding images from, 226–227
    importing, 58–59
    importing images from, 228–230
File compression, *def.*, 222, 279

Index

Index

Text selection methods, 51
Theme, built-in, 116–119
Theme, *def.*, 116, 281
    applying, 116–119
    creating custom, 119–127
    saving changes to, 122
    working with text in, 125–127
Theme graphics, using, 123–125
Theme text, modifying, 126–127
Thesaurus, 134
Titles, page, 183–184
Toolbar(s), *def.*, 9, 281
    standard buttons, 10
    working with, 9–11
Toolbar summary, 275–276
Top-level page, *def.*, 281
Touch-sensitive pad, *def.*, 4, 281
Trackballs, *def.*, 4, 281
Transition, adding page, 86–87
Transition effect, *def.*, 85, 281
    using, 85–90
Typeface, *def.*, 50, 281, *illus.*, 50
    sans-serif, *def., illus.*, 50
    serif, *def., illus.*, 50
Type size, changing, 53–54
Type styles, changing, 54–55

U

Uniform Resource Locator (URL), *def.*, 26, 90, 281,
    illus., 90
    page titles and, 183–184
    using relative and absolute, 92–93
Uploading, *def.*, 91, 281
USENET, 91

V

Verifying, *def.*, 282
Verifying hyperlinks, *def.*, 93
View
    Folders, 14–15
    HTML, 13–14
    Navigation, 16–18
    Normal, 13–14
    Page, 13–14
    Preview, 13–14
    Reports, 15–16
    using Web, 13–22
Views bar, *def.*, 13, 282

W

Web, *def.*, 4, 282
    applying a built-in theme to, 116–119
    closing, 25
    creating, from a template, 39–41
        with a Wizard, 166–174
    customizing, 171–174

    designing, 38
    editing a hyperlink in, 96–97
    finding Help on, 60–61
    linking to another, 102–103
    navigating, 72–103
    navigation structure of, *illus.*, 18
    opening, 11–12
    previewing, in a browser, 87–90
    replacing text in, 141
    searching text in, 137–139
    spell checking, 129–136
    surfing, 4
    using images in, 222–230
    viewing
        with a browser, 26–27
        in HTML view, 13–14
        in Normal view, 13–14
        in Preview view, 13–14
Web browser, *def.*, 4, 282
Webmaster, *def.*, 82, 282
Web page(s) *def.*, 4, 282
    adding
        from template, 44–46
        shared borders to, 77–79
        text to, 47–49
    creating, 43–46
        hyperlink to, 92–93
        from templates, 36–61
    editing, 41–43
    formatting text in, 50–57
    table of contents in, 75–77
    frames in, 205
    organizing, 74–77
    printing, 22–24
Web server, *def.*, 39, 90, 282
Web site
    modify and save changes to, 41–43
    using images from, 250–251
Web structure, *def.*, 16, 282, *illus.*, 38, 74
    viewing, in Navigation view, 17–18
Web views, using, 13–22
Web wizards, working with, 166–174
Windows clipboard, *def.*, 247, 282
Windows desktop, *illus.*, 6
Wizard, *def.*, 38, 282
    using a, 166–174
    working with Web, 166–174
Wizard dialog box
    elements of, 168
    using the, 167–168
World Wide Web, *def.*, 4, 282
    See also Internet.